T0391487

Indirect Speech Acts

To achieve successful communication, it is crucial to say clearly what we mean, but, at the same time, we need to pay attention to the form of our utterances, to avoid misunderstandings and the risk of offending our interlocutors. To avoid these pitfalls, we use a special category of utterances called 'indirect speech acts' (ISAs) that enable an optimal balance between clarity and politeness. But how do interpreters identify the meaning of these ISAs? And how does the social context influence the use of ISAs? This book attempts to answer these questions. It deals with the main theoretical and empirical questions surrounding the meaning and usage of ISAs, drawing on the latest research and neuroimaging data. Adopting a truly interdisciplinary perspective, it will appeal to students and scholars from diverse backgrounds, and anyone interested in exploring this phenomenon, which is so pervasive in our daily lives.

NICOLAS RUYTENBEEK specializes in experimental approaches to speech acts and politeness, using a combination of corpus data and psychophysiological methods. He is a postdoctoral researcher at the Faculty of Arts and Philosophy, Department of Translation, Interpreting and Communication, Ghent University.

KEY TOPICS IN SEMANTICS AND PRAGMATICS

'Key Topics in Semantics and Pragmatics' focuses on the main topics of study in semantics and pragmatics today. It consists of accessible yet challenging accounts of the most important issues, concepts and phenomena to consider when examining meaning in language. Some topics have been the subject of semantic and pragmatic study for many years, and are re-examined in this series in light of new developments in the field; others are issues of growing importance that have not so far been given a sustained treatment. Written by leading experts and designed to bridge the gap between textbooks and primary literature, the books in this series can either be used on courses and seminars, or as one-stop, succinct guides to a particular topic for individual students and researchers. Each book includes useful suggestions for further reading, discussion questions and a helpful glossary.

Already published in the series:
Meaning and Humour by Andrew Goatly
Metaphor by L. David Ritchie
Imperatives by Mark Jary and Mikhail Kissine
Modification by Marcin Morzycki
Semantics for Counting and Measuring by Susan Rothstein
Irony by Joana Garmendia
Implicatures by Sandrine Zufferey, Jacques Moeschler and Anne Reboul
The Semantics of Case by Olga Kagan
Attitude Reports by Thomas Grano

Forthcoming titles:
Frame Semantics by Hans C. Boas
Proper Names and Direct Reference by Gregory Bochner
Semantics and Pragmatics in Sign Languages by Kathryn Davidson Zaremba
Propositional Logic by Allen Hazen and Jeffrey Pelletier

Indirect Speech Acts

NICOLAS RUYTENBEEK

CAMBRIDGE
UNIVERSITY PRESS

University Printing House, Cambridge CB2 8BS, United Kingdom

One Liberty Plaza, 20th Floor, New York, NY 10006, USA

477 Williamstown Road, Port Melbourne, VIC 3207, Australia

314–321, 3rd Floor, Plot 3, Splendor Forum, Jasola District Centre, New Delhi – 110025, India

79 Anson Road, #06–04/06, Singapore 079906

Cambridge University Press is part of the University of Cambridge.

It furthers the University's mission by disseminating knowledge in the pursuit of education, learning, and research at the highest international levels of excellence.

www.cambridge.org
Information on this title: www.cambridge.org/9781108483179
DOI: 10.1017/9781108673112

© Nicolas Ruytenbeek 2021

This publication is in copyright. Subject to statutory exception and to the provisions of relevant collective licensing agreements, no reproduction of any part may take place without the written permission of Cambridge University Press.

First published 2021

A catalogue record for this publication is available from the British Library.

Library of Congress Cataloging-in-Publication Data
Names: Ruytenbeek, Nicolas, 1985– author.
Title: Indirect speech acts / Nicolas Ruytenbeek.
Description: Cambridge, UK ; New York : Cambridge University Press, 2021. | Series: Key topics in semantics and pragmatics | Includes bibliographical references and index.
Identifiers: LCCN 2021003161 (print) | LCCN 2021003162 (ebook) | ISBN 9781108483179 (hardback) | ISBN 9781108716482 (paperback) | ISBN 9781108673112 (epub)
Subjects: LCSH: Indirect speech acts (Linguistics) | Semantics (Philosophy) | BISAC: LANGUAGE ARTS & DISCIPLINES / Linguistics / Semantics
Classification: LCC P95.56.I53 R89 2021 (print) | LCC P95.56.I53 (ebook) | DDC 121/.68–dc23
LC record available at https://lccn.loc.gov/2021003161
LC ebook record available at https://lccn.loc.gov/2021003162

ISBN 978-1-108-48317-9 Hardback

Cambridge University Press has no responsibility for the persistence or accuracy of URLs for external or third-party internet websites referred to in this publication and does not guarantee that any content on such websites is, or will remain, accurate or appropriate.

Contents

Acknowledgements page viii
List of Tables x
List of Figures xi
Abbreviations xii

Introduction 1

1 Classic Speech Act Theoretic Approaches 5
   1.1 Introduction 5
   1.2 Generative Semantics 6
   1.3 Austin 11
   1.4 Grice 13
   1.5 Searle's Speech Act Theory 16
   1.6 Bach and Harnish 21
   1.7 Recanati 24
   1.8 Weak Literalism 26
   1.9 Brown and Levinson's Politeness Theory 29
   1.10 Conventionalized and Standardized ISAs 31
       1.10.1 Conventionality of Means 32
       1.10.2 Standardization 35
   1.11 Summary 41
   1.12 Discussion Questions 41
   1.13 Suggestions for Further Reading 42

2 The Semantics of Sentence-Types 43
   2.1 Introduction 43
   2.2 Imperatives 43
       2.2.1 Neo-Literalist Approaches to Imperatives 43
       2.2.2 The Features of Imperatives 46
   2.3 Interrogative Sentences 51
       2.3.1 What Is a 'Question'? 51
       2.3.2 Why Interrogative Requests for Information Are Direct 53
       2.3.3 Rhetorical Questions 66
       2.3.4 Interrogatives and Declaratives As Indirect Requests 69
   2.4 Deontic Modal Declaratives: Indirect Requests for Action? 75

v

2.5 Summary 79
2.6 Discussion Questions 80
2.7 Suggestions for Further Reading 80

3 **Cognitive and Relevance-Based Approaches** 81
3.1 Introduction 81
3.2 Cognitive Linguistic Approaches 81
  3.2.1 A Graded Notion of Speech Act Conventionality 81
  3.2.2 Illocutionary Force Salience 85
3.3 Relevance Theory 90
  3.3.1 Maximal Relevance 91
  3.3.2 Extra Processing for Indirect Requests? 94
  3.3.3 Extra Cognitive Effects in Indirect Requests? 98
  3.3.4 Standardized Indirect Requests and Speakers' Preferences 101
3.4 The Graded Salience Hypothesis 104
3.5 Summary 105
3.6 Discussion Questions 105
3.7 Suggestions for Further Reading 106

4 **The Comprehension of ISAs** 107
4.1 Introduction 107
4.2 Processing Differences between Sentences Used Directly or Indirectly 108
4.3 Processing Differences between Direct and Indirect SAs 111
4.4 Are Indirect Speech Acts Necessarily Secondary? 114
4.5 Three Linguistic Factors Influencing the Processing of ISAs 116
  4.5.1 Conventionality of Means 116
  4.5.2 Degrees of Standardization 120
  4.5.3 Illocutionary Force Salience 126
4.6 Measures of Cognitive Processing: Some Clarification 128
4.7 Eye-Tracking Experiments into the Interpretation of ISAs 132
4.8 Prosodic Aspects of ISA Comprehension 135
4.9 Summary 139
4.10 Discussion Questions 139
4.11 Suggestions for Further Reading 140

5 **Indirectness, Politeness and the Social Context** 141
5.1 Introduction 141
5.2 The Reasons behind Indirectness 141
  5.2.1 Face-Threat and Politeness 142
  5.2.2 'Communication' without Commitment 146
  5.2.3 Multiple Meanings, Immediacy and Intimacy 150
5.3 Face Concerns and Social Variables 151
  5.3.1 Status Asymmetries 153
  5.3.2 Degree of Imposition 160
  5.3.3 Social Distance 163

Contents   vii

        5.3.4 Status, Imposition and Distance   *164*
        5.3.5 Gender-Based Differences   *165*
        5.3.6 Individual Variables   *170*
  5.4 Explicitness and Face-Threat in Complaints   *172*
  5.5 Summary   *179*
  5.6 Discussion Questions   *179*
  5.7 Suggestions for Further Reading   *180*

6 Computational and Artificial Intelligence Approaches to Indirectness   *181*
  6.1 Introduction   *181*
  6.2 Computational Models of ISA Interpretation   *181*
        6.2.1 Plan-Based Approaches   *182*
        6.2.2 Specific Interpretation Rules   *183*
        6.2.3 Hybrid Approaches   *184*
        6.2.4 Indirect Directives and Reasons to Act   *185*
  6.3 Indirectness in Human–Robot Interactions   *186*
        6.3.1 Do People Use Indirectness with Robots?   *188*
        6.3.2 How to Make a Robot Disambiguate ISA Utterances   *189*
  6.4 Summary   *196*
  6.5 Discussion Questions   *197*
  6.6 Suggestions for Further Reading   *197*

  Conclusion   *198*

Glossary   *202*
References   *206*
Index   *221*

Acknowledgements

This book is the output of a successful collaboration with Helen Barton as editor and Izzie Collins as editorial assistant, whom I thank for their availability and responsiveness. It goes without saying that writing it would not have been possible without the help of the universities and, more specifically, the research labs where I have been working the last few years. I have also a sense of indebtedness to all the students who agreed to participate in my experiments in Brussels, Lille and Ghent. I thank my PhD supervisor, Mikhail Kissine, for giving me a taste for linguistic research, and my colleagues at the time, in particular, Gregory Bochner, Philippe de Brabanter, Philippe Kreutz, Philippine Geelhand de Merxem, Ekaterina Ostashchenko and Bob van Tiel, whom I worked with at the research centre in linguistics (LaDisco) of the Université libre de Bruxelles, for their helpful comments and suggestions. I am particularly grateful to the F.R.S.–FNRS for funding my PhD research for four years. I thank the Wiener Anspach Foundation for granting me a graduate visiting fellowship at the University of Cambridge, and Napoleon Katsos, who kindly agreed to supervise my work during my fellowship in 2013–14. This research has also benefitted from the coaching in experimental linguistics and advice offered by Benjamin Spector and Emmanuel Chemla during my Cogmaster program at the ENS in Paris in 2012–13, and by Steven Verheyen afterwards. These two international experiences determined to a strong extent the experimental orientation of my own work, which I pursued in 2018 as a visiting researcher at the LUCL in Leiden, stimulated by Marina Terkourafi's insightful ideas about speech acts and politeness research. I thank my current employer, Ghent University, for enabling me to complete the writing of this monograph in optimal conditions. I owe a special debt to

Acknowledgements

Herbert Clark, Sofie Decock, Ilse Depraetere, Thomas Holtgraves, Mathieu Lafourcade and Magali Norré, who provided constructive feedback on this manuscript. Last but not least, I thank my wife for her permanent support and her sharp, insightful remarks that helped me a lot when I had to clarify the content of this book.

Tables

1.1 Conventions of means for the performance of directives (with examples)   *page* 34
2.1 Syntactic, semantic and pragmatic notions of question   52
3.1 Predicted relevance of a *Can you VP?* IR in comparison with an imperative request   93
4.1 Prosodic cues for the interpretation of IR constructions in English   138
5.1 Frequency of one-, two-, three-, four-component combinations   175

Figures

2.1 Partition of the logical space corresponding to the meaning of the interrogative in example (43) *page* 59
2.2 Partition of the logical space corresponding to the meaning of the interrogatives in examples (44)–(45) 59
2.3 Continuum of informativeness/inquisitiveness for conceptualizing declarative and interrogative sentence-types (event: John's coming) 64
2.4 Continuum of informativeness/inquisitiveness for conceptualizing declarative and interrogative sentence-types (event: the closing of the door by the addressee) 66
3.1 Metonymic illocutionary scenario for requests (elaborated version, based on Panther and Thornburg 1998: 760) 82
4.1 Grid with geometrical coloured shapes and response buttons *133*

Abbreviations

A	Addressee
AI	Artificial intelligence
AOI	Area of interest
BNC	British National Corpus
CCSARP	Cross-Cultural Speech Act Realization Project
COCA	Corpus of Contemporary American English
DCT	Discourse completion task
DRT	Discourse representation theory
DSA	Direct speech act
ERP	Event-related potential
FTA	Face-threatening act
GSH	Graded salience hypothesis
HRI	Human–robot interaction
ICM	Idealized cognitive model
IFID	Illocutionary force indicating device
IR	Indirect request
IS	Inquisitive semantics
ISA	Indirect speech act
LPC	Late positive component
NLP	Natural language processing
NP	Noun phrase
RT	Relevance theory
S	Speaker
SA	Speech act
SAT	Speech act theory
SDRT	Segmented discourse representation theory
VP	Verb phrase

Introduction

Language is much more than a simple code for exchanging information. It is first and foremost used to interact with one another through the performance of actions such as warning about a state of affairs (*Your train is leaving in five minutes*), asking a question (*When does your train leave?*), wishing someone good luck (*Have a nice trip!*), telling someone what to do (*Show me your train ticket*). These actions, which are accomplished by means of written or spoken utterances, are called 'speech acts' (SAs), following the tradition in linguistic pragmatics and the philosophy of language.

When speakers and writers want to communicate clearly, when the meaning they purport to convey is explicit and unambiguous, they use 'direct' SAs, a category of utterances characterized by an association between a type of sentence and a type of SA. For example, a direct statement typically takes the form of a declarative sentence (*John is coming tomorrow*), a direct question the form of an interrogative sentence (*Is John coming tomorrow?*) and a direct request the form of an imperative sentence (*Come tomorrow, John!*). In all these cases, the meaning that the speaker or writer gets across is obvious.

However, in some situations, direct SAs are inappropriate, and, in using them, we face the risk of hurting our interlocutors and being considered impolite. This is where indirect SAs (for short, ISAs) come into play. They are considered 'indirect' in the sense that they are not the most straightforward way to perform a given SA, and they have different interpretations, depending on the contexts in which they take place. The utterance in (1), for example, is an ISA, because it involves a mismatch between the type of sentence used and the type of SA performed.

(1) It's cold in here.

It is a declarative sentence that, taken literally, is a statement about the temperature, but it can also be understood as a request that the

1

addressee close the window. It is therefore a safe alternative to the potentially rude imperative request (2), which is a direct SA.

(2) Close the window!

ISAs are pervasive in our daily lives, whether in private conversations, in commercial encounters, in emails, or in political discourse, to name only a few examples. But how are ISAs correctly understood despite the fact that they have different interpretations? What are the reasons why we perform ISAs in some situations? And what are the benefits of ISAs for ourselves and for our addressees? Exploring a whole variety of ISAs, this book attempts to answer these questions.

ISAs have been, and still are, a very popular research topic. Since John Searle's seminal paper called 'Indirect speech acts', published in 1975 and cited more than 4596 times (Google Scholar, 05/02/21), they have been the target of intense theoretical debate and considerable empirical investigation. Thousands of publications include 'indirect speech acts' or 'indirect requests' as keywords. They originate from various fields, such as philosophy of language, (intercultural) pragmatics, applied linguistics (e.g., second language acquisition), computational linguistics, social psychology and neurolinguistics. However, even though many researchers and disciplines are interested in ISAs, and a significant number of monographs deal with speech acts, imperatives, requests and questions, they are not specifically dedicated to indirectness. Another major issue in the available literature on SAs is that 'indirectness' is used with different meanings, and a clear definition of this notion is nowhere to be found. The present monograph aims to overcome these shortcomings and to complement previous work on this topic. It will cover both the theoretical and empirical issues raised by ISAs from a semantic/pragmatic perspective, offering a critical review of the literature on ISAs. Findings in experimental pragmatics, ranging from fieldwork on indirect requests carried out forty years ago to contemporary imaging and psychophysiological experiments, will be discussed. What will not be addressed in this book is the diachrony of ISAs, that is, how particular constructions gradually became associated with an indirect meaning. In addition, I will not be able to cover the bulk of experimental literature on ISA processing in atypical populations, and from the perspective of first- or foreign-language acquisition. I believe that these issues deserve a book on their own, and one written by specialists in these domains.

ISAs are very much worth investigating from the perspective of linguists, of course, as they challenge the division of labour between semantics and pragmatics. In the case of ISAs, it is sometimes difficult to disentangle the contribution of lexical items and contextual information in the output of interpretation. In addition, many notions and distinctions have been put forward in the theoretical literature, but it is unclear how the empirical data gathered thus far provides support for this or that notion. Furthermore, despite the considerable number of studies devoted to ISAs, much work remains to be done, in particular regarding the inter-individual variability in the use and understanding of ISAs.

The first three chapters of this book are theoretical. In Chapter 1, we will see that, in Searle's (1969) speech act theory, directness and indirectness were defined in terms of the semantic meaning of the types of sentences used indirectly. Building up on this opening chapter, Chapter 2 focuses on the semantics of the major types of sentences in English. In Chapter 3, I will consider the cognitive linguistic, relevance theoretic and graded salience approaches to utterance interpretation. What they have in common is that, unlike speech act theory, they see indirectness as a graded notion, not defined in terms of a relationship between a sentence and a type of SA, which offers more flexibility in the operationalization of ISAs. The second part of the book has a strong empirical and experimental orientation. In Chapter 4, I will provide a systematic overview of available studies on the comprehension of different types of ISAs. Empirical studies on politeness and other reasons for being indirect, such as commitment avoidance and the communication of multiple meanings, will be the topic of Chapter 5. In this chapter, I will also address studies exploring the role of the context and, in particular, the social dimension of language use, on the interpretation of ISAs. Chapter 6 will illustrate how computational models of ISA disambiguation have been improved and eventually applied to human-like robots in daily interactions, taking into account contextual parameters such as hierarchical status and politeness expectations. In the book's Conclusion, I will take stock of our current state of knowledge and outline directions for future work on ISAs.

When I was supervising students' experiments on indirect requests in Lille in 2015, they asked me whether there was any book on the topic available for them to read. Unfortunately, there was no such book on the market at the time. I am confident that the present textbook oriented monograph will be helpful to masters and PhD students in the linguistics program, as it provides a broad overview of pragmatic theories concerned with ISAs, with jargon-avoiding, accessible explanations, including discussion questions and applications. It can be used in semantics and pragmatics classes, but also in research seminars devoted to empirical approaches to utterance interpretation and production, and, of course, by semanticists and pragmaticians. Researchers working in other subfields of linguistics, such as second language acquisition, psycholinguistics, ethnolinguistics and in the fields of computer-mediated communication, cognitive science, social psychology and anthropology, and those who want to familiarize themselves with ISAs, will find food for thought.

To make abstract thinking as concrete as possible, I illustrate my discussions with examples: some of them are 'armchair' utterances, but, in order to achieve naturalness and reflect actual language use, the majority are authentic data collected on the Internet or retrieved in corpora. Most of these examples are in English, but I also provide attested spoken and written examples from other languages, such as French, Czech and Chinese. The theoretical approaches I outline and compare are not language-specific, and the ideas I propose, and the methods I have been using in my own research on ISAs, can be applied to many different languages.

1 Classic Speech Act Theoretic Approaches

1.1 INTRODUCTION

When we interact with one another, we perform 'illocutionary acts' or, more generally, 'speech acts' (SAs), following Austin's (1962) and Searle's (1969) seminal works. There are, of course, different ways to perform one and the same SA. For example, the imperative sentence *Open the window* can easily be used for requesting someone to open the window in a situation where the window is closed and the speaker would like some fresh air. In that case, the request is considered to be a 'direct speech act' (DSA), as it is the only possible interpretation of that sentence in that context. By contrast, an ISA is special: it is performed in addition to a DSA. For instance, when it is used for asking a question, the interrogative sentence *Can you open the window?* is a DSA, a request for information about the addressee's ability to open the window. However, it easy to think of a situation where this expression would be used as a request that the addressee open the window. In that case, the request would be an ISA, as it would be performed in addition to the DSA of a request for information.

This chapter offers an overview of the traditional accounts of ISAs. I am using 'traditional' in the sense that they are strictly speaking speech act theoretic or reminiscent of some aspect of speech act theory. It is also in these approaches that the very notion of an ISA has been introduced. I will first present generative semantic accounts of indirectness, which will lay the common thread in this chapter: the 'literalist' view that the syntax and semantics of sentences determines the pragmatics of utterances. We will also see how Austin's analysis of indirectness has been further developed in Searle's speech act theory, itself incorporating important insights from Grice's theory of conversational cooperation. More recent approaches with a speech act theoretic orientation will then be addressed, and I will close this chapter with a discussion of the relationship between indirectness and politeness, as well as make suggestions for how to deal with the variety of constructions that can be used in the performance of ISAs.

An important term used in SA literature, and throughout this book, is 'sentence-type'. As aptly proposed by Fiengo (2007), one can conceive of sentences as tools used in the performance of a range of verbal actions, including SAs. Sadock and Zwicky (1985: 156) define a 'sentence-type' as 'a regular association of form and the speaker's use of sentences'. In English, the three major, generic sentence-types would then be the declarative, the interrogative and the imperative. These generic sentence-types can be subdivided into different subtypes. For example, *yes/no* interrogatives, *wh-* interrogatives and disjunctive interrogatives are the three most common subtypes of the interrogative sentence-type in English. For Sadock and Zwicky, sentence-types are mutually exclusive: a sentence cannot instantiate more than one sentence-type. While Fiengo uses the term *sentence-type* to refer to the abstract notion of 'sentence' in opposition to a sentence *token*, which corresponds to the particular utterance of a sentence, I will use *sentence-type* as a shortcut for morpho-syntactic type, to refer to the distinction in terms of declarative, interrogative and imperative sentences.

As it is mostly indirect requests that have been, to date, discussed in theoretical work and used in experimental studies on ISAs, I will have more to say on indirect requests than on any other type of ISA. The same is true for the imperative sentence-type, prototypically associated with the performance of directive SAs. The common thread of the first theoretical chapters will therefore be the relationship between sentence-types and illocutionary types or 'SA types'. This perspective is actually more difficult to adopt for other SA types, such as promises, replies or compliments, which will nonetheless be discussed in my experimental chapters.

1.2 GENERATIVE SEMANTICS

The thesis that the illocutionary act performed with an utterance is directly predictable on the basis of the utterance's sentence-type is called literalism. This sort of approach is very important, because it lies at the origin of the notion of an ISA, and most accounts of indirectness either stand in line with or in opposition to this view. One of the earliest approaches that can be considered literalist is generative semantics. This approach is interesting, as it provides an attractive explanation of the relationship we observe between the three major sentence-types in English (as well as in other European languages, such

1.2 Generative Semantics

as Dutch, French and Spanish) and the three major SA categories. That is, it seeks to explain why declarative/interrogative/imperative sentences are commonly used in the performance of statements/questions/requests, respectively.

Following Chomsky's (1957) early work in generative syntax, the *surface* form of a sentence is the output of a set of transformations that affect the underlying syntactic structure or 'deep structure' of the sentence. Katz and Postal (1964), for instance, argued that the difference between the declarative sentence-type, on the one hand, and the imperative and interrogative sentence-types, on the other hand, arises from their deep structure. According to them, every sentence contains, at its deep syntactic level, a structure consisting of a pre-sentential marker of illocutionary force (the imperative marker 'I' for directives that are not questions, the marker 'Q' for questions) plus a proposition. For instance, (1a) and (2a) have (1b) and (2b) as their deep syntactic structure, respectively.

(1) a   Close the window.
    b   I [*you will close the window*].
(2) a   Can you close the window?
    b   Q [*you can close the window*].

Katz and Postal's analysis accounts for the fact that *You will* + verbal phrase (VP) can be used either with assertive or directive force. Because the imperative transformation applies optionally in the presence of the imperative 'I' marker, there is an ambiguity at the surface syntactic level.

According to this analysis, the surface form of (3) is ambiguous between the declarative and the imperative sentence-types.

(3) You will close the window.

For these authors, the possibility to add a tag such as *will you* in (4) indicates that the modal *will* is present in the deep structure of imperative sentences:

(4) Close the window, will you.

However, as Sadock (1974: 16) remarks, there is straightforward evidence against the claim that imperative sentences contain the modal *will* in their underlying syntactic structure. For instance, other, 'non-imperative' tags are compatible with imperative sentences without cancelling their illocutionary force of requests or commands (see also Bolinger 1977):

(5) Close the door, could you?

(6) Close the door, why don't you?

The pragmatic acceptability of these tags suggests that (5)–(6) contain a deep structure with *Could you VP?* and *Why don't you VP?*, respectively, instead of the alleged underlying *You will VP* structure.

Returning to (3), there is no reason why it should be considered an 'indirect' directive utterance in this approach. The command is not performed in addition to another SA of statement. In fact, (3) is a direct command because its deep syntactic structure is the same as that of an imperative sentence.

Things are more complicated for requests performed by means of interrogative sentences such as (2a).

(2a) Can you close the window? (repeated)

Unlike *You will VP* declaratives, here we have an incompatibility in terms of pre-sentential marker between the deep and surface structures of the utterance, and also a different modal verb included in the embedded propositional structure (*can* versus *will*) as in (7).

(7) Deep structure: Q [You can close the window]
    Surface form: I [You will close the window]

Saying that (2a) is an indirect request makes sense in this approach if one equates formal indirectness with a mismatch between the pre-sentential markers in the deep and surface structures. Instead of a simple imperative transformation, several moves must take place.

Another view, which Sadock (1974) calls the 'abstract-performative hypothesis' (APH), is based on Ross's (1970) performative analysis. Typical performative utterances, such as (8), take the form of a sentence with a main verb in the first person singular, in the simple present indicative active.

(8) I request that you make necessary revisions, publish an apology and take your mistakes into consideration for future coverage. (COCA, Davies 2008)

1.2 Generative Semantics

The semantic structure of (8), given in (9), includes a subject that refers to the speaker, a verb that indicates the illocutionary force of the sentence, a pronoun (i.e., *you*) that refers to the addressee, and a clause as the direct object of the verb.

(9) I REQUEST YOU [you will make necessary revisions, publish an apology, etc.].

The APH holds that sentences in which the illocutionary force is not explicit – sentences that are not explicit performatives – contain in their underlying syntactic form the semantic correspondent of a performative clause. One syntactic argument that supports the APH is the acceptability of parenthetical qualifiers such as *since I have my arms full* in imperatives, as in (10):

(10) Close the window, since I have my arms full.

These parentheticals are associated with the abstract performative clause in the deep structure of the imperative sentence, as in (11), and not with the embedded clause 'you close the window'.

(11) I request that you close the window, since I have my arms full.

However, as noted by several authors (Fraser 1974; Gazdar 1979; Searle 1975), the APH faces a good deal of problems, which make it empirically untenable.

First, remember that, according to the APH, the acceptability of *since I have my arms full* in a performative request explains why it is also acceptable in an imperative request. Implicit in the APH is the assumption that (10) and (11) are equivalent in meaning. But, as Sadock (1974) rightly points out, following the APH, (10) and (11) cannot be equivalent, because the deep syntactic structure of (11) is that of an assertion, that is, (12), and not (11) itself.

(12) I declare that [I request that you close the window since I have my arms full].

Because its deep structure is that of a declarative, (11) is specified for assertive force only and it should not be possible to use it with directive force at all. One therefore wonders why it is compared with the imperative (10) in acceptability judgements.

Second, data concerning non-directive uses of imperatives provide evidence against the APH. The examples below can easily be imagined in contexts where the directive meaning is missing: (13) is a threat and (14) a good wish.

(13) Hit me (and we all die). (COCA)

(14) Enjoy your trip. I'll take care of things here. (COCA)

Within the APH framework, the uses of imperatives exemplified in (13) and (14) should be set apart and considered deviant cases. A possible solution for the APH to explain why they lack directive force would be to include other performative verbs in the deep structure of these sentences, which boils down to postulating massive ambiguity at the deep structure level.

Finally, the acceptability of utterances such as (15), which, according to the APH, cannot have an abstract performative structure corresponding to the directive meaning of a request ('I REQUEST YOU [since I have my arms full you will close the window]), casts doubt on such an analysis of ISAs.

(15) Since I have my arms full, could you close the door?

This problem is reminiscent of Sadock's observation that parentheticals are licensed by the illocutionary force of an utterance rather than by its underlying deep structure. If the deep structure of utterances fully determines their actual illocutionary force, this poses a problem for a theory of ISAs.

The solution Sadock (1974) proposes is that *Can you VP?* indirect requests are linguistically ambiguous. For him, the illocutionary force of the utterance of a sentence is reflected in its surface structure. These syntactic cues, however, are sometimes ambiguous when it comes to illocutionary force identification. In fact, these syntactic properties are neither necessary nor sufficient for illocutionary force assignment. For instance, it is a well-known fact that imperative sentences can be used as requests, but also with several other illocutionary forces, each of which has distinct syntactic properties (Sadock 1974: 149).

Concerning the ambiguity of indirect request forms, Sadock illustrates the differences in syntactic markers of illocutionary force with the following three examples, which have in common the syntactic constituents of *Can you close the window?* (Sadock 1974: 123–4):

(16a) Can you close the window?

(16b) Can you close the window, please?

(16c) Can you please close the window?

Following Sadock's view, (16a) is ambiguous between a request for information, a 'survey requestion' (question asked as part of a survey) and a request for action. (16b) is also ambiguous, but it can only be used as a survey question or as an indirect request for action. The presence of *please* partially disambiguates this utterance, as *please* cannot co-occur with genuine requests for information. There is still some ambiguity, however, as sentence final *please* can originate from a clause whose main verb is TELL (i.e., 'S TELLS A to close the window'), but also from the clause with *close* as main verb (that 'A will close the window'). Finally, (16c) is not linguistically ambiguous, because the SA of requesting is the only one for which *please* is allowed to precede the main verb of the clause that is the direct object of the illocutionary verb.

To sum up, the generative semantic approaches reviewed in this section are able to account for speech acts typically associated with the deep structure of the sentences uttered, such as directives performed using imperative sentences and *You will VP* directives. However, they cannot satisfactorily explain non-imperative directives, and more generally mismatches between sentences' deep structures and SAs actually performed with these sentences. Sadock proposes a solution based on linguistic ambiguity, which accounts for the observation that *Can you VP?* sentences can be used with both a question and a request for action meaning. It is doubtful, however, that this solution can be applied, beyond the modals *will* and *can*, to other request forms and to other SA constructions.

1.3 AUSTIN

The notion of an ISA was first introduced by Searle's (1969) speech act theory (see Section 1.5), which is a direct development of the theory sketched by Austin (1962). Unlike Searle, Austin says very little on ISAs. For example, one case of indirect communication he discusses is (17) uttered by a player during a bridge session.

(17) I bid three clubs.

At first glance, if you are not well acquainted with the rules of bridge, you would think that all the player is doing with her utterance is bidding three clubs. This is the straightforward interpretation of a performative utterance. However, as Austin rightly points out, saying (17) amounts to performing, in addition to the SA consisting in bidding three clubs, another SA: conveying the information that one has no diamonds in one's game. This is an instance of an ISA insofar as the player informed the other player that she has no diamonds 'by means of' her bidding three clubs. Thus the performative utterance by means of which the SA of bidding is performed is used to convey something else in addition to the bid. To retrieve this extra informative content, other players will rely on the conventions associated with the game of bridge, that is, extralinguistic conventions. It is doubtful, however, that ISAs are produced and understood the same way in everyday communication as in card games. Unfortunately, Austin does not tell us much about the former sort of situations.

In fact, one might see any performative utterance as giving rise to an 'indirect' interpretation. Consider (18).

(18) I order you to leave the room.

There are other peculiarities of performative utterances, but it is important to stress that a description of an illocutionary act is not equivalent to the actual performance of that illocutionary act. After all, I could tell you that I am closing the door while opening it (making a mistake) or reassuring you that I am telling the truth while I am in fact lying. Thus, at the semantic level, (18) predicates of the speaker the property of issuing an order, and at the pragmatic level (18) can be a statement, an order, or even both – although this is a controversial issue. For instance, some propose that such utterances are understood both as a direct statement and as an indirect order, as in the speech act theoretic analysis (e.g., García Carpintero 2013; Recanati 1987: 143–50), while others argue against this view, claiming that these utterances are not statements (e.g., Jary 2007; Pagin 2004).

A working definition of indirectness can be achieved if we use Austin's (1962) distinction between locutionary and illocutionary acts. According to him, the performance of a 'locutionary act' amounts to uttering a meaningful sentence; an 'illocutionary act' (or 'speech act', for short) is necessarily performed by way of a locutionary act. For instance, in saying (19), S would perform the locutionary act of uttering a linguistic expression with some content.

(19) You can close the window.

As Austin (1962: 95) remarks, the locutionary act performed with a declarative sentence can be reported by using indirect speech, as in 'S said that A could close the window'. By contrast, for an imperative sentence such as (1), the locutionary act would be that 'S told A to close the window'.

(1) Close the window. (repeated)

The acts of 'saying' and 'telling to' thus correspond to the same level of analysis, that is, the locutionary level of the meaning of utterances. This suggests that, for Austin, the declarative, interrogative and imperative sentence-types express different types of locutionary meaning. At the illocutionary level, possible SAs performed with (19) are an assertion that A can close the window and a request that A close the window. It makes sense to consider that a request performed using (19) would be indirect inasmuch as there is a discrepancy between the locutionary act of saying, typically associated with the assertive illocutionary act type, and the directive illocutionary act performed with such declaratives. By contrast, direct realizations of SAs would be characterized by a typical association between the locutionary and illocutionary acts performed with the type of sentence uttered. However, Austin does not make it clear whether, in the case of ISAs, another SA is necessarily performed alongside the direct SA associated with the sentence-type of the utterance. Moreover, the interpretative processes that are necessary to understand ISAs fall beyond the scope of his work.

1.4 GRICE

Grice's contribution to the study of communication has been, and still remains, highly influential. Virtually any approach at the semantics–pragmatics interface includes a Gricean component.

A first tool that is useful to deal with indirect communication is Grice's (1975) distinction between what is explicitly communicated by an utterance ('what is said') and what is merely implied by that utterance ('what is implicated', the content of an implicature). While the former sort of meaning is closely tied to the meaning of sentences, the latter often arises from speakers departing from conversational expectations. An example of implicated meaning is the request interpretation of the utterance (20), the explicit content of which is the statement about the temperature; in contrast, the request meaning corresponds to what is said in (1).

(20) It's cold in here.

(1) Close the window. (repeated)

Conversational implicatures, as triggered by utterances such as (20), are differentiated from *conventional* implicatures. Unlike the former, the latter concerns the meaning of sentences. That is, a sentence that gives rise to a conventional implicature cannot be used without the implicature being triggered. For instance, the sentence *He is tall and, therefore, he could be a basketball player* cannot be used without triggering the implicature that 'he could be a basketball player because he is tall'. In this book, I will not assume that conventional implicatures give rise to cases of indirectness. I will only be concerned with conversational implicatures, which roughly speaking correspond to ISAs.

Grice's distinction between 'what is said' and 'what is implicated' bears some similarity to Austin's distinction between locutionary and illocutionary acts. However, for Grice, illocutionary acts can be performed both at the levels of what is said and of what is implicated. Thus in the case of a request performed with an imperative, the request meaning would be explicit (corresponding to what is said with the utterance). By contrast, at the level of what is said, (21) is a question, and its request meaning is implicit because it is conversationally implicated.

(21) Could you close the window?

Conversational implicatures are conceptualized against a background of linguistic cooperation between interlocutors. For Grice (1975: 45–6), it is rational and reasonable for speakers to adhere to a general 'Cooperative Principle', according to which one would be expected to '[m]ake a conversational contribution such as is required, at the stage at which it occurs, by the accepted purpose or direction of the talk exchange in which [one] is engaged'. This Cooperative Principle subsumes at least the following four conversational maxims: Quantity, Quality, Relation and Manner. According to the maxim of Quantity, speakers should say as much as, but no more than, required. The maxim of Quality relates to the fact that one should not say something one believes to be false or something for which one lacks evidence. The

1.4 Grice

maxim of Relation concerns the necessity to be relevant to the topic of the current situation of communication. Following the maxim of Manner, speakers should be clear, brief and ordered, and avoid ambiguities. Very often, communication is successful even though not all the conversational maxims are respected. Grice discusses several ways in which a maxim may be 'violated'. A typical case of a manifest violation of a maxim is when S strategically exploits a maxim in order to communicate something implicitly. In such cases, the only way to reconcile S's behaviour with her violation of the maxim is to assume that she follows the Cooperative Principle at the level of what she implicitly communicates. This sort of situation is quite likely to give rise to conversational implicatures.

As we will see throughout this book, ISAs mostly arise from the exploitation of the maxims of Relation and Quantity. To illustrate the fact that it can be difficult to tease a violation of Relation from a violation of Quantity, let me return to example (20).

(20) It's cold in here. (repeated)

From the perspective of the interpreter, (20) can be seen as a violation of Quantity. As a statement about the obvious, assuming everyone in the room is perfectly aware that it's pretty cold inside, S's utterance is not informative enough with respect to what is required as this stage of the conversation. However, if S had said *Because it's cold in here, you should close the window*, her utterance would have been sufficiently informative. On the other hand, (20) can be understood in terms of a violation of Relation, as in stating the obvious, S's utterance lacks conversational relevance. In fact, these two explanations are not mutually incompatible in the sense that they both provide a rational explanation of S's linguistic behaviour.

Grice himself was mainly concerned with assertive SAs, but the gist of his analysis can easily be applied to other illocutionary act types. Thus, according to him, cooperative speakers can exploit a maxim to convey information beyond what they say. This is what happens when a request such as (22) is produced.

(22) Can you leave now? (COCA)

Assuming a Gricean account of utterance interpretation, one should consider that it is not part of what is said that S requests that A leave the room. The request is not part of the conventional meaning, but, rather, it belongs to the speaker's meaning. To infer the request meaning, A should first reason that S blatantly violates the maxim of Relation insofar as the answer to the question about A's ability to leave the room is obvious. Assuming that S is nonetheless a cooperative speaker, A will try to identify the reason why S violates the maxim of Relation, which will lead him to the recognition of an implicated content – the illocutionary meaning of a request. We will consider a possible rational reconstruction of the inferential steps leading A to the identification of such a request meaning in Section 1.5.

Grice's theory of conversation helps draw a line between the meaning encoded by a sentence and the meaning that can be implicitly or 'indirectly' conveyed by an utterance of that sentence. At the same time, it accords with two intuitions. First, in many cases, A may not necessarily respond to the SA of questioning performed with (22) without being considered uncooperative (addressee's perspective). Imagine, for instance, that A complies with the request by just saying 'OK'. Second, (22) can be uttered without S actually requesting A to answer the question asked (speaker's perspective). This is because Grice defines non-natural meaning in terms of S's intention to make A believe what she says. Accordingly, in all the cases where (22) is used as a request, S does not necessarily intend A to believe that she is asking him whether he can leave the room. As a consequence, for Grice, the meaning of the ability question need not be part of what the speaker of (22) said. This can be a problem for this approach, because nothing would be said (or, rather, asked) by a speaker making a request using a *Can you VP?* sentence.

1.5 SEARLE'S SPEECH ACT THEORY

In line with generative semanticists, in Searle's speech act theory, ISAs are approached from a literalist perspective, assuming a systematic one-to-one correlation between sentence-types and speech act types. However, unlike Katz and Postal's (1964) and the APH literalist approaches, speech act theory (SAT) provides an account of non-imperative directive SAs based less on syntactic considerations than on general pragmatic principles of interpretation including Gricean cooperation. For Searle, the direct and literal SA performed by an utterance is determined by its morpho-syntactic structure or its 'illocutionary force indicators' (Searle 1979; Vanderveken 1990), a major such indicator being the formal properties of the sentence-type. According to this literalist view, sentence-types encode illocutionary forces. Declaratives encode assertive illocutionary force, imperatives

1.5 Searle's Speech Act Theory

directive force and interrogatives a subtype of directive force (requests for information). According to Vanderveken (1990: 126), '[the] directive force is realized syntactically in English in the *imperative sentential type*', and, therefore, '[a]ll simple imperative sentences serve to make an attempt with a medium degree of strength to get the [addressee] to do something'.

In SAT, 'the meaning of the imperative mood serves to determine that imperative sentences are used to give directives to the [addressee]' (Vanderveken 1990: 9). For instance, the utterance of the imperative sentence in (23) is literal if and only if the speaker who utters it 'means exactly what that sentence means in the context of [her] utterance' (Vanderveken 1990: 8), that is, if the felicity conditions for the performance of a directive SA are met.

(23) Leave now.

The conditions that are specific to the performance of a literal utterance of the imperative (23) are: that A is able to leave and would not leave otherwise (preparatory conditions), that S desires that A leave (sincerity condition), that S expresses the proposition that A will leave (propositional content condition), and that (23) counts as an attempt to make A leave (essential condition) (Searle 1969). Provided these conditions are met, S performs a literal directive SA.

This literalist view is compatible with holding that a directive illocutionary act can be performed without invoking an explicit illocutionary force indicator. In SAT, alongside the illocutionary force that can be predicted on the basis of its sentence-type, an utterance can have another illocutionary force. This is exactly where ISAs come into play. Take, for example, an interrogative sentence such as (22), which, according to SAT, encodes a subtype of directive force: the force of questioning or requesting information.

(22) Can you leave now? (repeated)

Imagine that (22), an utterance with a literal illocutionary force of questioning, is used by S as a request that A leave the room. In this situation, S does not seriously request that A give an answer to her question, but she expects that her request for action will be complied with. In SAT, the SA of request for action in (22) is 'indirect' insofar as it is performed by means of – and in addition to – another SA whose illocutionary force is determined by sentence meaning. To infer that S did not intend (22) to be taken as a mere literal question about his abilities, A must use Gricean principles of conversational cooperation, as well as background information. This reasoning enables him to reach the conclusion that the literal ability question is pointless in the context of the current conversation. He will then take the literal meaning of S's utterance as a device to identify S's illocutionary intent beyond this literal meaning (Searle 1975; 1979). Searle proposes a series of inferential steps describing how the interpretation of ISAs can be reconstructed (applied to the window example in (21)):

(21) Could you close the window? (repeated)
    a S asks A whether he could close the window.
    b A assumes S is conversationally cooperative and S's utterance has a purpose.
    c The context of the conversation (close friends having lunch) between S and A makes an interest in A's ability to close the window very unlikely.
    d S probably knows the answer to this question.
    e S's utterance is unlikely to be a question.
    f S's utterance therefore must have another illocutionary meaning: which one?
    g One preparatory condition for directive illocutionary acts is A's ability to carry out the expected action.
    h The fact that the answer to S's question is positive means that this preparatory condition is satisfied.
    i S and A are in a meeting, sitting comfortably, and A is closer to the window that S is (background information).
    j S has made a reference to the satisfaction of a precondition for a request which she probably wants A to satisfy (the compliance condition).
    k Therefore, in the absence of any other illocutionary act plausible, S is probably requesting that A close the window.

The speech act theoretic analysis of ISAs thus has a Gricean component as it is a rational reconstruction of possible inferential steps and it incorporates assumptions about linguistic cooperation, and, also, a literalist component insofar as the meaning of sentence-types is assumed to determine illocutionary forces. Furthermore, it complements the Gricean analysis presented above because it explains not only how, but also *which*, indirect meaning is inferred in terms of the preparatory conditions for the performance of the ISA in question.

In SAT, uttering an imperative sentence entails the performance of a *literal* directive SA. Whether this directive SA also corresponds to the full, intended meaning of the utterance is another matter. Let us, for

1.5 Searle's Speech Act Theory

instance, consider the expressive SA in (24), according to which S wishes her grandmother to have a good night.

(24) (He pressed a kiss to her forehead) 'Good night, Grandma. Sleep well.' (COCA)

Even though speech act theorists do not commit explicitly to this view, a standard SAT analysis of a good wish such as *Sleep well* in (24) would hold it that this expressive SA is 'non-literal' because it does not match the directive literal SA of 'requesting that A sleep well' that corresponds to the imperative sentence-type. There is, however, an undesirable consequence of the speech act theoretic analysis of imperatives. For imperatives used as directives, sentence meaning is sufficient for deriving their illocutionary force. But, in the cases of non-directive imperatives that we discussed, no semantic characteristic of the imperative is sufficiently reliable for the interpreter to access the intended meaning. In other words, additional Gricean inference based on S's intentions is required to access the meaning of imperative sentences used non-literally. From a psychological perspective, such an analysis is very implausible because, according to speakers' intuitions, understanding a good wish such as (24) is as straightforward as understanding an imperative command such as (23).

(23) Leave now. (repeated)

A similar reasoning applies to (7), but things are more complicated.

(7) Can you close the window? (repeated)

Depending on S's intention in producing her utterance, the SA corresponding to the literal meaning of the sentence uttered may or may not be part of the speaker's meaning. In the former case, this is because S has a genuine interest in knowing about A's physical abilities, and she expects A to close the window only if a positive answer is given to her question. In the latter case, the question is not seriously meant, and the only thing that matters to S is A's compliance with her request for action.

In SAT, the literal illocutionary force of an utterance is thus the force linguistically encoded by its sentence-type. It follows that a SA performed with (22), which is 'indirect' in the sense of SAT, is also non-literal because it departs from the meaning encoded by the sentence-type of the utterance. In contrast to (22), the request performed with (23) is 'direct' and literal.

(22) Can you leave now? (repeated)

(23) Leave now. (repeated)

Note, however, that the oppositions in terms of direct versus indirect, and literal versus non-literal do not fully overlap. Rather, indirect utterances would be part of the larger category of non-literal utterances. These are characterized by S meaning something different from what she literally says. Non-literal utterances include, for instance, ironical comments such as (25) said on a rainy day.

(25) What a lovely day for a picnic!

In prototypical ironical utterances, S communicates the exact opposite of what her utterance means: in (25) she is making a negative assessment about the weather on the day of the picnic. What ironical and indirect utterances have in common for SAT is that the illocutionary meaning of S's utterance is not identical with the meaning of the sentence uttered. But ISAs are distinct from ironical utterances because, in ISAs, S means, in addition to what she literally says, something else (Searle 1979). This analysis stands in sharp contrast to Grice's, who defines the notion of 'saying' in terms of non-natural meaning. Accordingly, for Grice, what S says is necessarily part of what she means (see Neale 1992: 522–5). According to Grice's analysis of irony, a speaker who produces an ironical utterance such as (25) when it is pouring outside does not really 'say' that it is a lovely day for a picnic; rather, she merely 'makes as if to say' that it is so.

The fact that the literal/non-literal and direct/indirect distinctions do not overlap entails that an utterance can have non-literal meanings in being both ironic and indirect. This could be a problem for a processing model based on the speech act theoretic analysis. Assuming such a model, one would expect an utterance that is both ironic and indirect to be inferentially more difficult to understand than an utterance only used non-literally or indirectly. For instance, imagine (26) uttered in a context where A is shouting at S.

(26) Can you speak louder?

With (26), S is actually requesting that A be quiet. According to SAT, an ironical request such as (26) is 'doubly' non-literal. This means that, from the perspective of a literalist processing model based on SAT, (26) would impose extra costs relative to both its direct and literal counterparts. First, (26) should be more difficult to process than the imperative request (27). Second, to this extra cost one should add additional extra cost relative to the non-ironic (28), that is, a series of inferential steps similar to those proposed by Searle (1975) for the derivation of IRs.

(27) Speak louder!

(28) Be quiet!

In Chapter 4, we will see that available experimental evidence does not support such a literalist model of utterance interpretation.

On the other hand, according to SAT, a directive SA that is not performed by means of an imperative sentence is necessarily non-literal. And, as we saw, performing an ISA always entails the performance of the literal SA that can be predicted on the basis of the sentence-type of the utterance. This follows from the literalist assumption that each sentence is associated, by virtue of its sentence-type, with a type of SA. Unlike in cases of non-literal utterances such as metaphors, for which, in some contexts, the literal meaning can be accessed and reflected upon (see Gibbs & Colston 2012 for a review), it remains unclear when, and why, the literal meaning of non-imperative sentences used as directives remains available for interpreters. For instance, is it plausible that the ability question meaning of *Can you VP?* IRs is accessed at some stage during interpretation? As we will see in Chapter 4, empirical evidence bearing on this question is scarce.

1.6 BACH AND HARNISH

Bach and Harnish (1979) propose an original theory of linguistic communication that retains several elements of Gricean cooperation. For instance, they assign a key role to mutual contextual beliefs of the conversational participants in utterance interpretation; these conversational presumptions, which are defeasible, are similar to Grice's maxims supplemented by maxims about politeness and morality. Bach and Harnish also use Austin's notion of a locutionary act, and their approach builds on Searle's (1969) speech act theory. Unlike in Searle's SAT, however, for them, inferential relationships are also involved in the interpretation of literal illocutionary acts. If the illocutionary act performed by uttering a sentence is literal, its propositional content is the same as that of the locutionary act of 'saying that' performed with the utterance. The locutionary act performed with a declarative sentence is 'S's saying that it is the case that p', where p is a proposition. Uttering an imperative sentence entails the performance of a locutionary act of 'S's saying that A is to VP (or to make it the case that p)'. In *yes/no* interrogatives, S is saying that A is to tell S whether or not it is the case that p. Literal illocutionary acts are defined in terms of a compatibility relation between locutionary and illocutionary acts.

For Bach and Harnish, the three main locutionary act types express different sorts of attitudes. When uttering a declarative sentence, S expresses the belief that p. The locutionary act performed with an imperative amounts to the expression of S's desire that A make it the case that p. For a *yes/no* interrogative, S displays her desire that A tell her whether or not p. Locutionary compatibility between an illocutionary act type and a sentence is achieved when the propositional content of the locutionary and illocutionary acts is identical. For an imperative utterance such as (1), the request that A close the window is L-compatible (locutionary-compatible) with the act of saying performed by S, here that 'S is saying that A is to close the window/make it the case that the window is closed'.

(1)   Close the window. (repeated)

The other requirement for locutionary compatibility is that the attitude expressed by the locutionary act is the same as that expressed by the illocutionary act; for example, S's desire is expressed by the locutionary act performed with an imperative sentence and by the illocutionary act of a directive. In such cases, these authors consider that the illocutionary act is performed literally.

Bach and Harnish acknowledge the existence of situations where S, in addition to performing one illocutionary act when speaking literally, performs another illocutionary act. They characterize indirectness in terms of 'an illocutionary act that is performed subordinately to another (usually literal) illocutionary act', the identification of the indirect act being mediated by the recognition of the first act (1979: 70). Following Searle (1975), Bach and Harnish consider that an indirect SA is performed 'by means of another illocutionary act' (1979: 60). Moreover, the success of the former is conditional on the performance of the latter. This view implies that the literal, direct SA cannot be bypassed during the interpretative process leading to the identification of the ISA. However, a difference with Searle's definition of ISAs, which entails that all ISAs are non-literal, is that, for them, there can be both literal and non-literal indirect SAs. For example, when S says to A that

1.6 Bach and Harnish

the bull is about to charge, she performs a literal SA of warning by means of a literal statement (relying on the mutual contextual belief that bulls are dangerous). Insofar as both the SAs of stating and warning are L-compatible with the locutionary act of saying that p, the warning is indirect and literal.

More generally, mutual contextual beliefs enable interpreters to know that the literal SA performed with S's utterance is not the whole point of her utterance; they help them determine what is indirectly communicated. When S makes a comment about the temperature, as in (20), A is expected to infer, on the basis of (a possible departure from) conversational presumptions, that this comment is not the only information contributed by S's utterance.

(20) It's cold in here. (repeated)

Having identified the locutionary act performed, A would reason that S could not merely make a statement about the fact that it's cold in the room, because it was already mutually known by the interlocutors that it is cold (and, e.g., a window has been left open); this would make S's statement uninformative. A would then hypothesize, assuming a principle of linguistic cooperation, the existence an illocutionary act related to this statement, so that in making a comment about the cold temperature S could also be performing that act. Insofar as it is mutually known that practical actions can be carried out when the temperature in a house is too low, A would understand that S is commenting about the cold and thereby requesting A to do something, a plausible candidate being, in these circumstances, the closing of the window left open.

In contrast to imperative requests, if one applies Bach and Harnish's definition of L-compatibility to an utterance of (7), the locutionary act of 'saying that A is to tell S whether or not it is the case that p' is not compatible with the attitude expressed by the utterance, that is, S's desire that A tell her whether or not p.

(7) Can you close the window? (repeated)

The request performed with (7) is, according to this criterion, non-literal. It is also indirect, as it is performed in addition to a literal question, and its success depends on the success of this literal SA. As Bach and Harnish rightly point out, some sentences such as *Can you VP?*, *I want you to VP*, *You should VP* are routinely used as directive ISAs, and they can be identified as immediately as if they were performed literally with an imperative. There are some regularities in the connections between the direct and indirect SAs associated with utterances of these sentences. A similar observation was made by Searle (1975), who was, as were Bach and Harnish, aware of the psychological implausibility of a fully detailed inferential process that interpreters should go through when processing these expressions. In Section 1.10, we will see which solutions have been proposed to account for the fact that ISAs such as *Can you VP?* seem very straightforward to understand.

1.7 RECANATI

Diverging from Bach and Harnish's locutionary-compatibility condition, Recanati (1980) revisited Austin's (1962) notion of a locutionary act. He proposed analyzing ISAs such as the request in (7) by distinguishing between the illocutionary act that is *indicated* by an utterance of a sentence (locutionary act), and the illocutionary act *actually performed* with the utterance (illocutionary act).

(7) Can you close the window? (repeated)

Thus, for Recanati, the illocutionary act indicated by a sentence can differ from the illocutionary act performed by uttering that sentence. In the case of (7), S would perform the locutionary act of 'asking whether A is able to close the window'. Accordingly, the interrogative (7) indicates the SA of *asking whether*. In some contexts, uttering (7) will also constitute the performance of the illocutionary act of 'requesting that A close the window', which is, unlike the SA of *asking whether*, not indicated by the sentence uttered. The distinction in terms of locutionary versus illocutionary points to another distinction based on propositional content. That is, the propositional content of the sentence uttered can be different from that of the illocutionary act performed with that utterance, a difference that led Kissine (2008; 2013) to propose an alternative distinction between *direct* and *indirect* SAs according to their respective propositional contents. Defining a locutionary act as the expression of a proposition under the scope of a certain mode or attitude, Kissine considers that a SA is *indirect* if its content differs from the content of the locutionary act performed with the corresponding utterance. For instance, despite the apparent mismatch between 'saying' and 'ordering', the directive SA performed with (3) would be *direct* in the sense that the content of the illocutionary act (of ordering 'that A will close the window') is identical to that of the locutionary act (of saying 'that A will close the window').

1.7 Recanati

(3) You will close the window. (repeated)

Even though this notion of 'propositional content indirectness' cannot be equated to the one assumed in the contemporary literature on SAs, it is reminiscent of the intuition, formulated by generative semanticists, that *You will VP* is syntactically ambiguous between an assertion and a command.

In addition to his distinction between direct and indirect SAs, Recanati proposes a distinction in terms of primary and secondary SAs, which concerns the cognitive processes involved in utterance interpretation. Before examining such a notion, I would like to warn against a possible confusion. In Searle's (1975) speech act theory, SAs are distinguished according to their relative importance from the speaker's point of view: *primary* refers to the ISA and *secondary* to the DSA performed with an utterance. For Searle, the request meaning of a *Can you VP?* request for action is primary because it corresponds to the primary motivation of S's utterance. Here, I will not use *primary* and *secondary* as Searle did but, rather, I will assume a distinction in terms of cognitive processing.

Unlike Searle, Recanati (2004) considers that a meaning is *secondary* if it is derived from a more basic, *primary* meaning, which it presupposes. The 'logically' secondary meaning is implied by the fact that S has said what she said, and it involves an inference from the logically primary meaning of the utterance. Secondary meanings meet the 'transparency' or 'availability condition' (Recanati 2004: 42–4). According to that condition, language users are aware of the distinction and the connection between the two layers of meaning; they are also aware of the inference from the primary to the secondary meaning. In other words, these meanings and their relationship are 'cognitively available' to interpreters. For instance, the 'request' meaning of (20) (that A is to close the window) can be accessed a posteriori by reflecting on the reasons why S commented on the temperature.

(20) It's cold in here. (repeated)

If all goes well, A will establish a link between S's observation about the temperature of the room and the action of closing the window that would remedy the negative state of affairs depicted in (20). Because the availability condition is satisfied, the request in (20) can be considered *secondary*. By contrast, it is all but obvious that the availability condition would be met in the case of a request such as (3).

(3) You will close the window. (repeated)

It does not seem intuitively plausible that interpreters are necessarily aware of both the assertive and the directive interpretation of that utterance. This suggests that the request in (3) should be considered *primary*.

Note that Recanati's notion of secondariness can be interpreted not only in terms of a logical relationship, but also in terms of a temporal relationship. This is the view adopted by Kissine (2013), who interprets the relationship between the primary SA and the secondary SA in the chronological sense: a primary SA is derived *before* possible secondary SAs. For him, the directive in (3) is primary because it is not necessary to interpret it as an assertion that A will leave the room to understand it as a command. According to Kissine, a SA is secondary if and only if its comprehension requires the utterance to be interpreted as another (primary) SA. He proposes that (20) is a secondary request that A close the window insofar as, in order to understand that the utterance is a request, A will first understand it as a statement about the temperature.

Now, if we return to typical examples of *Can you VP?* indirect requests, Recanati would agree that, in some situations, the request SA in *Can you close the window?* is conditional on (a positive answer to) the question about A's ability to close the window. In other words, in such contexts the request would be logically and chronologically secondary with respect to the primary SA of questioning. That being said, while it is plausible that Recanati's availability condition would be satisfied when the indirect request is conditional on a positive answer to the literal question, it need not be so in all situations. This question boils down to an empirical issue, and it will be dealt with in Chapter 4.

1.8 WEAK LITERALISM

Theories differ in terms of the extent to which information literally present in an utterance and its illocutionary force play a role in ISA interpretation. In particular, the view that the information literally contained in an ISA utterance enables the derivation of the ISA should not be confused with SA literalism. For instance, the view that sentence-types encode a component of illocutionary force – what could be called 'strong literalism' – was popular in the heyday of generative semantics and classic speech act theory. Nowadays, it has few defenders. Nevertheless, in the spirit of these early approaches, several contemporary authors propose that sentence-types should be defined

1.8 Weak Literalism

with a reference to illocutionary forces. These accounts, which I will call 'weak literalist', are interesting in that they do justice to some of the intuitions underlying strong literalism, while being compatible with the more recent theoretical developments on ISAs.

In a more recent version of speech act theory, Barker (2004) does not endorse the view that the declarative, imperative and interrogative sentence-types are distinct elaborations on a common sentential meaning, denying that these three sentence-types have the same propositional content. Rather, he considers that the meaning of a sentence resides in the specific SA type associated with the syntactic ordering of the constituents of the sentence. For him, the semantic interpretation of a sentence consists in the proto-illocutionary act performed by uttering the sentence. Accordingly, the semantic interpretation of the declarative (3) is a proto-assertion, (29) is a proto-request for information, and (1) is a proto-order.

(3) You will close the window. (repeated)

(29) Will you close the window?

(1) Close the window! (repeated)

When a speaker utters a sentence, she performs a proto-illocutionary act consisting in 'advertising' an intention (X) to represent a complex, and a communicative intention (Y). In the case of the imperative (1), S advertises an intention (X) to represent a complex of the form <S desires that the addressee see to it that the assertion that 'the addressee closes the window' is correct>. S also advertises an intention (Y) to make her addressee believe that she has such a desire. The proto-illocutionary order consists in S advertising these two intentions. However, to arrive at the illocutionary act of ordering A to close the window, one must complement the proto-illocutionary order with the assumption that S has the communicative intention (Y) she thereby advertises.

Unlike Searle, Barker does not hold that any utterance of an imperative sentence entails the (literal) performance of a directive SA. However, insofar as his proto-illocutionary acts are defined with respect to the prototypical illocutionary force associated with each sentence-type, this is a 'weak literalist' approach. Barker explicitly commits himself to the view that any utterance of a sentence (embedded or not) constitutes the performance of a proto-illocutionary act. However, he does not explain why imperative sentences, the utterance of which constitutes the performance of proto-illocutionary orders, are also frequently used in the performance of non-directive SAs. In the case of imperative directives, there is a straightforward connection between the proto-illocutionary acts and the SAs that requires some justification. Concerning ISAs, S advertises an intention she does not actually have: for example, in an interrogative indirect request for action (*Can you VP?*), the actual illocutionary act performed may diverge from the proto-illocutionary act of a request for information, as indicated by the syntax of the sentence. I consider that this proposal is literalist, because the proto-illocutionary act performed in uttering a sentence is defined in terms of the SA literally performed by uttering that sentence. However, while Barker assumes that there is a strong connection between sentence-types and 'proto-illocutionary acts', he does not claim that the actual illocutionary force of an utterance is encoded by its sentence-type.

Another semantic account of sentence-types that can be seen as literalist is Boisvert and Ludwig's (2006) proposal. According to Boisvert and Ludwig, close associations between sentence-types and illocutionary act types can be explained by a unified theory of sentence-types that is based on the notion of satisfaction conditions, in the spirit of McGinn (1977). Paralleling traditional analyses of declaratives in terms of truth conditions, they conceive of the semantics of non-declaratives in terms of another sort of satisfaction conditions: compliance conditions. More precisely, imperatives are defined in terms of obedience conditions and interrogatives in terms of answer conditions. These conditions correspond to the satisfaction conditions of 'requests for action' and 'requests for information' respectively associated with these two major English sentence-types.

For Boisvert and Ludwig, a directive SA is obeyed if the addressee acts according to the directive and 'does what is directed' because he has been so directed. They also propose that an imperative sentence is obeyed relative to a SA u if the addressee of the utterance performs the action expressed by the imperative on the grounds that he has recognized the obedience conditions of u. Thus, in these authors' account, sentence-types are apt for the performance of SAs of a certain type because they share the mode of evaluation of that SA type. Relative to some context of utterance, an imperative will be evaluated as obeyed or not obeyed and an interrogative as answered or unanswered. Note that, insofar as Boisvert and Ludwig's definition is semantic, it does not imply that any utterance will consist in the performance of the SA associated with the sentence-type of the utterance. Accordingly, imperatives, declaratives and interrogatives need not be uttered with a particular illocutionary force at all to receive a semantic evaluation.

I believe Boisvert and Ludwig's approach is a 'weak literalist' account in the sense that it defines sentence-types in terms of a concept associated with the performance of generic SAs: satisfaction conditions. I agree that the three major English sentence-types should be given a unified, semantic analysis. However, when utterances of these sentences give rise to SAs, the semantic analysis they propose does not always match the pragmatic analysis of the utterances in terms of illocutionary meaning. For Boisvert and Ludwig, in cases of indirectness such as *Can you VP?*, the interrogative sentence would – under some circumstances – be unanswered at the level of the direct, literal question (i.e., the satisfaction conditions for the SA of questioning do not obtain) while the utterance would be complied with at the level of its indirect interpretation. As we have seen before, there is a mismatch between the semantic and pragmatic meanings of utterances used as ISAs.

1.9 BROWN AND LEVINSON'S POLITENESS THEORY

We know, on the basis of available research concerning cross-cultural differences in the distribution patterns of request forms (see Flöck 2016: 61–74) that IRs, and *Can you VP?* interrogatives in particular, are preferred over imperative sentences in a variety of contexts. Brown and Levinson's (1987) politeness theory, which assumes a general speech act theoretic framework, establishes a direct connection between ISAs and politeness: indirectness enables speakers to alleviate the psychological and socio-emotional costs entailed by the performance of their SAs. In fact, social considerations such as linguistic politeness are often conceived of as the major reason for opting for these ISAs instead of DSAs (see also Chapter 5).

Building on Goffman (1955; 1967), Brown and Levinson define 'face' as a universal two-sided concept: negative face and positive face, both applying to the speaker and the addressee. For instance, the 'negative face' of an individual is their claim to be free to do only what they want to and their will that others do not impede their actions. The 'positive face' refers to an individual's want to be approved of by others. If, in theory, any utterance can have detrimental effects on a speaker and/or her addressee, several SA types are intrinsically associated with 'face-threat' (that is, the threat that an utterance constitutes for the face of conversational participants). For example, directive SAs constitute face-threatening behaviour because A's negative face is threatened when S exerts some degree of force towards her. Criticism and complaints pose a threat to the positive face of the recipient – providing he is also the target of the criticism and the person responsible for the situation being complained about – because the negative evaluation of the person compromises his claim to seek approval from other people.

Brown and Levinson's 'chart of strategies' offers a good overview of the various ways to perform a SA. If S's utterance is very unlikely to give rise to any threat to someone's face, she can perform it by going 'on record', with a direct SA. An example of this strategy is using an imperative request in the context of a conversation between good friends, in an informal setting. In the case of an 'on-record' SA, there can be no doubt concerning the intended meaning, whether direct or indirect, of the utterance. This meaning is said to be undeniable, that is, S cannot plausibly claim that she did not intend to perform that very SA. S's communicative intention is blatant, transparent. She is committed to the performance of the SA she performs. However, face considerations play a role on many occasions. In order to compensate for the face-threat entailed by the performance of their SAs, speakers go on record 'with redress', that is, their utterances include linguistic elements that contribute polite behaviour. Redressive action either belongs to positive or negative politeness strategies. Positive politeness amounts to displaying a favourable attitude towards the addressee, for example, by using familiarity (*come on*), nicknames (*Bob*), compliments (*you've always been a friend*), as in (30).

(30) Come on Bob, lend me 5 euros, you've always been a friend to me.

Negative politeness is illustrated by the use of linguistic expressions that mitigate the threat that the directive SA constitutes to A's negative face, such as apologies (*excuse me*), pre-requests (*Would you mind if...?*) and imposition minimizers (conditional forms *would* and *could*, *just*), as in (31).

(31) Excuse me, would you mind if I ask you if you could just lend me 5 euros?

In contrast to Brown and Levinson's (1987) on-record strategies, an 'off-record' SA is characterized by the fact that S's intention in producing her utterance remains to some extent ill defined. We saw that, if S is going on record, she can lessen face-threat by using linguistic expressions that will mitigate face-threat, that is, redressive action. For off-record strategies, according to Brown and Levinson, there is no need for redress. Rather, the idea is to trigger conversational implicatures and give a hint to the addressee, leaving to him the responsibility of the inferred meaning. As a consequence, S can deny the performance and the responsibility for the SA in question. She can hide behind the literal meaning of the utterance, as when saying that 'it's cold in here' (hoping that A will respond by closing the window while being prepared to deny having this intention in case A does not display readiness to comply).

In Brown and Levinson's (1987: 68–83) model, three variables determine expected politeness: the perceived power relationship between the conversational participants, the social distance between them, and imposition (the costs resulting from the performance of S's SA for A). A linear relationship is postulated between the degree of face-threat entailed by the performance of a SA and the amount of linguistic mitigation required. For them, the effects of each of these variables on face-threat and, as a result, on indirectness and politeness, are cumulative. Despite its intuitive plausibility, Brown and Levinson's account has been criticized on several grounds. One major problem faced by this approach is that the predicted effects of the three identified sociological variables are not always additive: as we will see in Chapter 5, they may interact in different ways. Another difficulty is that, in many different cultures, it is not off-record indirectness, but on-record indirectness including redressive action that is considered the most polite strategy (e.g., Blum-Kulka 1987). Furthermore, in some situations too much linguistic mitigation may cause one's utterance to be perceived as over-polite and sarcastic, which is at odds with the view that mitigation increases politeness. In fact, as Lakoff (1973b) argued, utterance production is regulated by a balance between clarity and politeness. That is, too much indirectness can render S's utterance difficult to understand, in which case A can miss the intended illocutionary meaning of S's utterance. In general, if S wants to avoid the emotional costs entailed by a directive SA for A, while at the same time making her communicative intention clear enough, the best option for her is to use constructions that express the requested action. These include *Will you VP?*, *Would you VP?*, *Why don't you VP?*, *Can/could you VP?*, and they are often called 'conventionalized' or simply 'conventional' in the literature.

1.10 CONVENTIONALIZED AND STANDARDIZED ISAs

At this stage, an important aspect of ISAs remains unaddressed: the variety of expressions that can be used with an indirect interpretation, and how one should account for this diversity. The solution I propose amounts to a combination of three notions, the first two of which I will describe in this section: conventionality of means (Section 1.10.1), conventionality of form (Section 1.10.2) and illocutionary force salience (presented in Chapter 3).

1.10.1 Conventionality of Means

A notion that helps account for differences in how utterances make their indirect meaning accessible is 'conventionality'. It is, however, important to differentiate between two sorts of 'conventions' involved in the performance of ISAs, and to clarify the connection between conventionality and another notion – 'standardization'.

A first definition of 'conventionality' associated with indirect SAs is the notion proposed by Searle. If we take the example of indirect directives, in SAT, the felicity conditions for directives consist in the preparatory condition (that A has the ability to do the requested action), the propositional content condition (that S expresses a proposition that A will perform a future action), the sincerity condition (that S has the desire that A do the requested action), and the essential condition (that the utterance counts as an attempt to make A perform the requested action). As Searle (1969; 1975) notes, the content of many sentences used in the performance of ISAs involves a reference to their felicity conditions. Searle points out that indirect requests (IRs) can be performed by asking whether, or stating that, A is able to do some action (*Can you VP?*, *You can VP*), by asking whether, or stating that, A will do the action (*Will you VP?*, *You will VP*), by stating that she wants A to do the action (*I would like you to VP*), or by presenting a reason to do the action (*You should/must VP*). This reasoning also applies to non-directive SA types, such as assertives. For instance, it is possible to make an indirect statement that 'it is raining outside' by stating that a preparatory condition obtains (*I believe that it's raining outside*). In some cases, general principles of rationality prevent some realizations of these ISAs. One cannot, for example, make an assertion that it is raining outside by stating that one's addressee believes this to be the case; in fact, if (I know that) he already believes this to be the case, my utterance would be pointless.

Most of these sentences have what Searle calls a 'generality of form'. Although Searle himself does not explain in detail what he precisely means by 'generality of form', utterances such as (22) share a core syntactic structure consisting in a second-person pronoun, a modal verb (*will, can, must, should*) and a VP denoting the requested action.

1.10 Conventionalized and Standardized ISAs

(22) Can you leave now? (repeated)

In contrast to sentences with a modal verb such as (22), many sentences referring to reasons to act do not have such a 'generality of form'. An example is (32), meant as a request to move away from the road.

(32) You're standing on a road, nitwit. (COCA)

Even though this label is not always adequately explained in the literature on SAs, IRs such as (22) are frequently referred to as 'conventional' (e.g., Blum-Kulka & Ohlstain 1984; Holtgraves 1994; Morgan 1978; Searle 1975). According to Searle (1975), the utterance in (22) is 'conventional' for the performance of requests for the reason that its 'generality of form' is typical of such IRs. That is, (22) is a token of an abstract *Can you VP?* construction, which exhibits such a generality of form; the *Can you VP?* construction itself instantiates the more abstract 'Modal *you* VP?' construction. I will come back to this approach in terms of constructions when I discuss cognitive linguistic accounts in Chapter 3.

According to Clark (1979), IRs such as (22) involve 'conventions of means', conventions 'about which sentences can be used for which indirect speech acts'. They concern the strategies used in the performance of SAs. For instance, one such convention relies on the SAT notion of preparatory conditions for the performance of an illocutionary act. Clark's conventions of means relate to Searle's (1975) classification of the sentences frequently used as directives. For instance, S can request that A do an action by asking a question about A's ability to do this action, as (33) illustrates – the content of S's utterance is in line with the preparatory condition for directives.

(33) Could you tell me the price for a fifth of Jim Beam?

By contrast, the sentence in (34) does not involve the convention of means concerning these preparatory conditions.

(34) Does a fifth of Jim Beam cost £5?

Clark nonetheless proposes that (34), which expresses the question whether a fifth of Jim Beam costs £5, could be used to request that A tell the price for a fifth of Jim Beam. However, he considers that such a request would not be conventional at all. Unlike Clark, I believe that this utterance actually is conventional. The utterance refers to the price of the item (to be precise, to the preparatory condition according to which there is an item such that one can make inquiries about its price), and thereby indirectly refers to the performance of the action of answering S's question. The link between the semantic content of the utterance and the convention is less straightforward than in the previous cases, but there is a link nonetheless. Table 1.1 offers an overview of the most common conventions of means for the performance of indirect directives.

For Searle and Clark, conventionality (of means) was conceived of as a binary criterion in the sense that an ISA either is conventional or non-conventional for the performance of some SA. In contrast to them, I propose that this criterion of conventionality of means is categorical: the possible values for this criterion correspond to the different strategies used in the performance of indirect directives. In fact, it makes sense to consider that any utterance used as a directive, whether

Table 1.1 *Conventions of means for the performance of directives (with examples)*

Convention of means	Examples
Question or refer to A's ability/possibility	*Can you close the window?* *You could close the window.* *It is possible to close the window?*
Question A's willingness	*Would you mind closing the window?*
State one's performance of a directive speech act (performative utterance)	*I suggest/request that you close the window.* *I order/command you to close the window.* *May I ask you to close the window?* (hedge)
Express an obligation	*You should/must close the window.* *Shouldn't you close the window?*
Refer to the action	*Close the window.* *You will close the window.* *Did you close the window?* *Don't you think you should do something?* (hedge)
Give a reason to act	*I want you to close the window.* *It's cold in here.* *There's a draught.*

1.10 Conventionalized and Standardized ISAs

indirect or direct, is produced in accordance to a convention of means. I fail to see why, on the basis of their semantic content, imperatives should be set apart from non-imperative directives. This view enables approaching direct and indirect realizations of directive SAs on equal terms. Accordingly, the semantic meaning of *I request that you close the window*, which can be used as a request, is that S performs a SA of requesting that A close the window. With an explicit performative utterance, S names the SA she intends to perform and, in so doing, she actually performs that SA. For other request forms, such as hedged performatives, several conventions of means are involved. (35), for instance, relates to permission and to A's ability/possibility to do the requested action.

(35) May I ask you if you could help me clean the dishes?

Once we have classified directive utterances in terms of conventions of means, we still have to account for the variety of request forms within a single convention of means, such as (7) and (36), which both express a question about A's ability to close the window.

(7) Can you close the window? (repeated)

(36) Are you able to close the window?

At first glance, the former seems more likely to give rise to the interpretation of an IR than the latter. But why is it so?

1.10.2 Standardization

The idea I explore in this section is that, in comparison with (36), the construction in (7) has developed, over time, a stronger association with its indirect request meaning. A possible empirical prediction is that it would be more frequently used as an IR than (36).

For Morgan (1978), the performance of IRs such as (7) involves a 'convention of use'. Such a convention amounts to the knowledge that some constructions can be used in a directive purpose. For Morgan, conventions of use give rise to short-circuited inferences between sentence meaning and the identification of the directive illocutionary meaning of the utterance. However, if the interpreter is not familiar with a convention (or if he is tired, distracted, has a pragmatic or hearing/reading impairment, etc.), he will have to follow a longer inferential path to access the indirect meaning. Thus, according to Morgan (1978), natural inferential schemes have 'conventionalized' over time, giving rise to short-circuited inferences. Even though Morgan is not very explicit on this point, no such short-circuited inference would be triggered by (35).

Unlike Morgan (1978), Bach and Harnish (1979) resist explaining the variety of sentences used for ISAs by one single 'convention'. The reason they give is that, for each and every construction that is regularly used indirectly with a directive meaning, such as, for instance, *Can you VP?*, one would have to hypothesize a distinct 'convention of use' associated with that construction. Postulating such conventions would go against the principle of economy of explanatory means (Occam's razor), according to which explanations should not be multiplied beyond necessity. Bach and Harnish therefore argue that the more general concept of 'standardization' is required to account for the variety of request forms. According to them, the frequency of use of, for instance, (7) with a directive illocutionary goal has led to the 'compression of the inference' from the literal meaning of *Can you VP?* (the meaning of a request for information about A's ability) to the indirect meaning. They thus consider that IRs such as (7) are 'standardized' inasmuch as the inferential route to the intended meaning has been short-circuited, leading 'the hearer ... [to identify] the speaker's requestive illocutionary intent without having to identify the literal intent of questioning' (1979: 198; see also Bach 1998). This analysis suggests the operation of a general cognitive principle that applies to an array of linguistic constructions with a diachronic dimension. Unlike the conventional/non-conventional distinction, Bach and Harnish's notion of standardization is also more representative of the variety of constructions used indirectly, some, such as *Can you VP?*, having a larger degree of standardization than others, such as *Are you able to VP?*. One possible way to objectivize differences in degrees of standardization is to compute the frequency of use of comparable expressions. Another prediction, in line with Morgan's (1978) idea of 'short-circuited inference' and Bach and Harnish's (1979) standardization hypothesis, is that the high degree of standardization of an expression enhances the likelihood that its indirect meaning will be primary. In other words, in highly standardized ISAs, the indirect meaning should not be inferred on the basis of another illocutionary meaning.

In a similar spirit, Clark (1979) contrasts 'conventions of means' with conventions concerning the wording of ISAs, which he calls 'conventions of form'. What Clark has in mind is that, for example, the request reading of (37) is more strongly associated with the words of the sentence relative to (38), a paraphrase of (37).

1.10 Conventionalized and Standardized ISAs

(37) Can you tell me the price for a fifth of Jim Beam?

(38) Is it possible for you/Are you able to tell me the price for a fifth of Jim Beam?

Conventions of form presuppose a diachronic process of standardization. Even though (37) and (38) follow from the same 'convention of means' (the preparatory condition of the directive SA), unlike *Can you VP?*, the forms *Is it possible to VP?* and *Are you able to VP?* have not been gradually associated with a request meaning over time (or less so). As a result, only in the case of (37) does the form of the utterance provide a clue towards the indirect meaning.

The distinction between standardized and non-standardized ISA constructions has given rise to some disagreement in formal pragmatics and in the philosophy of language. One example is the diverging views between Asher and Lascarides (2001) and Lepore and Stone (2015), who nonetheless both adopt formal semantic/pragmatic frameworks, that is, segmented discourse representation theory (SDRT), a recent development of discourse representation theory (DRT), and Hobbs's (1990) coherence theory, respectively. The co-occurrence patterns of IRs and *please* have been taken by Asher and Lascarides (2001) to support their dual account of ISAs. These authors start with the observation that only some IRs, such as (39a), can be responded to by a two-move answer, as in (39b).

(39) a Can you pass me the salt?
     b Sure (here you are). [Passes the salt]

For them, the appropriateness of responding both to the direct and the indirect meaning of an IR construction indicates that the utterance in (39a) performs 'two speech acts in one': it *both* has the illocutionary force of a request for information and that of a request for action. They propose that ISAs like *Can you VP?* are semantically incompatible types, as the semantic object of a question is a set of answers (more on this in Chapter 2), and that of a request is a relation between the world and action. Two necessary and sufficient conditions are given, which differentiate what I call 'standardized ISAs' from their non-standardized counterparts. The first condition is an incompatibility between semantic objects, and the second is a link between the direct interpretation and the indirect interpretation, grounded in Gricean principles of rationality and cooperation. To these conditions they add a principle of blocking, according to which possible paraphrases of (39a), such as

(40) and (41), for example, are not semantically requests, even though their IR meaning can be calculated in the Gricean sense.

(40) Are you able to pass me the salt?

(41) Is it possible for you to pass me the salt?

While some paraphrases are more natural than others, it is correct that not all of them are as standardized as (39a) is for the performance of IRs. The evidence they give in favour of their dual account consists in introspective data already discussed by Sadock (1974), who observed that the adverbials such as *please* and *since I have my hands full* cannot be added to any IR construction, and consider that *please* is not enabled by a syntactic type (i.e., the imperative), but by the semantic objects denoted by an utterance. They acknowledge that, on some occasions, the answer to the ability question in (39a) is already known by S, but they say that, even in these cases, the utterance both is a question and a request by virtue of the conventions of the English language. But note that the *Can you VP?* construction is only semi-productive, because it will not receive a request interpretation if the VP denotes a state instead of an action, as in (42).

(42) Can you hear at the back? (Asher & Lascarides 2001)

Asher and Lascarides thus make a strong case for a dual account of standardized IRs. However, a first problem with their proposal is that they infer, from the observation (based on acceptability judgements that are not always clear cut) that an utterance of *Can you VP?* 'behaves linguistically like both a request and a question', that it *is* both a request and a question. They determine its SA type on the basis of its semantic type. Another shortcoming of this approach, which heavily relies on the form of verbal responses to IRs, is that it does not explain why a positive answer to an interrogative used as an IR is optional. If a standardized IR utterance is both a question and a request, then why is it acceptable to respond only to the indirect meaning by doing the requested action? In my opinion, the optionality of responding to the direct meaning suggests that these utterances are *not* both a question and a request. At the semantic level, the utterance expresses a question, but, at the illocutionary level, it does not communicate a request for information. I will further substantiate this analysis in Chapter 2.

The same introspective data about the acceptability of *please* in ISA utterances has been taken by Lepore and Stone (2015: 98–106)

1.10 Conventionalized and Standardized ISAs

as evidence for the claim that *can* in *Can you VP?* is lexically ambiguous, a view also endorsed in Groefsema's (1992) account, which I will discuss alongside relevance theory in Chapter 3. Unlike Asher and Lascarides, Lepore and Stone do not consider that an IR such as *Can you VP?* is simultaneously a question and a request. Rather, they propose that IRs such as *Can you VP?* are ambiguous between these two interpretations. While acknowledging that the recognition of speakers' intentions plays a role in communication, they disagree with the traditional 'implicature' analysis of the relationship between the direct and indirect interpretations of ISA constructions. They argue that the fact that pragmatic principles of interpretation typified by Gricean implicatures are helpful for understanding creative uses of language, such as novel metaphors, is not a reason to apply them to highly routinized constructions such as *Can you VP?*. For them, the adverb *please* refers to a 'level of linguistic representation in which direct and indirect requests have the same status', as *please* can be added to imperative utterances and to highly standardized IR forms. For example, *Are you able to VP?*, a possible paraphrase of *Can you VP?*, cannot be modified with *please* (in a preverbal position), which shows that only the construction with *can* encodes the meaning of a request for action.

If I understand their proposal correctly, Lepore and Stone suggest that, if a particular IR construction modified with *please* is acceptable for native speakers, this is evidence that the construction is lexically ambiguous between a direct meaning and an indirect (request) meaning. It seems to me that such an account goes against the principle of economy of explanatory means (Occam's razor), according to which explanations should not be multiplied beyond necessity. In fact, if one tried to generalize these authors' analysis beyond *Can you VP?*, one would have to resort to ambiguity for a considerable number of constructions, including *Will you VP?*, *Would you mind VPing?* and *Shouldn't you VP?*, and also declarative constructions such as *I'd like you to VP* and *You should VP?* (providing they remain acceptable when *please* is included). I wonder whether the sort of ambiguity they attribute to *can* easily applies to ISA constructions that lack modal verbs.

Most of the examples I have provided relate to the preparatory condition about A's ability/possibility to carry out some action, which, in fact, often overshadows other conventions of means in the literature. We should not think, however, that differences of standardization only appear within this convention of means. For example, S's desire can be expressed using (43) or (44); in the latter case the indirect request meaning seems less easily accessible than in the former.

(43) I want you to close the window.

(44) I would be pleased if you would close the window.

The want statement in (43) is nonetheless different from the ability question in (39a), because a verbal response to the direct interpretation of the former, provided in (45), does not seem as appropriate as the positive answer in (39b):

(39) a   Can you pass me the salt? (repeated)
     b   Sure (here you are). [Passes the salt]

(45) That's right/indeed/sure you do.

In fact, even though empirical evidence is necessary to determine which of the aforementioned analyses is correct, it is not even certain that verbal responses to ISAs are reliable indicators of their actual illocutionary force. This is because a verbal response to an ISA that has the form of an interrogative does not entail that the ISA was understood as a literal request for information.

Summing up, in contrast with the binary distinction between so-called 'conventionalized' and 'non-conventionalized' ISAs (too often) assumed in the literature, I am endorsing a definition of *standardization* as a diachronic process by which a construction becomes more and more strongly associated with its indirect interpretation. This terminological choice enables me to avoid a recurrent problem in the literature, that is, that standardized ISAs are often referred to as 'conventional' ISAs. This notion of standardization is closely connected to the notion of frequency of use, and both can only be determined on the basis of a diachronic study complemented by a corpus analysis relativized to a context. Thus, indirect utterances such as (7) both are conventional and have a high degree of standardization qua directives.

(7) Can you close the window? (repeated)

While indirect directives may involve different conventions of means, only some of them, such as *Can you VP?* and *I'd like you to VP*, have a high degree of standardization. For the sake of readability, 'standardized' and 'non-standardized' will sometimes be used instead of 'highly standardized' and 'not very standardized', respectively.

1.11 SUMMARY

Historically, ISAs have been thought of as departures from conversational expectations such as Grice's maxims, while preserving cooperation between speakers and addressees. The idea of Gricean cooperation was retained in Searle's speech act theoretic approach, where a clear separation was assumed between the direct or 'literal' and indirect or 'non-literal' meaning of expressions such as *Can you VP?*. This chapter offered an overview of the variety of constructions that can be used with an indirect directive purpose, and several criteria that enable us to structure these constructions from a theoretical perspective. In addition to the formal criterion of indirectness proposed in speech act theory, we also considered that Recanati's cognitive distinction of primary versus secondary interpretation, and the difference between SA conventionality as a categorical criterion and the graded notion of standardization, are relevant to the study of ISAs.

In this chapter, we also saw that, following early generative semantic and speech act theoretic approaches, several contemporary accounts of the meaning encoded by the imperative sentence-type postulate a component of (directive) illocutionary force either at the syntactic or at the semantic level. These approaches make a reference – if only terminological – to the directive force in their definitions. What the processing models based on these literalist theories would have in common is the prediction that, at one level or another, the interpretation of any utterance of a declarative/interrogative/imperative sentence results in the activation of a component of the illocutionary force prototypically associated with each of these sentence-types. In Chapter 4, I will present evidence that this prediction is disconfirmed for interrogative and declarative sentences. Before that, however, I still have to unfold the semantic foundations of literalism, namely, why, unlike the interrogative and declarative English sentence-types, the imperative is strongly associated with the performance of requests for action. This is the topic of Chapter 2.

1.12 DISCUSSION QUESTIONS

- Ask someone who hasn't heard about ISAs before what ideas the words 'direct communication' and 'indirect communication' evoke for them. What theoretical distinctions would you relate these ideas to? What scientific disciplines?

- Would you say the literalist analysis of ISAs is a plausible option from a psychological point of view? Why so? What are, according to you, the main strengths/weaknesses of literalist approaches in general?
- So far we have mostly discussed indirect directive and assertive SAs. Do you think the literalist view of SAs could also be applied to other SA types, such as promises and expressive SAs?

1.13 SUGGESTIONS FOR FURTHER READING

For a very good discussion of early generative and speech act theoretic accounts of ISAs: Levinson (1983).

2 The Semantics of Sentence-Types

2.1 INTRODUCTION

While literalist accounts of ISAs provide a straightforward explanation of why imperative sentences give rise to the performance of directive SAs, they entail that any utterance having an illocutionary force that does not match the illocutionary potential of its sentence-type will be indirect or non-literal. The purpose of this chapter is to examine, instead, which features of the three main English sentence-types make these sentence-types compatible with the performance of (indirect) SAs. To do this, I will mainly be concerned with formal approaches to indirect communication. I will address, separately, the semantics of imperatives (Section 2.2), the semantics of interrogatives (Section 2.3) and the semantics of declaratives (Section 2.4). Unlike imperatives, a central feature of English interrogative sentences is that they can be conceived of as lying along with declaratives on a cline of informativeness. I will assume a semantic analysis of interrogative sentences that explains why they are used in the performance of direct requests for information and also why some of them can be used as indirect requests for action and rhetorical questions. Obligation declaratives *You should/must* VP used as directives will also be dealt with in Section 2.4, where I will draw a parallel between the imperative sentence-type and these obligation declaratives.

2.2 IMPERATIVES

2.2.1 Neo-Literalist Approaches to Imperatives

In the previous chapter I discussed 'weak literalist' approaches to ISAs, where SA types are defined in reference to the sentence-types typically associated with them. In line with 'strong literalist' accounts of ISAs, such as generative semantics and SAT, several scholars assume a biunivocal relationship between sentence-types and speech act types. In the case of the imperative sentence-type, for instance, they propose that requests for action performed with non-imperative sentences are indirect.

One such literalist account of illocutionary forces is Han's (1998, 2002). She postulates that the directive force of imperative sentences is directly encoded in their logical form. Like SAT, she explains away non-directive uses of imperatives by resorting to the notion of non-literalness. In the work on the morphosyntax of imperatives, such a literalist stance is actually one of the standard options (see, for instance, Isac 2015).

Han (1998) situates her account of imperatives within the framework of generative syntax. For her, imperative sentences have an 'imperative operator' encoded in their syntax. This imperative operator includes the [directive] feature, which encodes directive illocutionary force, and the [irrealis] feature, which contributes 'unrealized interpretation'. She takes it that the imperative operator contains a feature that encodes directive force – she calls this force 'directive' because this term reflects the canonical uses of imperative sentences. According to Han, the directive force of an imperative sentence turns the uttered sentence into a 'directive action'. This action amounts to instructing A to update his plan set, that is, the set of propositions that specify his intentions; these propositions represent the states of affairs that A intends to bring about. Uttering an imperative thus adds the action expressed by the imperative to A's plan set.

In line with her thesis that the grammar of imperatives encodes directive force, Han (1998: 156–57) considers that non-directive illocutionary acts performed with imperative sentences are necessarily non-literal. Let us consider, for example, a permission such as (1), in a context where A has made manifest his desire to come in.

(1) Come in, my dear! (COCA)

Because it is already known to the interlocutors that p is part of A's plan set, uttering the imperative (1) does not add p to A's plan set. In this case, contextual information blocks the directive interpretation grammatically encoded by the imperative. The illocutionary act of permission performed with the imperative (1) is therefore non-literal.

Another neo-literalist approach is that proposed by Portner (2004; 2007). Central to Portner's (2004) account is the notion of a 'to-do list', which resembles Han's plan set. A to-do list is the set of actions that an individual is committed to perform. For Portner, the participants in

2.2 Imperatives

a conversation mutually assume that each of them will try to perform the actions corresponding to his/her own to-do list. Furthermore, unlike in SAT, Portner (2004) considers that imperative sentences do not express propositions, but, rather, properties that can be true only of addressees. In that respect, imperatives contrast with declaratives, which encode propositions, and interrogatives, which encode sets of propositions. According to Portner (2004), the utterance of the imperative sentence *p!* by a speaker contributes to the addressee's to-do list by adding the property *p* to it. For instance, uttering *Leave!* adds the property of leaving to the addressee's to-do list by virtue of the 'conventional force' of imperatives. Portner calls such 'conventional force' of imperatives the 'force of requiring'. The differences between particular directive sub-types performed with imperatives can be explained by the pragmatic parameters underlying S's attempt to add a property on A's to-do list. For example, in the case of a command, what makes it possible for S to add *p* on A's to-do list is her power or social authority. By contrast, in a request, the grounds for adding a property on A's to-do list would be S's benefit. In the case of permissions, the property added to A's to-do list is one that is already desired by A.

An indication that Portner's proposal is literalist is that the only raison d'être of the properties expressed by imperatives is to become part of to-do lists. Another reason to consider that this proposal is literalist is that, in Portner's analysis, all imperative sentences share the 'force of requiring', the definition of which is similar to a definition of generic directive illocutionary force provided in SAT, but it is unclear whether the reference to 'requiring' is really meant as a subtype of directive force. That being said, as with Han's proposal, Portner's analysis comes close to SAT's analysis of the relationship between sentence-types and SA types.

A third neo-literalist analysis according to which imperatives encode properties of addressees is Mastop's (2005; 2011) proposal. Mastop develops a formal semantics of imperatives in the framework of 'update semantics'. A basic tenet of update semantics is that the meaning of a sentence should be understood as the change it can bring about in the cognitive state of the person who hears/reads an utterance of that sentence. Mastop proposes that, just as a declarative expresses an informative message, an imperative expresses a 'directive message', which he calls an *instruction*. Even though Mastop does not make any reference to Han's (1998) notion of instruction, the two notions seem equivalent. For Mastop (2005: 98–114), the goal of uttering an imperative is to expand the addressee's schedule with the action denoted by the verbal phrase (VP). If the addressee accepts the instruction expressed by the imperative, he will be committed to perform the action. For instance, accepting the imperative in (2) results in the addressee's schedule being updated with the commitment to close the window.

(2) Close the window.

Building on Hamblin's (1972; 1987) notion of a 'commitment slate', Mastop formally represents an instruction as an update function that transforms one commitment slate (set of rules that an individual is supposed to follow) into another commitment slate. Thus, in the case of (2), A's set of rules for his behaviour will be updated with the addition of a commitment, that is, his future closing of the window, resulting in a new commitment slate (set of rules).

Mastop's approach is a literalist proposal insofar as he resorts to the notion of instructions, a subtype of directives, to analyze the meaning of simple imperative sentences. His analysis also entails a terminological confusion: in what sense is the message expressed by an imperative sentence a 'directive' message? Even though further clarification is required, I would suggest that Mastop's notion of a 'directive message' should not be equated with 'directive force', and that these two notions refer to distinct levels of meaning: his 'instructions' belong to the semantics of utterances, and they have the potential of directive SAs.

Summing up, despite small differences in concepts and theoretical backgrounds, these three accounts share a literalist component: they all make a reference to illocutionary forces in their analysis of the imperative sentence-type. From their perspective, directive SAs performed with non-imperative sentences are indirect, as they depart from a pattern that is not necessarily encoded by (as SAT claims), but, at least, associated with the semantics of a particular sentence-type.

2.2.2 The Features of Imperatives

In contrast to the literalist approaches, I believe one should define the meaning of imperative sentences without referring to any component of (directive) illocutionary force. Such a stance would do justice to the variety of non-directive SAs that are performed with imperatives while keeping distinct the levels of sentence meaning (semantic) and illocutionary meaning (pragmatic). I will therefore ask which semantics features can, taken together, explain the pragmatic properties of imperatives and, in particular, why they are predisposed to the performance of directive SAs.

2.2 Imperatives

2.2.2.1 Imperatives Are Addressee-Oriented

A property that uniquely characterises imperative sentences concerns their subject: imperatives are understood in terms of a reference to an addressee which is typically identified with the referent of the subject. Katz and Postal (1964: 75) alluded to this when they claimed that English imperative sentences involve 'the necessity of a *you* subject'. Empirical evidence for this view comes from tag questions such as (3) and reflexive verbs as in (4).

(3) Be on time, will you/*he?

(4) Wash yourself/*herself.

An interesting issue about addressee reference concerns perspectival differences between declaratives and imperatives – what Mastop (2005: 32–3) calls 'perspectival dualism'. According to him, it is not totally correct to say that, for example, the declarative (5) and its imperative counterpart (6) depict the same situation or event.

(5) Mary buys a sports car.

(6) Mary, buy a sports car!

Let us imagine being Mary, the subject of (5) and the addressee of (6). She would be the person one is talking about in the case of (5), and an agent in the case of (6). Mastop argues that, whereas the declarative is about 'something that we can imagine perceiving', the imperative is about 'something we can imagine doing', the agent being part of what is imagined. The imperative (6) thus represents the event depicted by (5), but from the perspective of the agent. Imperatives are therefore addressee-oriented in a sense that declaratives are not.

Even though second-person subject imperatives are very common in English, they are not the whole story. Imperatives with generic subjects, such as (7), are also possible.

(7) Someone close the door.

As noted by Davies (1986), many expressions can be used as subjects of imperative sentences, including quantificational expressions as in (8)–(9), and bare noun phrases as in (10).

(8) Don't anybody move. (COCA)

(9) All competitors please note: dream tan is not allowed at this venue. (https://bit.ly/3f7AsNI)

(10) The man with the list come up here. (Davies 1986)

It is often held that 'third-person' imperatives such as (9)–(10) are understood as referring to a second person (Davies 1986; Takahashi 2012). The idea is that the definite description in (10) is used instead of a second-person pronoun to pick out which individual(s) in the audience is/are the addressee(s).

The introspective judgements discussed thus far suggest that the referent of the subject of an imperative sentence is not necessarily equivalent to the individual to whom the imperative is addressed. Two sorts of cases can be distinguished. On the one hand, in cases where the identity of the subject and that of the addressee do not coincide, the addressee(s) must be a subset of the subject's referents, as in (11).

(11) You and your friends get this mess cleared up before you go out. (Davies 1986: 140)

On the other hand, if the addressee is not included in the referents of the subject, as in the case of (12), the imperative will be understood as a directive that the addressee should perform by addressing the individuals concerned.

(12) Those children of yours keep out of my garden, or I'll set the dog on them. (Davies 1986: 141)

What these two sorts of examples indicate is that, even when the addressee of an imperative is not identical to the referent of its subject, the imperative is nevertheless addressee-oriented.

According to the theories addressed thus far, the properties of the subjects of imperative sentences are analyzed at the semantics–pragmatics interface. However, this need not necessarily be so. For instance, Zanuttini (2008) puts forward the view that the properties of imperative subjects are best explained by the syntactic representation of these sentences. According to her proposal, an imperative sentence encodes a reference to the addressee of the utterance by means of a functional projection – called 'Jussive phrase (JussiveP)' – with second-person features. The head of the JussiveP enters an agreement relation with the subject of the imperative, whereby the subject inherits the second-person features.

2.2 Imperatives

A related syntactic issue concerns the optionality of mentioning the subject of an imperative. Imperative sentences contrast with declaratives and interrogatives insofar as they 'need not and typically do not contain a subject at all' (Davies 1986: 131). The pair (13)–(14) illustrates how the possibility to perform a command with or without using the second person pronoun may cause differences in the pragmatic interpretations of imperatives.

(13) You leave!

(14) Leave!

For instance, according to Langacker (2008: 469), in (13), the second-person pronoun is used emphatically, and the addressee is encoded as an interlocutor and as a participant in the future event consisting in his leaving. By contrast, in (14) the addressee is only conceptualized as an interlocutor. For Langacker, mentioning a second-person subject will result in a distancing effect, and the command will therefore be perceived as more formal than when the subject is lacking.

2.2.2.2 Imperatives Depict Potential States of Affairs

The second feature that is, arguably, part of the semantics of imperative sentences is the notion of potentiality. While imperative sentences do not depict states of affairs in a speaker's world, that is, in her actual world, they nonetheless refer to states of affairs in alternative, possible worlds.

In Davies's (1986: 47–8) words, an imperative sentence presents a potential state of affairs. The view that imperatives encode potentiality makes it possible to account for examples in which the state of affairs referred to, already settled in the actual world, is presented as unsettled from S's perspective. In a similar vein, Wilson and Sperber (1988) take 'achievability' and 'desirability' to characterize imperative sentences. Imperatives are, according to them, specialized for descriptions of states of affairs in potential and desirable worlds (see also Sperber and Wilson 1995). Consider, for example, (15) said by a mother to her child:

(15) Oh please, don't have said anything rude!

In (15), the state of affairs referred to is potential relative to S's states of information; as far as she knows, it is potential for her that A has not said anything rude on that specific occasion.

According to Takahashi (2012: 71–2), there is a feature of the imperative, distinct from potentiality, which is 'non-past'. For him, the imperative is future-oriented, as the contrast between (16) and (17) illustrates:

(16) Talk with your doctor now/tomorrow/next month. (Takahashi 2012: 71)

(17) Talk with your doctor *yesterday/*last month.

While it is true that many imperatives refer to prospective states of affairs, Takahashi's point here is that the state of affairs alluded to by the imperative is non-past with respect to S's particular point of view, but not necessarily with respect to the time of utterance. For instance, in the case of (15), it is not the state of affairs evoked by the sentence but, rather, S's knowledge about what happened that is presented as 'non-past'. One should therefore avoid equating potential with 'non-past'. Because the states of affairs evoked by imperative sentences may belong to the past, but nonetheless are always presented as potential, 'non-past' should not be considered a specific property of imperative sentences and the notion of potentiality should be preferred instead.

If imperatives indeed refer to potential states of affairs, the conjunction of an imperative and a clause that denies the potentiality of the state of affairs depicted by the imperative should be pragmatically inconsistent. Examples (18)–(20) suggest that this is the case.

(18) ? Open the window, but you can't.

(19) ? It's impossible to do that, but open the window.

(20) ? Sleep well, but you won't sleep.

The second part of these utterances would cancel the 'pragmatic implication' of the first part, that is, the assumption that it is possible for A to open the window or to sleep well, which would be irrational for S to do (sadistic readings set aside).

Because they encode potentiality, imperative sentences cannot be used to represent actual states of affairs – in other words, they lack assertoric potential (Jary & Kissine 2014: 89–91; Mastop 2005: 44–54). For instance, the propositional content of the imperative cannot be said to be true of false, even if one believes that it will never be actual, as

(21)–(24) respectively illustrate. This is a major difference between imperatives and declaratives.

(21) S: Open the window. – A: #Yes, that's true, I will.

(22) S: Open the window. – A: #No, that's not true, I will never do that.

(23) S: You will open the window. – A: Yes, that's true, I will.

(24) S: You will open the window. – A: No, that's not true, I will not do that.

To conclude, I believe that the combination of these two features, namely, 'addressee-oriented' and 'referring to a state of affairs presented as potential' help explain why the imperative sentence-type can be used in the performance of directives. As it semantically encodes these two features, it lends itself straightforwardly to the ascription of future actions (directives) or future properties (expressives) to addressees.

2.3 INTERROGATIVE SENTENCES

2.3.1 What Is a 'Question'?

Before addressing the relationship between the meaning of interrogative sentences and the direct and indirect illocutionary forces of interrogative utterances, a terminological clarification is in order.

The term *question* has several definitions, depending on the level of meaning involved (Aloni et al. 2007). This polysemy is responsible for some confusion in the literature. From an epistemological perspective, a *question* is something people can be concerned with – an issue. At the syntactic level, the word *question* can be used to refer to a linguistic entity with certain features such as inverted word order, *wh*- expressions (*what, who, where, when,* etc.), a question mark (property of written sentences), and rising intonation. For the sake of convenience, I will call such entities *interrogative sentences*. At the semantic level, question refers to the semantic denotation of interrogative sentences. To keep things as clear as possible, I will follow Groenendijk and Stokhof (1997) and Aloni et al. (2007) and use *question* only in this latter sense. Finally, at the pragmatic level, the term *question* can be understood as 'asking someone to answer a question', something I will be referring to as the speech act of *questioning* (Table 2.1).

Table 2.1 *Syntactic, semantic and pragmatic notions of question*

Syntactic notion	Interrogative
Semantic notion	Question
Pragmatic notion	Questioning
	(= 'S asking a question to be answered by A')

In Chapter 1, I endorsed a purely formal definition of the three major English sentence-types (imperative, interrogative and declarative). In this chapter, following, for instance, Sadock and Zwicky (1985) and Fiengo (2007), I will assume the existence of several, formally distinct, interrogative sentence-types such as (25)–(28).

(25) Er Miss (– – –) what did you do next? (BNC)

(26) Did you close the door? (COCA)

(27) Did you or did you not lie to me? (COCA)

(28) So you didn't see anything ... didn't hear anything? (COCA)

The interrogative (25) expresses a *wh-* or 'open' question; the set of possible answers to the question is potentially infinite. (26) expresses a polar question, as the answer typically has the form of 'yes' or 'no'. (27) is a disjunctive question, which is typically answered either with 'yes, I did' or 'no, I did not'. (28) is a non-inverted interrogative (also called 'rising declarative'), with a confirmation as typical answer. I will use the question mark as a conventional shorthand to indicate the rising intonation of (28), which contrasts it with the declarative in (29), where the period signals falling intonation.

(29) So you didn't see anything ... didn't hear anything.

In English, open, polar and disjunctive interrogatives are characterized by inverted word order, but this feature does not apply to 'rising declaratives' such as (28).[1] Despite this label, sentences such as (28)

---

[1] Note that non-inverted open interrogatives such as *I could do what?* are also possible, albeit mainly in 'echo' contexts. Unlike in English, French polar questions are generally asked with non-inverted interrogatives, as in *Tu as mangé ?* ('You have eaten?'). Another possibility is the interrogative particle *est-ce que* as in *Est-ce que tu*

2.3 Interrogative Sentences

belong to an interrogative sentence-type insofar as they have an interrogative component – rising intonation – which makes them a convenient means to perform the SA of questioning. As we will see, there are arguments for thinking that, on a cline of 'questionhood', such constructions represent intermediate cases between prototypical declaratives and prototypical interrogative sentences as they share features of both sentential categories. However, in what follows, I will be focusing on polar interrogatives such as (26).

(26) Did you close the door? (repeated)

One such polar interrogative construction, *Can you VP?*, is frequently used in the performance of IRs.

2.3.2 Why Interrogative Requests for Information Are Direct

A possible starting point to address the semantics of interrogatives is to consider the literalist view that interrogative sentences encode the directive force of questioning, which makes them the most convenient tools for requesting information.

2.3.2.1 *Interrogative Sentences versus Speech Act of Questioning*

In Searle's (1969) SAT, questioning is a special case of request for action, that is, a request for an answer. In line with SAT's literalism, interrogative sentences are said to encode the force of questioning, whereas imperative sentences encode the force of other directives except questioning. In the same vein, in line with her literalist analysis of imperatives, Han (1998; 2002) considers that, in their syntax, interrogative sentences contain an operator that indicates the force of questioning. For Searle and Vanderveken (1985: 199–200), since directives in general constitute attempts to get A to do some action, asking a question amounts to 'request[ing] that [A] perform a speech act to the speaker, the form of which is already determined by the propositional content of the question'. For instance, asking whether *p* is asking A to perform a true assertion with the propositional content that *p* or that ¬*p*. A similar view is endorsed by Schiffer (1972: 85–6, 103). Bach and Harnish (1979: 47–9) too consider that questioning is a subtype of directives. For them, questioning consists in the expression of (a) S's desire that A tell S what is the answer to the question and (b) of

---

as mangé ? ('Did you eat?') In everyday French, both constructions are much more common than the corresponding inverted interrogative *As-tu mangé ?* ('Did you eat?'), which is restricted to more formal settings.

S's intention that A tell S what is the answer to the question because of S's desire.

Unlike SAT, some authors consider that questioning should not be conceived of as a type of directive. For instance, for Groenendijk and Stokhof (1997), a crucial difference between questioning and other directives is that questioning does not require a change in the world, but, rather, a change in *information about* the world. These authors acknowledge that (obviously) information about the world is also part of the world, but they stress that it is so only in a secondary sense, and that one should therefore keep these two levels apart. I agree with Groenendijk and Stokhof that one should not confuse the physical world with the second-order information about the physical world. However, even on the definition of directive SAs they assume (i.e., as requests for action), questioning still belongs to the category of directives, as providing information by answering a question is still a sort of (motor) action. I will therefore assume, in line with Searle and Vanderveken (1985), that questioning is a special type of directive because it amounts to requesting A to perform an action, that is, to provide some piece of information.

In SAT, the SAs of requests for action in general and the SAs of questioning differ in several respects. For requests for action, the propositional content condition is that S refers to A's future action. For questioning, the propositional content is less constrained (it must be a proposition or a propositional function), and it is necessary that S does not know the answer to the question. Another preparatory condition for questioning is that A is able to answer the question asked (albeit not necessarily to provide the exact information). Rather than counting as an answer to the question, expressing ignorance would be an appropriate response in such cases. 'Real' questions are distinguished from 'exam' questions (*What happened at Waterloo?*), in which S does not want or need to know the answer, but, rather, wants to know whether A knows it. For SAT, all other possible uses of interrogative sentences are considered non-literal.

It is true that, in many cases, when people utter an interrogative sentence, such as (30), they are intending that their addressee provide them with an answer.

(30) What's your name? (BYU–BNC, Davies 2004)

However, one can utter an interrogative sentence without necessarily requiring an answer (Wilson and Sperber 1988). As there is no biunivocal relation between interrogatives and the SA of questioning, the SA

2.3 Interrogative Sentences

of questioning can be performed with an imperative or a declarative sentence, as (31)–(32) illustrate, respectively.

(31) 'Tell me your name, boy! Quick!' he said, still holding me. (BYU–BNC)

(32) Come on young man, I want to know your name. (BYU–BNC)

In addition, uttering an interrogative sentence can perform a variety of illocutionary acts distinct from the SA of requesting an answer to the question asked, such as the following (Wilson and Sperber 1988; the list is not exhaustive):

(33) Peter has made a New Year's resolution to give up smoking. As he lights up on New Year's Day, Mary says to him: What was your New Year's resolution? (rhetorical question)

(34) Mary hides a sweet in her hand, puts both hands behind her back, and says to John: Which hand is it in? (guess question)

(35) Peter: The president has resigned.
Mary: Good heavens. Has he? (surprise question)

(36) How are non-declarative sentences understood? (expository question)

(37) What is the best analysis of interrogative sentences? (speculative question)

In fact, expository and speculative questions do constitute attempts by S to arrive at some information, albeit in a tentative manner: an expository question indicates that the information that will follow consists in a possible answer to the question, and asking a speculative question may initiate a reasoning process which leads the addressee (or, rather, the recipient) towards an answer to the question. Interrogative sentences can also be used to inform by means of a presupposition, as in (38), and, of course, to request A to perform an action (and not to answer the question), as in (39), an example I will analyse in some detail in Section 2.3.4.

(38) Did you know that Bill is getting married? (informative SA)

(39) Will you close the window? (request for action)

It also makes sense to consider that, when an interrogative is used as a title for an article, as in (40), even if the recipient is presented with a question, he is not requested to answer it. In fact, it is almost as if the author of the question herself proposes to provide it with an answer.

(40) What is a speech act?

According to SAT, the variety of SAs performed by interrogatives such as (33), (34), (35), (36), (37) and (40) would count as non-literal because, in all these cases, the essential condition for the SA of questioning is not met, that is, S's utterance is not an 'attempt' to get A to answer the question asked. A search for a non-literal interpretation will then be triggered. Possible literal counterparts of (33), (34), (38) and (39) are, respectively, *Your New Year's resolution was to give up smoking*, *Guess which hand it is in!*, *Bill is getting married*, and *Close the window*. Furthermore, these examples suggest that postulating the force of requesting information in the meaning of interrogatives does not do justice to the polyvalence of this sentence-type. More generally, outside the framework of SAT, one fails to see why it is the force of questioning rather than any of the other illocutionary forces illustrated in (33)–(40) that interrogatives are taken to encode.

A more decisive argument against the view that interrogative sentences encode the force of questioning relates to typology. Implicit in SAT is the claim that basic SAs correspond to basic sentence-types. However, there is evidence that typologically diverse languages do not treat interrogative sentences as a special case of imperative sentences, but, rather, that all languages have distinct interrogative and imperative sentence-types, whether distinct by means of syntax or intonation (e.g., Zaefferer 1990). This actually makes the claim that interrogatives encode the force of questioning counter-intuitive.

In sum, theoretical and empirical considerations suggest that it is preferable to analyze the meaning of interrogatives independently of considerations about illocutionary force. What, then, makes interrogative sentence-types convenient tools for performing directives?

2.3.2.2 What Do Interrogative Sentences Encode?

Several theories of the meaning of interrogatives have been proposed, and I will not attempt to address all of them here. Rather, I will concentrate on two major contemporary frameworks: relevance theory and inquisitive semantics. According to these approaches, the meaning of interrogative sentences is best captured by taking into account their 'answerhood' conditions, that is, the conditions defining the possible

2.3 Interrogative Sentences

answers to the question. Under such conceptions, understanding an interrogative sentence is possible only if one knows what counts as an answer to it. As we will see in Section 2.4, this view parallels the view that, to know what a declarative sentence means, it is necessary to know under which conditions it is true.

2.3.2.2.1 Relevance Theory. The notion of 'desirability' is central to Wilson and Sperber's (1988) analysis of the meaning of interrogative sentences. In relevance theory (RT), a conceptual representation (a thought) or an assumption (a thought about the actual world) is desirable only if it yields enough contextual effects for the addressee to make this representation worth processing (Sperber & Wilson 1995: 250–51). According to them, an interrogative is a representation that itself represents another thought in virtue of a resemblance between the two representations. In such cases, the first representation is used 'interpretively' to represent what S takes to be relevant answers to the question expressed by the interrogative. That is, interrogatives are doubly interpretive in the sense that they represent a thought of the speaker's, which is itself a representation of another thought or utterance. For these authors, a *wh-* interrogative represents the completions of the incomplete logical form it expresses. In addition, the most relevant completion, that is, the most relevant answer, which minimizes cognitive effort for the interpreter while maximizing the cognitive effects, would be the one corresponding to the truth of the proposition expressed by the interrogative. Thus, positive polar interrogatives such as (26) indicate that a positive answer would be more relevant than a negative one.

(26) Did you close the door? (repeated)

For a negative polar interrogative such as (41), the negative answer would be more relevant, and for disjunctive interrogatives such as (27), both answers would be equally relevant.

(41) Didn't you feel the same? (https://bit.ly/38UlkSw)

(27) Did you or did you not lie to me? (repeated)

Wilson and Sperber (1988) do not discuss non-inverted interrogatives such as (42).

(42) John will close the window?

Assuming that (42) indeed is an interrogative, a positive answer to the question should be considered as being the most relevant. This would be in line with the view that the typical move following (42) would be a confirmation.

According to RT, in order to resolve the semantic under-determinacy of interrogative sentences, A must make an assumption about the individual to whom S is suggesting that an answer to the question expressed would be regarded as desirable. Thus, at the pragmatic level, S may be taken as indicating that she regards the answer to the question as relevant either to herself or to A. The cases where the answer is regarded as relevant to S are 'ordinary' questions (requests to answer questions), exam questions, requests for action in general, guess questions, surprise questions, self-addressed questions; further contextual assumptions are needed to distinguish between this variety of interpretations. For instance, exam and guess questions differ from ordinary questions in that they involve S's being manifestly in a better position than A to know the answer. The cases where the answer is regarded as relevant to A encompass expository and rhetorical questions. In expository questions, S makes it manifest that she knows the answer and is prepared to provide it, while in the case of rhetorical questions S expects A to know the answer or to be in a position such that he can infer it by himself.

A central tenet of RT, which is shared by other recent approaches, is that what interrogatives are taken to encode involves a reference to the notion of answer. In addition, RT's account of the meaning of interrogatives is compatible with the view that interrogatives are the expression of a lack of information. We will see that, at the semantic level, such an incompleteness of the propositional content is sufficient to characterize the meaning of interrogatives, and to differentiate it from that of imperatives.

2.3.2.2.2 Interrogatives, Declaratives and (In)Completeness. Contemporary approaches to interrogatives assume that interrogative sentences express questions, understood as semantic objects. One influential approach to the meaning of questions is Groenendijk and Stokhof's (1984) partition theory. According to partition theory, interrogative sentences denote a function that partitions the logical space of possibilities. Each block within the partition stands for one possible answer. To be more precise, each block stands for the set of possible worlds in which a given answer is true, while only one block of the partition contains the actually true answer to the question. For instance, in the case of *wh*- interrogatives, assuming that, in the universe of the model,

2.3 Interrogative Sentences

| John will (but Mary won't). | Mary will (but John won't). |
| Mary won't and John won't. | Both John and Mary will. |

Figure 2.1 Partition of the logical space corresponding to the meaning of the interrogative in example (43)

| John is closing the window. | John is not closing the window. |

Figure 2.2 Partition of the logical space corresponding to the meaning of the interrogatives in examples (44)–(45)

there are only two individuals, John and Mary, the sentence (43) returns the partition in Figure 2.1.

(43) Who will close the window?

The idea of partition theory is that, in using interrogative sentences, speakers express an interest in knowing in which block of the partition the actual world resides. A distinction can then be made between a 'potentially complete answer', which is a proposition corresponding to one single block of the partition, and a 'partial answer', which is a proposition that eliminates at least one block of the partition, but on the basis of which one cannot locate the actual world in a single block. A 'true complete answer' singles out the block of the partition to which the actual world belongs. For polar interrogatives such as (44), a bipartition of the space of possibilities is returned (Figure 2.2); it is reasonable to suppose that things would not be different for (45), the non-inverted counterpart of (44).

(44) Is John closing the window?

(45) John is closing the window?

Thus, according to partition theory, what interrogative sentences encode makes them a convenient means to convey ignorance on the part of the speaker as to which block of the partition expressed by the question the actual world belongs to.

Another recent framework concerned with the meaning of interrogatives, and which includes later elaborations on and criticism of standard partition theory, is inquisitive semantics (IS) (see, e.g., Ciardelli et al.

2013; 2015; Groenendijk 2007). IS follows the trend of dynamic semantics, that we have already discussed in relation to Mastop's 'to-do list' account of imperatives, according to which the meaning of a sentence resides in its update potential, that is, in the possible changes the sentence can cause in the informational states of interlocutors or in the 'common ground'. For instance, according to IS, the declarative sentence (46) expresses the proposition corresponding to all the worlds in which it is true that the president will attend the meeting.

(46) The president will attend a memorial service in Newtown later today. (COCA)

The set of possibilities expressed by (46) contains only one alternative, namely that the president will attend the meeting. In IS, a sentence is informative if, at least in some context, it eliminates some worlds from the set of worlds the actual world belongs to. Sentence (46) is therefore informative because it proposes only one possible update to the information mutually shared by the interlocutors. This explains why declaratives such as (46) are useful tools to perform 'assertive' SAs such as statements and predictions: they provide information without requesting any further completion.

In contrast to an informative sentence, a sentence is inquisitive if it distinguishes between two worlds. For instance, according to IS, the polar interrogative (47) expresses a proposition consisting in two alternatives, which correspond to the set of worlds in which the president will attend the meeting and to those in which he will not attend the meeting, respectively.

(47) Will the president attend a memorial service in Newtown later today?

Because the IS framework aims at capturing both informative and inquisitive contents, it addresses not only interrogatives such as (47), but all inquisitive constructions in general, including 'hybrid' declarative sentences – sentences that have both an informative component and an inquisitive component – such as (48).

(48) I forgot my keys somewhere. (https://bit.ly/3ny49dJ)

In IS, lexical items such as indefinite noun phrases (e.g., *somewhere*) are taken to encode inquisitiveness. For example, while (48) can be used by S to convey a piece of information about her keys and her

2.3 Interrogative Sentences

forgetfulness, it can also be used to raise an issue about her keys ('Where are my keys?'), which is a possible way for S to request information about her keys. Interestingly, in IS, interrogative sentences are considered on a par with declarative sentences. To the best of my knowledge, imperative sentences are excluded from the IS framework. As the discussion in Section 2.2 made clear, it is theoretically untenable to define the meaning of imperatives as a call for propositional completion or as an offer of such completion. If an imperative sentence calls for completion, it is by way of the lexical meaning of the main verb or because of its embedded interrogative propositional content, as in *Tell me what's your name*, not by virtue of any feature of the imperative sentence-type.

Thus, according to the IS framework, interrogative sentences are a convenient means for displaying ignorance because they have an inquisitive content. Albeit in a less standard approach to meaning, Fiengo (2007) too builds on the observation that interrogative sentences are tools that are incomplete in one respect or another. He proposes that displaying such incompleteness enables speakers to get missing information from addressees, and that different interrogative sentence-types are associated with different sorts of incompleteness.

First, in *wh*- interrogatives, there is an incompleteness in what is expressed, which is reflected by the logical form (49b) of a sentence such as (49a).

(49) a   Who is John talking to?
      b   [who$_x$ [John is talking to x]]

According to Fiengo, interrogatives do not encode requests for information, but there is a convention of use according to which speakers use incomplete sentences so that their addressees provide them with some information.

Second, in a polar interrogative such as (26), the proposition expressed is incomplete in that what joins the predicate and the subject – what Fiengo calls the 'glue' – is lacking.

(26) Did you close the door? (repeated)

In (26), it is not the case that the closing of the door is predicated of the subject 'you'; rather, such a predication relationship is presented as being at issue. For Fiengo, using an interrogative sentence is a way of signalling that one questions whether a predicate applies to an item. As in the IS framework, for him, (in)completeness is a graded notion that is also relevant to the analysis of declarative sentences. For instance, (51) involves a higher degree of completeness relative to (50) because it contains more information about Jack's action.

(50) Jack ate.

(51) Jack ate an apple.

The same analysis applies to interrogatives: (52) is less complete or 'more inquisitive' than (53), as the worlds in which Jack ate an apple are a subset of the worlds in which he ate (something).

(52) Did Jack eat?

(53) Did Jack eat an apple?

According to Fiengo, in the case of interrogatives, the standard of completeness is given by declaratives; accordingly, (5) is the complete version of (26).

(5) You closed the window. (repeated)

(26) Did you close the window? (repeated)

Third, Fiengo also analyzes English interrogatives such as (54), which consist in non-inverted declarative sentences with rising intonation or, for the sake of simplicity, 'non-inverted interrogatives'.[2]

(54) You closed the window?

This is because they pattern in some respects with declaratives, and in other respects with inverted interrogatives (Gunlogson 2002: 126–30). On the one hand, like inverted interrogatives, non-inverted interrogatives do not commit the speaker to their propositional content. For instance, non-inverted interrogatives may be used to convey the information that the addressee is in a better position than the speaker to

---

[2] The interrogative in (54) is what Fiengo (2007) calls a 'confirmation interrogative'. Contrary to what this label suggests, it is by no means obvious (especially in French) that the only possible use of a sentence such as (54) is to ask a confirmation question. For instance, the French equivalent of (54), *Tu as fermé la fenêtre ?*, can be used to remind A that he was supposed to close the window.

2.3 Interrogative Sentences

know whether the proposition expressed is true. On the other hand, non-inverted interrogatives resemble their declarative counterparts because both of them are unacceptable in contexts where S is expected to remain neutral as to the question under discussion. For instance, the rising (55b) cannot be used to request information without committing S to some prejudice about A to the same extent as (55a) (Gunlogson 2002: 126).

(55) (in a job interview)
    a   Have you been convicted of a felony?
    b   #You've been convicted of a felony?
    c   #You've been convicted of a felony.

For Fiengo, the sort of incompleteness characterizing non-inverted interrogatives resides in the using of the sentence, that is, at the SA level. In uttering (54), S would represent herself as having not enough confidence to perform an assertive SA. That being said, it is unclear whether Fiengo assumes that non-inverted interrogatives also involve incompleteness at the level of the propositional content of the sentence.

Let me sum up the crucial assumptions about the meaning of interrogatives that are shared by the theories I have discussed. The meaning of an interrogative sentence involves some kind of ignorance either relative to some information that is lacking in the proposition expressed (open interrogatives) or relative to the truth/falsity of the proposition expressed (polar interrogatives). Non-inverted interrogatives are special in that they do not encode ignorance at the propositional level, but, rather, at the SA level, which makes them a convenient means for asking confirmation questions. We saw that the assumption that interrogatives express S's ignorance is particularly salient within the IS framework. According to partition theory, with interrogatives, the logical space of possibilities is divided up in blocks; such a partition implies S's ignorance as to which block of the partition the actual world belongs to. For Fiengo, interrogative sentence-types are characterized by their incompleteness. Likewise, in a neo-Gricean approach such as the relevance-theoretic framework, interrogatives are taken to express a lack of information.

Following the insights of IS and Fiengo's (2007) approach, it is thus a safe bet to conceive of both the declarative and the interrogative sentence-types in terms of degrees of informativeness and inquisitiveness. Bolinger (1977) had already suggested that the variety of declaratives and interrogatives could be regarded as a cline ranging, at one end, from sentences typically used to perform the SA of questioning,

THE SEMANTICS OF SENTENCE-TYPES

Figure 2.3 Continuum of informativeness/inquisitiveness for conceptualizing declarative and interrogative sentence-types (event: John's coming)

such as the open interrogative (56), to, at the other end, prototypical assertions performed with declaratives such as (57).

(56) Who came?

(57) John came.

Examples such as (58)–(59) illustrate intermediate positions. I have ordered them in Figure 2.3 along their degree of semantic informativeness, with (57) being the most informative.

(58) Did John come?

(59) John came?

I leave aside the issue of how variations in the form of declaratives and interrogatives modulate the resulting illocutionary forces of asserting and questioning. What is important for my purposes is that, unlike imperatives, interrogatives and declaratives are best conceptualized in terms of relative degrees of (in)completeness in their informational content. I have therefore translated Bolinger's question-to-assertion cline into a scale of informativeness/inquisitiveness corresponding to different degrees of (in)completeness. Declarative sentences are located at the left end of the cline, and open interrogatives at the right end; non-inverted interrogatives and polar interrogatives occupy intermediate positions (Figure 2.3). Bolinger's cline is discussed – and further developed – by Levinson (2012). However, unlike Levinson, I interpret this cline in semantic terms. That is, I analyze the degrees of (in)completeness associated with these sentence-types regardless of the illocutionary acts performed with them.

This cline also makes sense from the perspective of Groenendijk and Stokhof's (1984) partition theory, where open interrogatives such as (25) entail polar interrogatives such as (26).

2.3 Interrogative Sentences

(25) What did you do next? (repeated)

(26) Did you close the door? (repeated)

This is because in (25) more information is lacking than in (26), where the range of questionables is narrowed to two alternatives (A closed the door, A didn't close the door). Thus (56) is located at the right end of the scale because it expresses a maximal range of alternatives (a plurality of possible worlds), and (57), which expresses no alternative at all (the only possible world is the actual one), is located at the left end.[3]

(56) Who came? (repeated)

(57) John came. (repeated)

Just like (56)–(57), the interrogatives (25) and (26) can be situated on a cline of informativeness/incompleteness (Figure 2.4).

Conceiving of declaratives and interrogatives according to a gradual change in the informative and inquisitive aspects of their meaning also applies to languages other than English and French. Typological evidence for this view is that not all languages make clear formal distinctions between declarative and interrogative sentences. First, in some languages, the notion of declarative or interrogative corresponds to a distinction in terms of degrees of 'interrogativity', as statements and polar questions are only differentiated by their intonation, as in Spanish and colloquial Italian, for instance (Dryer 2013). Second, in many languages in the south-east of Asia, for instance in Lao (Enfield 2014), the structures corresponding to the English open interrogatives are declaratives with indefinite quantifiers, such as *Someone came* (meaning 'Who came?').

Despite the fact that the cline of informativeness/inquisitiveness provides an adequate analysis of the semantics of interrogatives, it doesn't explain why at the pragmatic level interrogatives can be used to indicate

---

[3] The existence of hybrid constructions should be acknowledged. For instance, it is debatable where sentences such as (i)–(ii) should be located on the informativeness/inquisitiveness conceptual cline.

(i) He closed the window, didn't he?
(ii) He closed the window, did he?

A commonsensical way to analyze (i)–(ii) would hold it that the interrogative tag, by adding to a declarative sentence, results in higher inquisitiveness, which moves the two constructions some way towards the right end of the cline.

Figure 2.4 Continuum of informativeness/inquisitiveness for conceptualizing declarative and interrogative sentence-types (event: the closing of the door by the addressee)

that the answer to a question is obvious, as in 'rhetorical questions' such as (60) uttered by a commander-in-chief to new recruits.

(60) Who's in charge here? (COCA)

And interrogatives can also be used to perform indirect requests for action, regardless of whether the answer to the question asked is obvious or not, as in (61).

(61) Would you mind closing the window?

I will address these two pragmatic interpretations of interrogative sentences in turn.

2.3.3 Rhetorical Questions

One of Wilson and Sperber's (1988) examples I used to illustrate the variety of SAs that can be performed with interrogatives was the rhetorical question in (33):

(33) Peter has made a New Year's resolution to give up smoking. As he lights up on New Year's Day, Mary says to him: What was your New Year's resolution? (repeated)

A typical feature of such 'rhetorical questions' is that speakers who produce them do not thereby request their addressee(s) to answer them. In asking a rhetorical question such as (33), Mary does not expect Peter to give an answer to her question; rather, the utterance functions as a reminder.

In line with Wilson and Sperber (1988), Fiengo (2007: 61–3) conceives of rhetorical questions as questions asked not to request an answer, but to produce other effects. He differentiates two sorts of rhetorical questions: questions that have no answer, which he calls 'open rhetorical questions', and questions with an obvious answer. On the one hand, 'open rhetorical questions' are characterized by S's use of an

2.3 Interrogative Sentences

incomplete sentence that she does not intend to be completed, as in (62), which indicates that 'there is nothing S could do'.

(62) (In a context where S's car has broken down and A complains that S is late, S says:) What could I do?

Fiengo includes non-inverted interrogatives such as (63), which, if uttered in the same context as (60) and attributing to someone the thought that there is 'something S could do', can be used as rhetorical questions.

(63) I could do what? Build an airplane?

With (63), S fails to make the assertion that there is something she could do, and she challenges A to perform such an assertive SA, while signalling that performing that SA is impossible. In a similar fashion, polar interrogatives such as (64), which at the semantic level indicate ignorance as to whether the proposition expressed is true or not, can be used as rhetorical questions to imply that the answer (here, negative) is obvious.

(64) Is there something/anything I could do?

As Fiengo (2007) argues, uttering a sentence that indicates a lack of information does not always entail that S is ignorant. The incompleteness in the proposition expressed or the incompleteness in the use of the sentence can be a pointer towards such a completion. Accordingly, rhetorical questions can be used to perform SAs of the assertive type. The propositional content of the assertion would be obtained by saturating the variable in the question expressed, as in (65).

(65) Who are we as human beings if we ignore the suffering of others? (Anonymous, Internet)

This rhetorical question amounts to an assertion that we are bad people if we ignore other people's pain.

Han (2002) proposes an explanation of why the illocutionary force of a rhetorical question such as (66a) amounts to an assertion of the opposite polarity.

(66) a Did I tell you to speak? (COCA)
     b Didn't I tell you to speak?

In line with partition theory, she considers that the meaning of polar interrogatives is a function that partitions the set of possible worlds into two blocks: one block containing the worlds in which the positive answer is true, and another block containing the worlds in which the negative answer is true. In line with pragmatic considerations of informativeness, uttering a polar interrogative such as (66a) implies that S believes that the negative answer is more likely to be true than the positive answer. In such a case, the negative answer would be more informative. If the positive answer was more likely, S would have framed her question with a negative polarity, that is, she would have said (66b), which would be a reminder about something it was obvious A should have done. The answer to (66a) that is consistent with the pragmatics of polar interrogatives expresses a negative proposition: A wasn't told to speak.

Even if Han's (2002) proposal is appealing and capable of accounting for the meaning of rhetorical questions such as (66a, b), it raises two issues. First, it is hard to see how Han could account for the meaning of some polar interrogatives such as (67) – she herself acknowledges this problem is a footnote (2002: 216).

(67) Is the Pope Catholic?

This example was discussed by Morgan (1978), who pointed out that speakers using rhetorical questions in order to answer questions seem to follow a general schema such as: 'answer an obvious *yes/no* question by replying with another question whose answer is very obvious and the same as the answer you intend to convey' (1978: 278). However, according to Han's analysis, in the same way as (66a), (67) should convey a negative answer to the question asked. Morgan's (1978) analysis suggests that some rhetorical questions do not have the meaning Han predicts them to have.

Another problematic issue with Han's approach, which is not specific to rhetorical questions, concerns confirmation questions performed with non-inverted interrogatives such as (54).

(54) You closed the window? (repeated)

According to Han (2002: 215), 'a declarative sentence with a rising intonation expresses question force rather than assertive force'. Yet a non-inverted interrogative such as (54) can be used not only to perform the SA of questioning, but also to express one's surprise at the fact that A closed the window, as a reminder to close the window, or even to

2.3 Interrogative Sentences

echo A's alleged closing of the window, and, in so doing, express scepticism as to whether A actually closed the window. In such examples, S's use of (54) would have both informative and inquisitive pragmatic components. A consequence of this observation is that the 'rhetorical' use of questions such as (54) can no longer be explained purely in terms of the semantics of interrogatives because, in Han's view, (54) is not an interrogative. The challenge for Han, then, would be to reconcile the semantics of declaratives with the pragmatics of rhetorical confirmation questions. By contrast, examples such as (54) and (67) do not pose any special challenge to the informativeness/ inquisitiveness approach, which has two advantages: it applies both to interrogatives and declaratives, and, as it concerns the semantics of these sentences, it is compatible with a pragmatic approach according to which interrogative sentences can be uttered with illocutionary forces distinct from that of questioning.

Now, an important question concerns how people recognize that an interrogative sentence is used rhetorically. A plausible rational reconstruction of this interpretation is that an interrogative will be understood as a rhetorical question once its most plausible answer is inferred in the particular context of utterance. After inferring the answer to the question, the addressee would go through the following two stages. First, he would understand that the answer is obvious. Next, he would discard the possibility that the interrogative was meant as a question to be answered, and he would search for another interpretation. As discussed above, a possible SA performed with a rhetorical question is an assertion. It would be 'indirect' insofar as it departs from the declarative sentence-type associated with assertive SAs.

2.3.4 Interrogatives and Declaratives As Indirect Requests

The semantics of interrogative sentences makes them a convenient means to perform the SA of questioning, and also, as rhetorical questions, to perform assertions. Here, we will see that interrogatives can also be used to perform indirect requests (IRs) for action by means of – and/or in addition to – the SA of questioning. First, I explain why asking a question can be used to perform an IR for action. Second, I will address whether and, if so, to what extent, the semantic meaning of interrogatives and declaratives is compatible with the directive illocutionary force.

Among the interrogative sentence-types that can be used to perform requests for action, polar interrogatives seem to be the most frequent (see Flöck [2016] for evidence from written and spoken English data). Arguably, a request to close the window can easily be performed with one of the examples (68)–(70):

(68)   Can you close the window?

(69)   You can close the window.

(39)   Will you close the window? (repeated)

(70)   You will close the window.

The use of polar questions such as (68) and (39) and statements such as (69)–(70) in the performance of IRs for action requires an explanation. We saw, in Section 2.3.2, that, according to Fiengo, because of their incompleteness, interrogatives are convenient tools that can be used by speakers to reveal their lacks and to try to remedy these lacks. The prototypical lack associated with the use of interrogative sentences is ignorance, but interrogatives can be used to express the lack implied by a desire, as with (71).

(71)   Would you pass the sugar? (COCA)

For Fiengo, the directive interpretation of (71) can be inferred because the interrogative sentence (71) expresses S's desire that the predicate 'pass the sugar' apply to the addressee. In uttering (71), S does not expect A to indicate whether the proposition (you would pass the sugar) is true or false. Rather, she would expect the lack implied by her desire to get the sugar to be remedied by A's passing her the sugar.

Within the framework of conversational analysis, utterances such as (68) are analyzed as 'pre-requests', that is, requests for information that are performed prior to requests for action (Clark 1996: 306–10; Levinson 2012; Sacks 1992: 685; Schegloff 1980).

(68)   Can you close the window? (repeated)

Provided A gives an affirmative answer to the question asked (*Yes, of course*), in her next conversational turn S could very well perform a direct request that A close the window (*Close it, then*). Other interrogatives, which question the availability of an item, such as (72), are very convenient for requesting this item. If the item is available, (72) will

2.3 Interrogative Sentences

easily be understood as a request to serve an enchilada. The request for information in (72) thus makes it possible for S to check whether the preparatory condition for her request applies, so that she can order her meal.

(72) Do you have any enchiladas? (Gibbs 1986b)

A plausible explanation of the form of IRs such as (68), which follows the conversational analytic approach, is proposed by Francik and Clark (1985). According to these authors' obstacle hypothesis, speakers phrase their requests so as to deal with the obstacles that would prevent their addressees from complying with their requests. For instance, S would utter (73) if she believes that the greatest obstacle for A to provide the requested information is that John did not tell A where he will go on holiday.

(73) Did John tell you where he will go on holiday?

Francik and Clark's explanation applies not only to IRs for information, but also to IRs for action in general. According to the obstacle hypothesis, *Can you VP?* requests such as (68) are used to remove very general or ill-defined obstacles to compliance. This is a possible reason why they are frequently used to make requests. In such situations, A would understand that S is trying to remove an obstacle to the satisfaction of her forthcoming request. In so doing, A would anticipate S's request when the answer to a question such as (68) is obvious.

Requests, however, cannot always be anticipated, as the composition of conversational exchanges involving pre-requests indicate (Merritt 1976). A first type of question–answer sequence Merritt identifies in her corpus of customer–merchant service encounters is called 'chaining'. In (74), the customer is not in a position to formulate an accurate request, as she does not have all the information she needs for her purchase. She therefore questions, in Q1, the availability of the items she would like to purchase and, as the preparatory condition for the successful performance of her request is satisfied, she orders, in Q2, four size C flashlight batteries.

(74) Customer – Q1 – Hi. Do you have uh size C flashlight batteries?
Merchant – A1 – Yes sir.
Customer – Q2 – I'll have four please.
Merchant – A2 (turns to get)
(Merritt 1976: 324)

It can be considered that, in (74), the customer's request is distributed over two conversational turns, Q1 and Q2, in the sense that Q2 builds on the information exchanged in Q1–A1 and the conversational relevance of Q1 is justified by Q2. The second type of question–answer sequences that is particularly relevant to the discussion of ISAs is 'coupling'. As illustrated in (75), a coupling sequence consists of a request for information that functions as a pre-request (Q1), followed by an answer by the merchant (A1), after which the same person asks the customer a question (Q2), which replaces, so to speak, the request the customer could have performed in Q1:

(75) Customer – Q1 – Where's the water?
      Merchant – A1+Q2 – Back here. Would you like some?
      Customer – A2 – Yes, please.
                                            (Merritt 1976: 337)

What is interesting with the utterances of *Do you have NP?* and *Where's NP?* in (74)–(75) is that they initiate a conversational sequence, and serve as preliminaries to the performance of another SA. Provided a bit more information is included (e.g., if the customer specifies the number of batteries), they could themselves be understood as (indirect) requests in their own right. Combined with the discussion of the obstacle hypothesis, examples such as (74)–(75) show that an utterance that functions as a pre-request can also be understood as an IR, in which case there is a short-circuiting from Q1, the pre-request, to the typical move following a request (compliance or non-compliance).

As Clark (1996: 213; 301) claims, from the researcher's perspective, the point is not to decide whether utterances such as (72), (73) and Q1 in (74)–(75) were initially meant as a pre-request or as an IR by S. Rather, an analysis of these examples should focus on A's construal of these utterances, which indicates his uptake and is evidenced by his verbal response. These conversational exchanges demonstrate that the meaning of ISA utterances is shaped both by S and A. They also show that SAs in general, and ISAs in particular, can only be properly understood in the light of the responses they give rise to, as part of situated conversational sequences – a point Merritt (1976) made forty-five years ago.

We have just seen why it is convenient to use the SA of request for information (performed with interrogative sentences) in order to additionally perform IRs for action. We still need, however, an explanation of what, in the semantic meaning of interrogatives such as *Can you VP?* and *You can VP?* makes them a convenient means to perform such IRs.

2.3 Interrogative Sentences

Following the theories of interrogatives discussed in this chapter, at the semantic level (68) and (39) express the question whether the addressee of the utterance is able to or will close the window, respectively. They have a higher degree of incompleteness than the corresponding declaratives (69)–(70), which can also be used to request that A close the window.

(68) Can you close the window? (repeated)

(69) You can close the window. (repeated)

(39) Will you close the window? (repeated)

(70) You will close the window. (repeated)

To put it in the terms of Talmy's (2000) force dynamics, the interrogative (68) expresses a representation of A as an agent capable of performing the action of closing the window. A is conceptualized as an entity capable of exerting a force with the consequence that the window be closed. This representation of A as an entity capable of force exertion is compatible with, and entailed by, the force dynamic representation of a directive (Johnson 1987; Ruytenbeek 2017b, 2019a). In a similar vein, Sweetser (1990: 52–3) analyzes the meaning of *can* in terms of the force dynamic pattern of enablement. By contrast, in (39) and (70), *will* refers to a future state of affairs. The inverted word order in (68) and (39) indicates S's ignorance as to whether this representation depicts an actual state of affairs.

Assuming that declaratives and interrogatives are conceptualized together on a cline of degrees of (in)completeness (Figure 2.3 and Figure 2.4), the only difference between the interrogative (68) and the declarative (69) is that (69) expresses not an incomplete representation, but a complete representation according to which A is able to close the window. Since they need no 'yes' answer to get completed, the semantic representations expressed by declaratives have a closer connection to the conceptual representation of a directive SA. That is, unlike (68) and (39), (69)–(70) express, with a complete representation, A's power to act and A's future action, respectively.

For other declaratives, such as (76)–(77), the connection between the meaning of the sentence uttered and the meaning of a request is less straightforward.

(76) I would like you to close the window.

(77) It's cold in here.

As is the case in (69)–(70), by virtue of their sentence-type, (76)–(77) express a complete representation. By virtue of their compositional semantics, they both express a reason for A to close the window. Such reasons can be thought of as forces urging the speaker to the performance of a request that someone close the window.

Assuming that the relationship between the meaning of interrogatives/declaratives and the meaning of a directive SA can be explained in terms of degrees of incompleteness (taking into account the force dynamic pattern of enablement encoded at the lexical level, that is, the meaning of the modal *can*), I will distinguish two possible ways for A to arrive at the request interpretation of (68).

(68) Can you close the window? (repeated)

First, A may sincerely be asked about his ability to close the window, with the result that he is prompted (in case the answer to the question is positive) to perform the requested action. In such a case, the directive would be a secondary SA conditional on the performance of the logically primary SA of questioning. Second, it may be mutually manifest to S and A that A is able to close the window, in which case it makes little sense to assume that S questions A about his ability to close the window. In both cases, the incompleteness of the interrogative sentence is resolved at the pragmatic level, that is, a 'yes' answer (whether implicit or explicit) makes the representation expressed by the interrogative complete. This positive answer, however, does not constitute a satisfactory response to the utterance, as it is the indirect meaning that needs to be inferred for the communication to be successful.

In fact, the use of interrogatives such as (68) in the performance of directives resembles the use of interrogatives such as (64) in the performance of assertions.

(64) Is there something/anything I could do? (repeated)

I suggest that, on some occasions, requests for action are performed like rhetorical questions. We might therefore consider that (68) functions as a rhetorical question about A's ability to close the window in the sense that its answer is obvious: 'yes, of course, A is able to close the window'. As it is indirectly conveyed through the rhetorical question, A's ability is presented as a reason for A to perform this action, in a way that is similar for the declarative (69).

(69) You can close the window. (repeated)

The inferential process linking the question meaning and the IR meaning is thus short-circuited (cf. Morgan 1978). As there remains the possibility that, in some situations, A is really asked about his ability, the IR can either be performed in addition to a SA of questioning or as a rhetorical question – in which case no questioning SA takes place. However, while it is fairly uncontroversial that *Can you VP?* interrogatives can be used as IRs for action, whether one or two SAs are inferred in such cases is an important empirical issue, and a largely unsettled one, which I will discuss in Chapter 4. Yet before doing this, I have to address a type of modal declaratives that, unlike declaratives involving the ability modal *can*, are predisposed to the performance of directives.

2.4 DEONTIC MODAL DECLARATIVES: INDIRECT REQUESTS FOR ACTION?

Are statements of obligation direct or indirect directives? From the perspective of SAT, *You must/should VP* constructions are literal assertions. They would be considered ISA expressions because they are declarative sentences potentially used with the illocutionary force of requests and commands. The issue, however, is more complicated if we consider SA types other than requests and commands. For Searle (1969: 66–7), requesting, advising and warning constitute three distinct illocutionary types, but he does not make clear whether all of them fall under the category of directives. Even though they both concern a future act of A, requesting is distinguished from advising on the basis that, for requesting, S wants A to do some action, whereas, for advising, S does not necessarily have such a desire, but she has the belief that the action will benefit A. Even though they note that advising and warning can be either assertives or directives, Searle and Vanderveken (1985: 202–3) and Vanderveken (1990: 197) classify these two SAs as directives, arguing that the aim of issuing advice (or warning) is in general to get A (not) to do some vaguely defined action (see also Bach & Harnish 1979). However, it makes little sense to consider that a warning or advice can be successfully performed without ipso facto conveying some information. This accords with the observation that, in English, advising and warning can be performed with both imperative and declarative sentences. This is illustrated in (78a, b) for advising and in (79a, b) for warning.

(78) a Make an appointment with the stylist.
     b You should make an appointment with the stylist who works in a nice environment.
                                                              (https://bit.ly/38UiIo0)

(79) a Don't eat mushrooms alone and also eat them on days where it's easy to walk around outside.
                                                              (https://bit.ly/3lMgQ48)
     b You shouldn't eat mushrooms with insect grubs in.
                                                              (https://bit.ly/2UCAnYT)

With these examples in mind, it is no surprise that modal declaratives are sometimes considered alongside imperatives in the literature. For instance, Mastop's (2005; 2011) notion of instruction also applies to modal declarative sentences such as (80).

(80) All of you boys and soldiers, you must go and attack and kill. (COCA)

(81) All of you boys and soldiers go and attack and kill!

What distinguishes a modal declarative such as (80) from an imperative such as (81) is that imperatives grammatically indicate that they cannot be interpreted as expressing a proposition. This is because imperatives merely express properties that can be true – but are not predicated – of addressees. By contrast, in (80), the obligation to 'go and attack and kill' is predicated of the addressees.

Concerning modal declaratives with *must*, such as (82)–(83), on their deontic reading, they express the existence of a strong obligation to close the window.

(82) The window must be closed.

(83) You must close the window.

A possible interpretation of deontic *must* is that S lays an obligation on someone (Coates 1983: 31–41; Palmer 1986: 98). In some situations, by saying *You must VP*, S makes it necessary for A to do some action, which amounts to performing a 'strong' directive SA, for example, in (84), a strong recommendation:

(84) Though many new risks are indeed external to your enterprise, you must pay more attention than ever to threats from insiders – including highly placed insiders. (Broadbent & Kitzis 2005)

2.4 Deontic Modal Declaratives: IRs for Action?

Unlike for declarative sentences in general, the directive interpretations of *You must VP* can be considered a direct specification of the meaning of the modal in the sense that the notion of obligation is part of the semantic meaning of the utterance. It is thus possible for S to utter a *You must VP* declarative and mean it as a directive SA, in which case S is the source of the obligation, that is, she imposes an obligation upon A by means of her utterance. Such examples, where S is involved in the creation of an obligation, contrast with examples such as (85), where S is merely reporting the existence of an obligation for A to act.

(85) You must attach three separate Daily Mirror Tokens, printed this week, to take up the special offer. (BNC)

This suggests that, at the semantic level, the meaning of *must* should include a reference to the notion of force exertion, but no specification of the source of the exerted force. Interestingly, regardless whether S is the source of the obligation, one cannot assert that A must p and, at the same time, deny that A will p, as in (86) (Ninan 2005).

(86) # You must go to confession, but you're not going to.

To account for the oddity of such examples, which is expected if *must* refers to strong obligations, Ninan (2005) proposes a semantic analysis of *must* that is close to Portner's analysis of imperative sentences in terms of to-do lists. Accordingly, it would be odd for S to put p on A's to-do list if she believes that A will not make p true. The unacceptability of (86) thus parallels that of (87).

(87) # Close the window! You're not going to close the window.

The view that *must* can be defined in terms of the notion of obligation is also in line with force dynamic semantics. In fact, Talmy (2000: 440) suggests that force opposition constitutes the core of the meanings of modals. According to his semantic framework, force dynamics is directly involved in the meaning of some grammatical categories, such as modals (2000: 409–70). He analyzes the construction X *must* VP in terms of a force-interaction pattern in which an antagonistic authority, whether actual or virtual, exerts a psychological pressure on the agonist. What Talmy also has in mind is that *must* encodes a negative compulsion: the agonist's tendency to perform whatever action he wants is overridden by the stronger antagonistic force's tendency, with the result that the action referred to by the VP will take place instead of the action desired by the agonist. Sweetser (1990: 52–4) follows Talmy and considers that *You must VP* sentences are conceptualized in terms of a compelling force directing an addressee towards an action. In the same vein, Furmaniak (2010: 19) defines the obligation or 'deontic necessity' expressed by *You must VP* as a concept involving an agent 'who is under socio-physical pressure to act in the way described by the VP'. This view is compatible with the standard formal semantic analysis of modals, according to which *must (p)* expresses the necessity that *p*, and the different interpretations of *must* depend on the conversational background assumed in the context of utterance (Kratzer 1977; 1991; see also Portner 2009: 47–85 for a discussion).

Like *must*, *have to* can be used to express obligations. But, unlike *must*, it cannot be used by a speaker to impose an obligation on her addressee. This is because, with *have to*, S dissociates herself from the obligation, and the source of the obligation is necessarily external to S (Coates 1983; Palmer 1986). The directive interpretations of *You have to VP* are rather unlikely because S cannot be the source of the obligation. Another difference between *must* and *have to* would be that, while *must* denotes an irresistible force, *have to* denotes a resistible force (Sweetser 1990: 54). This feature of *have to* accords with the view that *You have to VP* is unsuitable to the performance of commands, which involve a strong degree of force exertion.

Another modal that is associated with the notion of obligation is *should*, as in (88)–(89).

(88) The window should be closed.

(89) You should close the window.

Most scholars agree that, unlike the construction *You must VP*, *You should VP* denotes a weaker obligation (Coates 1983; Palmer 1986; Papafragou 2007). As the following contrast (90)–(91) illustrates, in saying *X should VP*, S 'admits the possibility that the event may not take place' (Palmer 1986: 100).

(90) He should/ought to close the window, but he won't do it.

(91) #He must close the window, but he won't do it.

S would use *must* if she has a high degree of certainty that the obligation will be fulfilled, but she would use *should* if she thinks that the obligation may not be fulfilled. From a force exertion perspective,

You should VP is weaker than *You must VP* in two respects. First, unlike in the case of *must*, the agonist (addressee) is stronger than the antagonist (source of the obligation). Second, since *should* involves weak obligations, there is no certainty that A will act as suggested. To summarize this comparison between *must* and *should*, I will say that, in their deontic readings, *must* refers to the existence of strong obligations and *should* to the existence of weak obligations. Accordingly, the constructions *You must VP* and *You should VP* predicate an obligation for the addressee to act, and, if S presents herself as the source of the obligation, the utterance should be understood as a directive SA. Despite the strong association between their literal meaning (existence of some degree of obligation for A to act) and their possible directive meaning (S puts A under such an obligation), however, utterances of these modal constructions would not constitute direct but indirect SAs according to Searle's speech act theoretic definition.

2.5 SUMMARY

In line with the major theories of interrogatives and declaratives, unlike imperatives, these two sentence-types are best conceptualized in terms of a cline of informativeness and incompleteness. Such a cline imposes a constraint on the semantic theories of interrogatives and declaratives, and it makes them compatible with a range of SAs, including questions and requests for action.

As in the case of imperative sentences and directive SAs, we saw that there is not a one-to-one correspondence relationship between interrogative sentences and the SA of questioning (a similar observation applies to declarative sentences and assertive SAs). That is, one can request information with non-interrogative sentences, and interrogatives can be used in the performance of SAs other than questioning. Semantically, the meaning of an interrogative sentence amounts to an incomplete representation of a state of affairs, as in open interrogatives, or to a representation of a state of affairs as being not actual (polar interrogatives). This analysis also applies to non-inverted interrogatives, where the rising intonation signals that the actuality of the representation expressed by the utterance is presented as being at issue. Interrogatives, which semantically express questions, are prototypically used to get an answer to these questions, that is, to perform the SA of questioning. However, the picture is more complex. In some cases, a question is asked and another, additional and indirect, SA is performed, such as a request for action. In some other cases, the interrogative expresses a question but it lacks the directive force of questioning. In such cases, the interrogative is used as a 'rhetorical question', and the SA performed is an assertion or a directive. As for the meaning of declarative sentences, even if the declarative sentence-type lacks force dynamics, force exertion can be expressed at the lexical level. In particular, *You must/should VP* encode strong/weak obligations, respectively, and they are predisposed to the performance of indirect directives.

2.6 DISCUSSION QUESTIONS

- Building on the sort of 'semantic' analysis of ISA constructions proposed in this chapter, one can consider the relationship between a particular SA type, for example 'promising', and the three major English sentence-types in order to assess the (in)directness of several realizations of a promise. From that perspective, promises that are performed using 1st-person future declaratives and explicit performatives would be considered 'direct'; any other realization would constitute an ISA. Can you think of another example to illustrate such a relationship between a sentence-type and a SA type?

2.7 SUGGESTIONS FOR FURTHER READING

Peter Siemund provides a very interesting analysis of the English sentence-types, including exercises devoted to the case of ISAs: Siemund, Peter. 2018. *Speech Acts and Clause Types: English in a Cross-Linguistic Context*. Oxford: Oxford University Press.

3 Cognitive and Relevance-Based Approaches

3.1 INTRODUCTION

Up to now, I have assumed a definition of indirectness as a formal binary notion, the performance of a given SA being either direct, as in the case of a statement performed with a declarative and a request with an imperative, or indirect when the SA performed does not match the so-called 'literal' force associated with the sentence-type of the utterance. This binary notion stands in sharp contrast to the graded notion of indirectness frequently encountered in the literature (see, for instance, Brown & Levinson 1987; Blum-Kulka 1987; Blum-Kulka & Olshtain 1984; Blum-Kulka et al. 1989; Leech 1983). According to this view, 'direct' and 'indirect' refer to the endpoints of a scale of (in)directness. For instance, in the case of directives, imperatives are the most direct request forms, and negative state remarks (*It's cold in here*) the most indirect request forms. In this chapter, I consider the view that 'direct' and 'indirect' are, at best, abstract labels referring to endpoints of a continuum of (in)directness or, in more appropriate terms, a scale of explicitness. In addition, in these frameworks, there is strictly speaking no such things as 'ISAs', and the notion of a SA itself has little theoretical significance.

3.2 COGNITIVE LINGUISTIC APPROACHES

3.2.1 A Graded Notion of Speech Act Conventionality

The notion of conventionality associated with indirectness has been reconsidered by cognitive linguists to explain differences among utterances used as directives. While I assumed a categorical notion of conventionality in the preceding chapters (i.e., there exists a variety of conventions of means for different SA types), for cognitive linguists conventionality is a graded notion, some utterances being

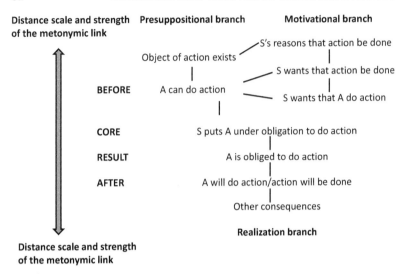

Figure 3.1 Metonymic illocutionary scenario for requests (elaborated version, based on Panther and Thornburg 1998: 760)

more conventional than others for the performance of such and such SA. An illustration of this graded notion is proposed by Panther and Thornburg (1998; 2004; 2005), who conceive of the relationship between utterances and their use in the performance of SAs in terms of 'metonymic illocutionary scenarios'. The components of Panther and Thornburg's request scenario, which actually is a reinterpretation of SAT's felicity conditions, include those shown in Figure 3.1. In the case of directives, the 'before' component concerns the conditions that have to be fulfilled before the SA can take place, namely, that S believes that A can do the action and S wants A to do the action. The 'core' refers to S's putting A under a more or less strong obligation to do the action, and the 'result' to A's being under a more or less strong obligation to act. Panther and Thornburg thus distinguish between an action (S's producing an obligation for A to do an action) and a state (A's being obliged to do an action). The 'after' component encompasses the relevant consequences of the SA performed.

For instance, from the perspective of Panther and Thornburg's metonymic illocutionary scenarios, when an utterance such as (1) is used as a request that A close the window, A's ability to close the window 'stands for' the request SA.

(1) Can you close the window?

3.2 Cognitive Linguistic Approaches

The utterance in (1) bears a 'metonymic' relation to the request SA because A's ability to do some action is part of the illocutionary scenario for requesting. When (1) is used as a request, two metonymic mappings are necessary. First, the ability question activates the 'before' component of the scenario. Second, the 'before' component activates the 'core' of the scenario, that is, that S puts A under some obligation to do the action. This is not explicit in their account, but I believe that the likelihood of an utterance being used in some SA positively correlates with the strength of the metonymic link between the component of the SA scenario expressed and the core of that scenario.

IRs such as (1) thus illustrate a metonymic relationship between the utterance and the SA scenario for requesting. If we compare different request forms, a request performed with (2) would have a higher degree of conventionality than the request in (1) because of the smaller number of metonymic links required to reach the core of the scenario.

(2) You must close the window.

Only one metonymic mapping is necessary for (2) to be understood as a request: the statement that A is obliged to do the action activates the core of the scenario, that is, that S puts A under some obligation to do the action. Because the utterance straightforwardly activates the core of the scenario, it stands for the request scenario as a whole. Panther and Thornburg's conceptualization of IRs does not straightforwardly translate into claims about how these expressions are processed. That being said, to put it in terms of cognitive processing, there is an expectation that the indirect directive meaning of, for example, (2) is more likely to be primary than secondary because the component of the request scenario is, conceptually speaking, very close to the core of the scenario.

Metonymic or 'stand for' relationships illustrated by examples such as (1)–(2) contrast with 'point to' relationships, where the utterance's conceptual content is much more distant from the core of the SA scenario (motivational branch in Figure 3.1). An IR such as (3) illustrates a 'point to' relationship.

(3) It's cold in here.

In a request such as (3), several metonymic links are required between the parts of the scenario to activate the core of this scenario. The utterance in (3) is a statement about the temperature, which is the starting point of the metonymic chain leading to the identification of an indirect directive meaning. These metonymic links connect the source meaning (statement about the cold) with the target meaning (request that A close the window). The assertion that p ('it is cold in here') suggests that p is undesirable (it is a reason for A to close the window). In turn, it activates S's wanting not-p, which activates the assumption that 'S wants that A do the action of closing the window'. This scenario component, which concerns S's desire that A do the action, then activates the core of the scenario, that is, that 'S puts A under the obligation to do the action so that not-p'. Speaking in terms of expected differences in processing, as we did for *You must VP* and *Can you VP?* above, the indirect directive meaning of negative state remarks such as (3) is more likely to be secondary (inferred on the basis of another SA interpretation) rather than primary.

Panther and Thornburg's distinction between 'stand for' and 'point to' relationships is best understood as a graded notion. This accords very well with their view that the conventionality of an utterance for the performance of a given SA is a matter of degrees. For them, conventionality is operationalized in terms of the conceptual distance between the component activated by the utterance and the core of the scenario. According to their notion of conventionality, the closer an utterance is to the core of the scenario, the more conventional it is qua directive. This graded notion stands in contrast to Searle's (1975) and Clark's (1979) notion of 'conventions of means'. We saw that, for Searle and Clark, an utterance is conventional for the performance of some SA inasmuch as it is produced according to some strategy such as, for instance, referring to A's ability to do some action, or referring to the action expected from A.

This approach in terms of 'metonymic illocutionary scenarios' is, however, not incompatible with one based on convention of means. First, the components of the request scenario overlap, to a large extent, with Searle's felicity conditions for the performance of directives. Second, Panther and Thornburg (1998) classify the components that can be used to evoke a request scenario according to three axes: presuppositions related to the content of the request and its preparatory conditions, motivations (reasons for action and sincerity condition), and realization (satisfaction conditions and consequences of the SA) (see Figure 3.1). In fact, these three axes correspond to three superordinate conventions of means for the performance of directives. That is, one can perform a request by using a sentence questioning or referring to the possibility to perform the action (presuppositional branch), by using a sentence concerning A's obligation to do some action or concerning A's future action (realization branch), or by using

3.2 Cognitive Linguistic Approaches

a sentence expressing S's motivations for performing the request (motivational branch).

Summing up, Panther and Thornburg's cognitive linguistic approach to the conventionality associated with directive utterances revisits Searle's (1975) generalizations about the sentences frequently used as IRs. More precisely, these authors propose a definition of conventionality based on metonymic links between components of illocutionary scenarios. They provide conceptual motivations for Searle's generalizations, but the relationship between imperative and non-imperative constructions used as directives remains unaddressed in their approach.

3.2.2 Illocutionary Force Salience

The notions of conventionality (of means) and standardization are not sufficient to account for the whole variety of forms used as indirect directives. For instance, it is obvious that (1) and (4) involve the same convention of means about A's ability, because they are both specifications of the *Can you VP?* construction.

(1) Can you close the window? (repeated)

(4) Can you just close the window for me, please?

Even though their linguistic content is in part identical, these two utterances differ in terms of the degree to which they make their indirect directive meaning salient to the interpreter. Pérez Hernández and Ruiz de Mendoza (2002) propose that (1) and (4) have not the same degree of prototypicality as members of the illocutionary category for directives. Uttering (4) would result in a more prototypical request than uttering (1) because, relative to (1), (4) contains three additional expressions – *just, for me, please* – which refer to components of the conceptual scenario for requesting. The phrase *for me* refers to the fact that the action is beneficial to S, a component that differentiates requests (and commands) from other directives such as advice and suggestions, which are performed in the addressee's benefit. Regarding *just*, it is plausible that, as these authors suggest, it is used in (4) to indicate that the requested action is less costly for A than otherwise expected. In fact, this mitigation effect is only possible because of the semantic meaning of *just*, which, like *only*, signals the existence of alternatives to a given state of affairs while urging A to discard these alternatives and focus on only the state of affairs expressed by the utterance. By contrast, in the following example, it makes little sense to consider that S is trying to mitigate the intensity of the directive force of her utterance.

(5) Oh, just shut your trap! (https://bit.ly/36MAAhJ)

In (5), the state of affairs selected by S is that A stops talking. S sets aside other possible states of affairs (that A switches to another conversational topic, that A apologizes for something, etc.).

In a similar vein, I have no worries with the idea that the optionality of A's expected action may be a central component of requests, but it is not certain that the adverb *please* in an IR such as (4) achieves optionality or mitigation.

(4) Can you just close the window for me, please? (repeated)

As proposed by Sadock (1974), *please* can be considered an indicator of directive illocutionary force. This suggestion is in line with empirical data such as the two-part utterance in (6), in which *please* is unlikely to indicate mitigation.

(6) Please, I have five children.

Imagine (6) said by a speaker who is begging for money. Further assume that, with (6), S is presenting the fact of having five children as a sufficient reason for the recipients of her utterance to give her some money. Does S use *please* to mitigate the force of the request for money she performs with the declarative *I have five children*? Such a view is rather implausible. Even though *I have five children* could be used as a request for money, this request would have been more tentative, hence less likely to be understood as a request at all. It makes more sense to consider that S is primarily concerned with making explicit the directive illocutionary force of her request for money. Note that one could also perform a request for money with the one-word utterance *please*, in which case it would be difficult to maintain that the use of *please* mitigates anything. In both cases, the existence of S's children would constitute a reason not only for begging for money, but also for the addressee to comply with the directive.

This analysis strongly suggests that the notion of illocutionary force mitigation should not be thought of as part of the semantic meaning of *please*. Rather, it is necessary to identify two pragmatic uses of *please* that do not necessarily go together: the indication of directive force and the indication of optionality of the requested action (which also results

3.2 Cognitive Linguistic Approaches

in the mitigation of the strength of directive force). On the one hand, the mitigating effect of *please* is only possible because *please* is associated with directive force in the first place. On the other hand, *please* can be used in a directive utterance without achieving any mitigation. This explains why, in cases where the form of the utterance is already specified for the performance of directives, such as imperatives, the addition of *please* will be interpreted in terms of a mitigation effect.

Let us return to examples (1) and (4), which, according to Pérez Hernández (2013), differ in terms of prototypicality qua members of the category of directives.

(1) Can you close the window? (repeated)

(4) Can you just close the window for me, please? (repeated)

Pérez Hernández and Ruiz de Mendoza (2002) and Pérez Hernández (2013) build on the view that SAs are best conceived of in terms of graded categories defined with respect to a prototype (cf. Rosch 1973). In cognitive linguistic approaches, an idealized cognitive model (ICM) is a mental structure of conceptual representations (Lakoff 1987). As Glynn (2006) puts it, an ICM is not necessarily present in a speaker's mind, but it is an abstract generalization that can be used by any member of a given speech community. ICMs for SA types have an ontology (the set of elements used in the model) and a structure (the properties of these elements and the relations between these elements). For Pérez Hernández (2013), the prototypicality of an utterance used as a request depends on two properties. The first one is the number and centrality of the attributes that are activated in the illocutionary ICM. The second property is whether the metonymic operation between the utterance and the core of the illocutionary scenario is launched from an external or an internal layer of the ICM ontology. For Pérez Hernández (2013), the more central the attributes (and the larger the number of attributes) of the ICM that are linguistically expressed in an utterance, the more prototypical the SA. Accordingly, (4) would be a very prototypical request because its content refers to several central components of the request ICM: optionality, benefit for S and mitigation. In these respects, (4) contrasts with (1), the content of which is under-specified for the performance of a request. (1) only activates a component about A's ability and it is addressee-oriented.

In line with Pérez Hernández and Ruiz de Mendoza (2002) and Pérez Hernández (2013), I propose, in addition to the categorical criterion of conventionality of means and the graded criterion of standardization, a graded criterion of 'illocutionary force salience'. This criterion consists in the degree to which the illocutionary force (for instance, directive) of an utterance is linguistically 'specified'. For instance, (4) is a prototypical request because the presence of the expressions *just*, *for me* and *please*, which refer to the components of the scenario for requests, result in the construction in (4) having a specific illocutionary meaning, that is, that of a request. Without these three markers, the construction would be 'illocutionarily unspecified'.

Note that illocutionary force salience can involve both downgraders, that is, linguistic devices that decrease the strength of a SA, and upgraders, that is, items that reinforce illocutionary force, as in the example of command in (7).

(7) I want you to leave immediately! (https://bit.ly/3pE7pWF)

The utterance in (7) is specified for the performance of a particular subtype of directive, namely a 'strong' directive. Following Pérez Hernández's (2013) scenarios, the following two conceptual elements are part of the scenario for commands: the state of affairs alluded to is in S's benefit (*I want you to VP*, see also *for me* in example (4) above) and the state of affairs should be brought about with no delay (*immediately*). The presence of these two explicit markers increases the salience of the force of commanding. Another feature of commands, which is illustrated by the form of (7), is that they lack downgraders.

The examples of illocutionary force salience discussed above include only indirect directives, but the criterion of degree of illocutionary force salience applies to any SA realization, whether direct or indirect, including, in the case of directives, utterances of imperative sentences:

(8) Close the window.

(9) Please close the window, would you?

In line with Pérez Hernández's (2013) analysis, I consider that (9) is more specified qua directive subtype than (8) for the reason that (9) involves two markers of the force of requesting (*please* and *would you*). The force of requesting is therefore more salient in (9) than in (8), which can also be used as a command, as an offer, or as a suggestion.

Just as with the criterion of degrees of standardization, I expect differences in illocutionary force salience to have an influence on how ISAs are processed. In particular, degree of illocutionary force salience should positively correlate with the likelihood that the ISA

3.2 Cognitive Linguistic Approaches

will be primary. For example, in (4), the indirect directive meaning is very likely to be primary because of the presence of several expressions making this indirect meaning highly salient, while making the direct question meaning of the utterance non-salient.

(4) Can you just close the window for me, please? (repeated)

The upshot of this discussion is that it is necessary to include, alongside the criteria of conventionality of means and degree of standardization previously adopted, a criterion that is able to account for the difference between, for example, *Can you VP?* and *Can you please VP?*. This criterion concerns degrees of illocutionary force salience. One should, however, avoid equating the synchronic notion of illocutionary force salience with the notion of 'conventionality of form', which involves a diachronic process of standardization.

As we have seen, according to these cognitive linguistic accounts, each SA type is defined in terms of a conceptual scenario that consists in a set of features; some of these features are more central to an utterance being an instance of that SA type than others. Support for this position can be drawn from Coleman and Kay's (1981) empirical investigation of the semantics of the word *lie*. Coleman and Kay defined lies according to three features: (a) S makes a false statement; (b) S believes that she makes a false statement; and (c) S intends to deceive A. They presented participants with stories and asked them to rate the extent to which they considered that a given utterance consisted in a lie. They found a positive correlation between the ratings and the summed weights of the features satisfied by the utterance; the most important feature was (b). The results of Coleman and Kay's study suggest that the notion of a lie refers to a fuzzy category defined with respect to a prototype that satisfies some of the three features proposed.

Van Tiel (2020) extended Coleman and Kay's (1981) approach, and tested the predictions of prototype theory on the 'genuine' SA categories of promise, apology, claim, complaint, question and suggestion. The example I will focus on is a request for information. It can be considered that, like suggesting, requesting information belongs to the category of directives because it amounts to requesting A to answer a question. Van Tiel used (10b) as a prototypical question in the context of (10a) and (11b) as a prototypical suggestion in the context of (11a).

(10) a Susan and Mark are leaving the cinema. They just watched a movie together. Susan turns to Mark and says,
 b Did you like the movie?

(11) a Mark just failed his exam. He wasn't able to study properly because he had a serious cold. Susan says,
     b Maybe you can ask your teacher for a resit.

First, the participants were asked to rate the extent to which a SA is a representative member of its category, and they were successful in doing so. For instance, they considered that 'question' is an appropriate label for (10b), but that (12b) in the context of (12a) is not appropriately described as a 'question'.

(12) a Susan sees Mark. Mark is carrying a sports bag with a squash racket sticking out. Susan walks up to Mark and says,
     b So you play squash.

Moreover, in a forced categorization task, they classified (10b) more often as a question than they did (12b). Second, their representativeness ratings correlated positively with the likelihood that the SAs are classified as genuine members of a category. Third, the speed of forced categorization correlated positively with the representativeness ratings: positive categorizations were faster for prototypical exemplars of the category such as (10b) relative to less prototypical ones such as (12b) (see also Rosch and Mervis 1975). Fourth, the representativeness ratings correlated positively with the summed weights of the features that the participants proposed to define the SA categories. Taken together, the results of van Tiel's (2020) experiments suggest that SA categories are fuzzy, with more prototypical members and less prototypical members depending on the features that are satisfied. In line with this view, one also expects that the more features of a SA category an utterance satisfies, the more likely it is that the utterance will be understood as an instance of that particular SA type.

3.3 RELEVANCE THEORY

Like cognitive linguistic approaches in general, relevance theory is interested in the cognitive processes underlying utterance interpretation. Another important similarity is that, for both, the difference between so-called 'direct' and 'indirect' SAs is reinterpreted in terms of a continuum of explicitness. However, relevance theory differs from cognitive linguistics in that it analyzes communication in terms of intention recognition and expectations about the processing costs and cognitive effects of utterances. Considerations of costs are reminiscent of the traditional speech act theoretical view according to which, relative to DSAs, ISAs involve more complex inferential processes and, as a result, it is plausible that these indirect constructions take longer to understand. Such possible extra costs also raise the question why these constructions are used at all, another issue I will address in this chapter.

3.3.1 Maximal Relevance

Sperber and Wilson's (1995) relevance theory (RT) conceives of human cognition as geared towards the minimization of processing costs and the maximization of cognitive effects (cognitive principle of relevance). RT regards linguistic communication as a form of ostensive-inferential communication. It defines a *thought* as the conceptual representation communicated by means of an utterance; an *assumption* is a thought that an individual considers as being about the actual world. In RT, an ostensive stimulus (for example, the utterance of a sentence) is a stimulus designed by an individual in order to attract another individual's attention. Building on Grice's theory of communication, RT distinguishes two kinds of intentions involved in this process. First, the informative intention is S's intention to modify A's cognitive environment, for instance to make (more) manifest a set of assumptions (the manifestness of an assumption being the degree to which an individual is able to mentally represent this assumption as being true). Second, S's communicative intention amounts to making her informative intention mutually manifest to S and A. To understand the meaning conveyed by an utterance, A takes the utterance as a piece of evidence about S's intention to convey some information. More technically, A infers S's informative intention from the communicative intention he attributes to S. In order to process the linguistic input efficiently, the interpreter must focus on an interpretation that will satisfy his expectations of relevance. According to the communicative principle of relevance, A assumes that the processing efforts required from him are counterbalanced by S's utterance's effects on the set of assumptions that are manifest to him (his 'cognitive environment').

In the RT framework, A thus expects from S's contribution that the information she intends to convey will have a substantial cognitive effect that should compensate for additional interpretative effort required to process the utterance in question. For instance, if I tell you something like (13), as a cooperative and benevolent speaker I shouldn't expect you to make unnecessary effort trying to make sense of my utterance.

(13) It took me many working days to complete this book.

And indeed it shouldn't be too difficult for you to understand the communicated content of this utterance. By contrast, if I utter (14), you will probably take some time reflecting on what I meant, spending considerable effort with little guarantee to recover the intended meaning of my utterance.

(14) My dog wrote this book.

You would perhaps take (14) as a joke, or as a metaphor meaning that my dog was often sitting next to me when I was writing, but you would certainly struggle to ascertain my illocutionary intent. In RT terms, unlike in the case of (13), which yields its cognitive effects without unnecessarily increasing processing effort for you, my addressee, in the case of (14) your expectations about the relevance of my conversational contribution would not be fulfilled. This is because processing one's utterances should be worth its while, and this is what we expect our utterances to make manifest.

The degree of relevance associated with an utterance might thus be conceived of as a ratio between the utterance's effects and the processing costs of that utterance for A – I will use the expression 'effects/costs ratio' to refer to this relevance-theoretic notion. *Maximal* relevance is achieved, for any given level of effort, when the effects resulting from that effort are maximized, or, for any given level of effects, when the effort required for deriving those effects is minimized. Accordingly, S should choose the utterance that would achieve the highest ratio – a stimulus that achieves maximal relevance.

To illustrate the relevance-theoretic analysis of IRs in terms of processing costs and cognitive effects, I will compare the two IRs in (16)–(17) with the corresponding imperative request in (15).

(15) Close the window.

(16) Can you close the window?

(17) You can close the window.

For the sake of the argument, I assume that non-imperative sentences such as (16)–(17) and imperative sentences such as (15) are plausible alternative ways to perform one and the same request. In fact, I am making some simplifying assumptions, as there are insuppressible

3.3 Relevance Theory

Table 3.1 *Predicted relevance of a* Can you VP? *IR in comparison with an imperative request*

		Which alternative is maximally relevant?
A	More costs, same effects	Imperative
B	**More costs, more effects**	**Imperative or *Can you VP?***
C	More costs, fewer effects	Imperative
D	**Same costs, same effects**	**Imperative or *Can you VP?***
E	**Same costs, more effects**	***Can you VP?***
F	Same costs, fewer effects	Imperative
G	Fewer costs, same effects	*Can you VP?*
H	Fewer costs, more effects	*Can you VP?*
I	Fewer costs, fewer effects	Imperative or *Can you VP?*

differences between these three expressions such as, for instance, their sentence-type and the fact that the imperative construction is syntactically – at least at the surface level – shorter than the other two. My point here is that the three of them can be used for requesting that A close the window in a set of contexts of utterance that should be, of course, determined empirically.

Following the definition of maximal relevance, a request such as (16) would be more relevant than an imperative request only if the IR causes extra cognitive effects absent in the imperative (15) while entailing no extra processing costs (see Table 3.1). Equivalently, relative to (16), (15) would be maximally relevant if it reduces the processing costs while triggering the same (and no more) cognitive effects as the IR in (16) does. Thus, to determine which alternative is maximally relevant, one needs to take into account both the processing costs and the cognitive effects associated with the interpretation of an utterance in a particular context.

At the theoretical level, it is quite difficult to conceive how an utterance of *Can you VP?* intended as a request could yield a smaller number of cognitive effects for the addressee than an imperative request. In addition, the option according to which an imperative request would be more effortful to process than a *Can you VP?* request is very unlikely and it has, to date, never been suggested in the pragmatic literature. This is why only the four possibilities in bold (i.e., in rows A, B, D and E in Table 3.1) will be considered seriously in this chapter. I first deal with the issue whether more costs are entailed by IRs such as *Can you VP?* in Section 3.3.2, and, in Section 3.3.3, I address the question whether these IRs trigger more cognitive effects than imperatives.

3.3.2 Extra Processing for Indirect Requests?

In order to see whether, all other things being equal, from RT's effects/costs perspective, IRs such as (16)–(17) are likely to involve extra processing costs relative to imperative requests such as (15), let us have a look at the standard RT account of the interpretation of imperative sentences.

(15) Close the window. (repeated)

(16) Can you close the window? (repeated)

(17) You can close the window. (repeated)

According to RT, the imperative sentential mood encodes two propositional attitudes: desirability and potentiality (Carston 2002; Clark 1993; Wilson & Sperber 1988). That the content of an imperative sentence is potential and desirable is where the semantic, incomplete, interpretation of the utterance leaves A. The pragmatic interpretation is delivered by resolving this semantic indeterminacy. In the case of imperative requests such as (15), this means understanding that the represented state of affairs is desirable to S and from S's point of view. This may lead to the explicature that <'the window will be closed immediately' is desirable to S and potential>. In RT, an *explicature* is a communicated assumption that is fleshed out by pragmatic enrichment and/or modulation of the logical form (LF) of the utterance. Other possible explicatures inferred from an utterance of the imperative in (15) are given in (18). In *higher-order explicatures*, the LF is embedded within a higher-level description, for example, in speech act terms, as in (18d).

(18) a   It is desirable to S and potential that the window will be closed immediately.
 b   It is desirable to S and potential that A close the window.
 c   S is telling A to close the window.
 d   S is requesting that A close the window.

Under such a view, although the imperative does not encode directive illocutionary force (but only desirability and potentiality), it gives A the direction in which to seek relevance. The imperative mood can thus be conceived, at most, as a cue that gives probabilistic indication as to which higher-order explicature is being communicated.

Now, according to RT, how do people infer the indirect directive meaning of utterances such as (16)–(17)? Do their interrogative and declarative sentence-types act as cues to their IR meaning?

3.3 Relevance Theory

(16) Can you close the window? (repeated)

(17) You can close the window. (repeated)

To the best of my knowledge, the only detailed treatment of standardized IRs such as (16)–(17) in RT is Groefsema's (1992) account of IRs involving the modal *can*, which resembles Lepore and Stone's (2015) proposal that I discussed in Chapter 1, as they both postulate lexical ambiguity of the modal *can*. For Groefsema, *can* has a 'direct' request interpretation in such examples, the 'request' meaning being a direct development of the unitary meaning of *can*, guided by the communicative principle of relevance. That is, if Groefsema is right, there is nothing special to (16)–(17): the higher-order explicature in (18c) is derived after enrichment of the LF of the sentence uttered, much in the same way as (15) yields the assumption in (18c).

(15) Close the window! (repeated)

(18c) S is telling A to close the window. (repeated)

Following Wilson and Sperber's (1988) analysis of the interrogative mood, Groefsema (1992) conceives of the utterance of (16) as communicating that the thought <The addressee can close the window> would be relevant if true. According to Groefsema, the LF of the interrogative (16) is (19), in a situation where it is mutually manifest that P is relevant if true.

(19) S is asking whether $<_P <_Q$ A closes the window$_y >$ is compatible with the set of all propositions which have a bearing on Q>.

She points out that, in the context of a typical household interaction between intimates, it is mutually manifest that A is able to close the window, and, as a consequence, that (16) cannot be about A's physical ability to close the window but 'achieves relevance as an instantiation of her ability of [closing the window]'. Groefsema further argues that, since S and A are having a conversation in a specific place (here and now), the only 'relevant' enrichment of the LF of (16) is that the instantiation of A's ability be immediate. Thus (20) is fleshed out of (19).

(20) S is asking whether $<_P <_Q$ A closes the window$_y$ *immediately*> is compatible with the set of all propositions which have a bearing on Q>.

A is then invited to focus on all the evidence concerning the proposition that <A closes the window immediately>, that is, the evidence supporting his closing of the window (that there is a window open, that windows in general ought to be closed, that A is closer to the window than S is, etc.). If at least one element in the context is incompatible with the proposition Q, A should give a negative answer to S's question (e.g., if the window in question is blocked, or cannot be closed). If there are no such elements incompatible with the proposition Q, A should give a positive answer to the question, but this 'yes' answer would not achieve relevance. Since the proposition Q describes a state of affairs that does not hold at the time of utterance, the only relevant way for A to provide evidence for Q is to make sure that the state of affairs described by Q will hold immediately. That is, the only way A can respond to the question in (16) while being conversationally cooperative is to close the window.

When she proposes that the IR meaning of utterances of *Can you VP?* is 'directly' inferred, Groefsema suggests that these requests come at no extra cost relative to their imperative counterparts. However, a closer look at her analysis points to the contrary. In fact, Groefsema's (1992) explanation of how the higher-order explicature of a request can be inferred from the interrogative (16) resembles very much the kind of rational reconstruction postulated by Searle (1975). Groefsema's analysis implies that a possible interpretation of (16) that would not consist in a request would be discarded as inappropriate relative to the context at hand. This strongly suggests that, at some point in the comprehension process, the discarded interpretation and the correct, 'request' interpretation compete. This does not make her analysis, strictly speaking, an alternative account of IRs than Searle's. Furthermore, her account raises an important issue. She focuses on requests involving the modal *can*, but, in English, other constructions are used in standardized requests, such as *Would you like to VP?*, *Will you VP?*, *Why don't you VP?*, *Why not VP?*, to mention just a few. Arguably, if used in appropriate circumstances, these could be understood as requests in a very straightforward way. I fail to see how an approach based on claims about lexical meanings, such as Groefsema's, could account for these cases. Assuming that all of these utterances would be formulaic requests, would she be willing to postulate for each of them – in a rather ad hoc fashion – the same kind of analysis she proposes for *can*?

That being said, Groefsema's (1992) account is well in line with Wilson and Sperber's (1988) analysis of mood in terms of potentiality and desirability. Both predict semantic differences between an IR

3.3 Relevance Theory

performed with an interrogative such as (16) and the corresponding IR performed with a declarative such as (17).

(16) Can you close the window? (repeated)

(17) You can close the window. (repeated)

From a psychological perspective, all other things being equal, a declarative IR such as (17) is expected to impose extra processing effort relative to its interrogative counterpart (16). Let me explain why. We saw that, according to RT, interrogative sentences are interpretively used to convey desirable answers, that is, answers that cause positive effects for the interpreter. Likewise, at the semantic level, the assumption expressed by an imperative sentence is potential and desirable. Thus both the requests performed by means of imperatives and interrogatives can, rather straightforwardly, be explained in terms of the relevance-theoretic notions of potentiality and desirability. By contrast, for RT, declaratives do not encode desirability, let alone potentiality. At most, the potentiality of the assumption expressed by the declarative in (17) would be a consequence of the lexical meaning Groefsema (1992) defines for *can*, but this has nothing to do with the declarative qua sentence-type. The consequence is that, as interrogatives, and not declaratives, encode desirability, there should be extra inferential work associated with the declarative IR in (17) relative to the interrogative IR in (16).

Returning to the contrast between imperative requests and IRs, from the perspective of cognitive processing, the question is whether, following the standard RT analysis of moods, the imperative mood facilitates the request interpretation in comparison with other constructions used in IRs that lack imperative mood. Roughly speaking, there are three options regarding the competition between the 'direct' and 'indirect' interpretations of *Can you VP?* and *You can VP* utterances, all of which entail extra costs for the expressions with an IR meaning relative to imperative sentences (and to corresponding direct questions/ statements).

In the first option, the 'ability' meaning of *Can you VP?* and *You can VP* requests is 'default'. Such an option is neo-Gricean in the sense that it builds on the theories of utterance interpretation in line with Grice (1957; 1975), who conceives of inferential understanding in terms of a reasoning based on S's communicative intentions. The second option amounts to considering that the meaning of a request for action is the default. This option is closely related to views held by researchers in grammaticalization, who consider that the literal meaning of a given construction can be replaced over time by another literal meaning (e.g., Traugott 1988; Traugott & Dasher 2005). For instance, Terkourafi and Villavicencio (2003) argue that *Can you VP?* IRs are able to provide, in some contexts, a default directive illocutionary force that can be overridden by another, inferentially derived force. In this case, the request interpretation of these constructions would not involve more effort than the corresponding imperative. However, a possible problem with this view is that the 'question' meaning would be non-literal, and therefore expected to be costlier to process than the request meaning, which lacks plausibility. According to the third option, which is the one assumed by relevance theorists, both interpretations of an ISA utterance are inferred in parallel. This suggests that IRs are costlier than imperative requests because a decision must be made to know which interpretation is the correct and the most relevant one. However, as Vega Moreno (2007: 116) points out, 'recurrent selective processing of a familiar stimulus [for instance, a token of *Can you VP?*] may lead to the development of a more or less automatic cognitive procedure or inferential route to process this stimulus'. Her notion of 'pragmatic routine' reinterprets standardization as a reduction of the number of inferential steps required to understand the (indirect) meaning of an utterance. In the same vein, Escandell-Vidal (2004: 357) proposes that a higher accessibility of background assumptions can guide the addressee towards the correct interpretation. From her perspective, social representations 'are ready to be used in the inferential processing' (2004: 360). Assuming pragmatic routines would thus rule out the possibility that standardized IRs impose extra processing costs relative to their imperative counterparts, making them after all maximally relevant, just as are imperative requests.

3.3.3 Extra Cognitive Effects in Indirect Requests?

If, in some contexts, standardized utterances such as (21)–(22) make the higher-order explicature of a request costlier to access relative to their imperative counterparts, from the perspective of RT this extra cost should be counterbalanced by extra cognitive effects.

(21) Can you give me a few examples? (BNC)

(22) You can give me a few examples.

If it is the case that the extra costs are compensated for by extra effects, the standardized utterances would be maximally relevant, just as

3.3 Relevance Theory

imperative requests are. But what effects exactly? By means of such standardized IRs, S would communicate to A her intention to be polite, that is her concern for A's face needs. She could opt for (21)–(22) instead of uttering (23).

(23) Give me a few examples.

An intuitively appealing hypothesis is that, in standardized IRs, the indication that S wants to be polite would compensate for the extra processing of the utterance in comparison with the imperative in (23). A similar rationale applies to impolite utterances. Consider, for instance, (24), which can receive a rather impolite reading, such as the implication that A is a non-cooperative person.

(24) Can't you give me a few examples?

Heinemann (2006) demonstrates that, in Danish, *Couldn't you VP?* requests are more assertive and more powerful than their affirmative *Could you VP?* counterparts. As a consequence, one expects that they would be perceived as a less polite means of requesting. As in the case of (21)–(22), the assumption about S's (im)politeness would constitute an extra effect that compensates for extra processing costs associated with (24).

Appearances notwithstanding, it is doubtful that politeness and impoliteness are plausible compensations for the extra costs that would arise from IRs: saying that a standardized IR is considered more polite than an imperative request is different from claiming that it communicates a politeness assumption. As Jary (1998b) points out, very often politeness does not attract attention; in fact, in many cases, linguistic politeness does not belong to the intended message, so that a politeness assumption has not the status of a conveyed propositional content. For a politeness (or impoliteness) assumption to be communicated, this assumption must be both intentional and manifest. Under such a view, it makes little sense to assume that (21)–(22) systematically communicate politeness or impoliteness assumptions. Like Jary, Escandell-Vidal (1998; 2004) considers that politeness assumptions are optional. Although she acknowledges that inferential judgements of (im)politeness are possible for any utterance, she argues that politeness is rarely communicated. In other words, in many contexts, the implicature in (25) will not be derived for (21)–(22).

(25) S told me to give her a few examples, and she did it politely.

According to Escandell-Vidal (1998), an IR such as (21)–(22) can give rise to the higher-level explicature (25). Alongside the decoding and the inferential modules assumed in the relevance-theoretic framework, Escandell-Vidal (2004) proposes a 'social module'. This module would yield a set of representations on socially accepted behaviour while operating an online analysis of perceived pieces of behaviour. Empirical evidence indicates that, despite the impression of rudeness that is traditionally associated with them, imperative requests are not perceived as particularly impolite in all contexts (see Freytag 2020 for evidence from business emails). Thus higher-level (im)politeness explicatures can also be derived in the case of imperative requests. The upshot is that, as (im)politeness assumptions are not specific to standardized IRs, their status as a possible compensation for the extra costs entailed by these constructions cannot be generalized across contexts.

In the same spirit, Terkourafi (2003; 2008) considers politeness, impoliteness and rudeness as perlocutionary effects of S's utterance. Accordingly, a politeness or impoliteness assumption can – but need not – be achieved as a consequence of S's utterance. Additional arguments against the view that 'polite utterances' result in the generation of 'politeness implicatures' are discussed in Haugh (2015: 149–58), who considers that politeness is best defined as an evaluation of the attitude conveyed by an utterance, rather than as a level of meaning of an utterance. In the words of Terkourafi (2015), rather than being communicated by speakers, the politeness of standardized IRs is a by-product of utterance interpretation. For instance, a standardized IR such as *Can you VP?* is considered polite because, in the speakers'/addressees' mental lexicon, the expression *Can you VP?* is represented as contextually appropriate. *Can you VP?* contributes to politeness judgements across contexts because interpreters have the 'meta-knowledge' that *Can you VP?* is a common and acceptable request form in a variety of contexts. Assuming such a view, in some contexts, such as formal interactions, imperatives would be considered marked relative to standardized expressions, which are the 'baseline' for pragma-social appropriateness.

From an empirical perspective, the results of Culpeper's (2011: 186–93) experiments provide support for the idea that standardized IRs are unmarked in terms of (im)politeness. Culpeper asked graduate students to rate utterances such as (26) (direct request), (27) (standardized IR) and (28) (non-standardized IR) on a scale of increasing impoliteness.

(26) You be quiet.

3.3 Relevance Theory

(27) Could you be quiet?

(28) You aren't being quiet.

In these examples, the request SA was the same. Telling someone to be quiet is face-threatening not only because of its illocutionary force (it restricts A's freedom of action), but also because making such a request implies that A's behaviour was inappropriate at the time of utterance. Three basic scenarios were displayed in the high–low (H–L) power condition: a boss speaking to an employee, a judge to a defendant and a sergeant-major to a recruit. In the low–high (L–H) power condition, the speaker and addressee roles were reversed. In the H–L condition, the mean ratings for direct, standardized indirect utterances such as (27) and non-standardized indirect utterances such as (28) were all below 'neither agree nor disagree', with lower impoliteness ratings for standardized IRs such as (27). In other words, *Could you VP?* was evaluated as being neither polite nor impolite in situations where face-threat was involved, for example, when addressing a higher status person. This finding is not surprising if, as Terkourafi (2015) proposes, the expression *Could you VP?* is perceived as being polite *all other things being equal*.

All these analyzes accord very well with the view that standardized IRs do not always trigger extra cognitive effects absent in their imperative counterparts. They mark a clear departure from Brown and Levinson's SA based analysis of indirectness, according to which politeness comes into existence as a propositional content intended to compensate for the face-threatening aspects of our SAs. Now if, in some situations standardized IRs performed with *Can you VP?* and *You can VP* do not cause additional effects in comparison to imperative requests, one wonders why they are preferred to imperatives in the first place. A possible reason is that they are more in agreement with the speakers' preferences. In RT terms, unlike imperative requests, standardized expressions are 'optimally relevant' stimuli.

3.3.4 Standardized Indirect Requests and Speakers' Preferences

In line with the presumption of optimal relevance, (a) A assumes that S's utterance is relevant enough for it to be worth A's processing effort and (b) A expects S to choose an utterance that matches as much as possible her preferences and her abilities. The stimulus that satisfies the presumption of optimal relevance, that is, which is *optimally* relevant, may thus be a stimulus that is not *maximally* relevant. If one applies this line of thought to ISAs, the idea is that, if an utterance of *Can you VP?* or

You can VP is not *maximally* relevant in a particular context (because its effects/costs ratio is lower than that of an imperative), it is plausible that this construction was used by virtue of its *optimal* relevance. According to the presumption of optimal relevance, if an interrogative/declarative sentence such as (21)–(22) is more in agreement with S's preferences and abilities than the imperative in (23), then, if S is a rational and benevolent speaker, S should perform her request that A give her some examples by using (21)–(22) instead of the imperative.

(21) Can you give me a few examples? (repeated)

(22) You can give me a few examples. (repeated)

(23) Give me a few examples. (repeated)

This should be so whether or not (21)–(22) have a higher effects/costs ratio than (23) – that is, whether (21)–(22) or (23) is the maximally relevant stimulus. Conversely, if the imperative in (23) matches S's preferences or abilities better, she should opt for (23) rather than for (21)–(22) regardless of whether (23) has a higher effects/costs ratio than (21)–(22).

One such preference concerns S's desire to avoid being impolite. Discussing the difference between imperative and indirect requests, Jary (1998a) argues that in communicating her desire by means of an imperative utterance, S makes manifest her belief that this desire be relevant for A. The recognition of this premise is required for A to access the intended request interpretation. For Jary, the choice of indirect constructions for the performance of requests is motivated by S's desire to avoid conveying hazardous implications such as the assumption that, because her desire is relevant for A, S is 'superior' to A. Thus, according to Jary, the reason that IRs are preferred to imperative requests in some situations is that they match S's preferences better than imperatives would do. Standardized IR constructions help speakers save their positive face while minimizing the threat to their addressees' negative face. The problem with this argument is that A's compliance with a standardized IR implies that S's desire is relevant for A, just as it is when the imperative counterpart is used as a request. That is, even though only imperative requests encode S's desire through the propositional attitude of desirability, such a desire will be relevant for A whether the uttered sentence is imperative, interrogative or declarative. In all such cases, understanding that a request has been made implies that S's desire has been perceived by A as a reason to

3.3 Relevance Theory

comply. Thus, as soon as the directive force of the utterance is inferred, both an imperative request and an IR may convey the implicature that S is superior to A. There must therefore be something else in utterances of *Can you VP?* and *You can VP* that explains why they match S's preferences better than imperatives do. I believe IRs are less likely than imperatives to convey unwanted implicatures because of their interrogative sentence-type and the meaning of modal *can*, that is, their semantic incompleteness and the enablement pattern lexically encoded by *can*. Taken together, these two features of *Can you VP?* provide an explanation why this construction is often considered polite.

Jary's idea was that S can choose to perform a request by using a standardized utterance such as *Can you VP?* rather than an imperative sentence because the former matches her preferences better than the latter would. Such motivations are relevant to discuss because they provide an explanation why *Can you VP?* and *You can VP* are used in the performance of requests despite their being not necessarily more relevant than imperatives. Instead of considering that these expressions are used to convey politeness assumptions, I propose that they enable avoiding being perceived as impolite. According to Jary (1998b: 2–3), the choice of 'polite' forms such as standardized IRs is, above all, explained by S's desire to preserve her status within a social community. In a similar vein, Davis (1998: 119) points out that central matters for S regard, first, the degree of cognitive effort *she* produces in conveying her assumptions and, second, the possible consequences of the utterance's form for her reputation (see Lee & Pinker 2010; Pinker et al. 2008).

Summing up, the politeness associated with utterances of *Can you VP?* and its declarative counterpart can be analyzed in at least two respects. On the one hand, it can be thought of as an implicature of the utterance. On the other hand, it is best seen as a by-product of interpretation or a perlocutionary effect that is frequently associated with the performance of these IRs. From the latter perspective, such standardized IRs are preferred to imperatives because they are often optimally relevant stimuli. This is so not because utterances of *Can you VP?* give rise to extra effects for A – which imperatives would lack – (in which case *Can you VP?* stimuli would be maximally relevant), but because this construction makes it possible to avoid undesired impoliteness effects. This explanation accommodates the view that *Can you VP?* is considered polite qua expression, unlike the imperative sentence-type. The view that *Can you VP?* corresponds to a 'baseline' for politeness evaluations explains why it is commonly used as IR, regardless of considerations of processing costs and cognitive effects that also apply to imperative utterances.

3.4 THE GRADED SALIENCE HYPOTHESIS

Rachel Giora's Graded Salience Model has elements in common with cognitive linguistic and relevance theoretic approaches. Although it was originally designed for the study of figurative language interpretation, I believe that this theory has something to say about ISA processing. Giora (2002; 2003) puts forth a notion of 'salience' that is a function of frequency of use, familiarity, conventionality (contextual appropriateness), prototypicality and probably other factors such as 'what is on one's mind at a particular moment'. The Graded Salience Hypothesis' (GSH) proposes that, in the initial phase of comprehension, salient meanings will always be activated, even if they do not fit the context. In the ensuing integration process of comprehension, salient meanings can either be retained or rejected. Crucially, not only the meanings of lexical items can be salient: salience also applies to longer linguistic units, such as phrases, and to propositional meanings as well. ISA expressions can therefore be approached from the perspective of this theory.

Importantly, salience is not a theoretical property of meanings. Rather, the salience of a given meaning must be established empirically. Thus, if we intend to test the GSH's predictions for ISA interpretation, we first should establish empirically which meaning of our target expressions are the most salient ones. This is best done with very specific constructions, such as *Can you stand up?*, instead of the more abstract construction *Can you VP?*. For instance, a quick survey for *Can you stand up?* on the COCA corpus suggests that it is more frequently associated with a request interpretation: I found three tokens of this sentence with a 'question' meaning and five with a 'request' meaning, which indicates that the latter interpretation should be considered as the most salient one. For another specification of *Can you VP?*, such as *Can you bring me* + noun phrase (NP)?, the only plausible interpretation of the eleven relevant occurrences on the COCA corpus was the IR. Assuming that frequency of occurrence is indicative of meaning salience, these results strongly suggest that the indirect meaning of *Can you bring me NP?* is the most salient one. Using this method, it would be time-consuming to determine whether the direct question of the indirect request meaning of the abstract *Can you VP?* is the salient one for English speakers. To have an estimate of IR meaning salience, any specific instantiation of this construction by means of a VP should be taken into account. Therefore, only specific constructions, such as the ones I have given as examples, should be examined in comparable linguistic environments before making any claims as to the salience of IR interpretations in general. In line with the idea that the indirect meaning of *Can you VP?* is more salient than its direct meaning of an ability question, Gibbs (1983) has shown that *Can you VP?* utterances are read faster when they convey a request than when they are used as a literal question. These results too suggest that the indirect meaning of *Can you VP?* takes less time to be derived than the direct one, and possibly that the indirect interpretation is activated before the direct interpretation, even when it is not the relevant or intended meaning. The more salient meaning associated with this construction would thus be the 'request' meaning; we will see in the next chapter whether this prediction is verified.

3.5 SUMMARY

In this chapter, I discussed approaches of utterance interpretation that do not conceive of indirectness as a particular type of SA realization or as a feature of the relationship between a sentence-type and a SA type, but, rather, in terms of a cline of explicitness of the communicated meaning. This amounts to saying, in cognitive linguistic (CL) terms, that constructions with a possible indirect meaning activate this meaning by virtue of SA scenario components linguistically expressed in the utterance. In RT terms, the request meaning of, for example, *Can you VP?* is an implicated assumption derived on the basis of a combination of linguistic meaning and contextual information. While direct and indirect utterances can be studied in terms of their respective processing costs and cognitive effects, the explicitness of the request meaning would be higher in the case of the imperative *VP!*, as the imperative mood encodes a propositional attitude of desirability distinct from that encoded by interrogative constructions. A major difference with Brown and Levinson's (1987) theory is that these cognition-oriented approaches do not view the politeness of ISAs as a propositional meaning. Like the CL and the RT approaches, the graded salience hypothesis is interested in the cognitive processes involved in ISA interpretation, and it offers predictions that can be tested on the basis of empirical data such as relative frequency of use associated with different ISA constructions.

3.6 DISCUSSION QUESTIONS

- In the most recent cognitive linguistic analyses of IRs, the higher the number of components of a SA scenario that are expressed in an utterance, the more salient and the more prototypical the SA.

Accordingly, a prototypical request takes the form of an addressee-oriented preparatory interrogative, which displays optionality, and includes a linguistic marker of mitigation. By contrast, a prototypical command lacks mitigation and optionality, and emphasises the benefits of A's action for S. Use the examples of IRs such as those given in this chapter and rank these constructions, first, in terms of their degree of prototypicality qua requests, and, second, in terms of their degree of prototypicality qua commands. Then compare your ranking orders. What is the picture that emerges?
- Relevance theory is sometimes criticized for not being amenable to falsification. Consider the possible costs and effects of ISAs in different contexts, and think of testable predictions that would refute such a criticism.

3.7 SUGGESTIONS FOR FURTHER READING

For a discussion of the cognitive linguistic approaches to SAs, with a focus on English foreign language studies: Pérez-Hernández, Lorena. (2020). *Speech Acts in English: From Research to Instruction and Textbook Development*. Cambridge: Cambridge University Press.

An excellent introduction to relevance theory: Clark, Billy. 2013. *Relevance Theory*. Cambridge: Cambridge University Press.

4 The Comprehension of ISAs

4.1 INTRODUCTION

The three previous chapters offered us a general picture and several frameworks useful for conceptualizing indirect communication. They were, however, mainly theoretical, and, to have a better idea of what it is for a SA to be 'indirect', it is necessary to take into account experimental data. This chapter therefore proposes a review of experimental work concerning the comprehension of ISAs. Most available empirical and experimental data concern the category of directives, in particular IRs, which have been the focus of a considerable number of studies. This is the reason why IRs are also central to this book.

The main issues that have been addressed in the experimental literature on the comprehension of IRs can be grouped under two main headings. A first issue concerns differences in processing between imperative and indirect requests, and a second issue the differences between the IR uses and the literal/direct uses of IR constructions. Two further questions, which have been at the origin of the early studies of IR comprehension, are whether the understanding of an utterance as an IR necessarily implies the derivation of the direct meaning of the construction, and what properties of the construction used make such a direct meaning more or less likely to be inferred. Three properties are expected to influence the comprehension of IRs – conventionality of means, degree of standardization and degree of illocutionary force salience – although the latter has been largely under-researched. It will also be necessary to clarify what are the different measures of the processing costs associated with indirectness, and how they should be interpreted. The results of two eye-tracking experiments involving the interpretation of pragmatically ambiguous IRs will shed new light on the processing correlates of IRs.

4.2 PROCESSING DIFFERENCES BETWEEN SENTENCES USED DIRECTLY OR INDIRECTLY

One possible way to experimentally investigate indirectness is to compare the indirect use of an IR construction, such as *Can you VP?*, to the same construction used as a direct SA, such as an ability question, to see how the IR use and the direct use of the construction differ in terms of cognitive processing (Ruytenbeek 2017a). The basic assumption underlying this approach is that there are contexts where ISA constructions are ambiguous between a direct and an indirect interpretation. For instance, in Abbeduto et al.'s (1989) experimental setting, IR constructions such as *Could you open the scissors?* and *Could you roll the shoebox?* were actually ambiguous between their direct and their indirect readings; the participants responded only to their direct meaning when they were not sure if they could perform the action.

Exploring the relationship between direct and indirect meanings, Shapiro and Murphy (1993) started their study by teaching their participants the difference between these two types of meaning. The participants were then presented with a series of interrogative utterances such as (1)–(2) and asked to decide whether they contained a plausible direct meaning (i.e., ability question), while ignoring possible indirect meanings.

(1) Can you stop whistling?

(2) Do you have any money?

In the case of (1), the 'ability question' meaning is very unlikely, because anyone is able to stop whistling (as long, of course, as they are able to whistle). By contrast, for (2), the direct, 'request for information' meaning according to which S is asking A whether he has any money is quite likely (the conveyed – and indirect – meaning being S's request that A give her some money). These authors found longer decision times when a plausible indirect meaning was also present, as in (2). In another version of the experiment, participants were asked to answer questions such as (1)–(2). The response times associated with their answers were similar when only one meaning was plausible (e.g., 1) and when both meanings were (e.g., 2). In addition, these response latencies were similar when the direct meaning or the indirect meaning was the only plausible meaning. This indicates that it is not the indirectness of an interpretation, but, rather, its likelihood that should affect its processing times. This sort of experimental study,

4.2 Processing Sentences: Direct versus Indirect

however, is far from being ecological, and it remains to be seen whether its findings would be replicated in real-life conversational interactions. Moreover, in explicitly telling participants the difference between direct and indirect interpretations, the authors collected metapragmatic data unlikely to be informative about the actual interpretative processes involved in ISAs. It is also difficult to conclude anything concerning the activation of the direct meaning of ISA utterances.

Using a comprehension task, Coulson and Lovett (2010) compared the processing of another type of ISA expressions: negative state remarks such as (3) either uttered as a direct SA (statement) or as an ISA (request for another bowl of soup).

(3) My soup is too cold to eat.

They used event-related potentials (ERPs), a non-invasive technique consisting in measuring, with a low spatial, but high temporal resolution, electrical brain activity as a response to a stimulus. Participants read a scenario on a computer screen, followed by a target remark (either used as a direct statement or as an IR) and, after a blank screen, a possible continuation of the scenario. They were then asked to decide whether the continuation of the scenario was expected or not. The results of Coulson and Lovett's experiment indicate that a remark such as (3) induces a distinct electrical brain activity whether it is uttered as a DSA or as an IR. As an IR, it elicited more positive waveforms than the direct statements between the second word (e.g., *soup*) and the sixth word (e.g., *to*) of the sentence, which is interpreted by the authors as an indication that the processing of the utterance's content was less effortful in the IRs. A possible reason for this is that the IR meaning of the remarks was more natural in these scenarios. In addition, by the second and third words of the sentences, the IRs elicited larger 'late positive components' (LPC) of ERPs, that is, positive waveforms towards the end of the individual words, relative to the direct statements. As the participants' task consisted in assessing the (un)expectedness of scenario continuations, this latter finding may indicate higher memory effort for the IRs.

Following Coulson and Lovett's (2010) insights, van Ackeren et al. (2012) were interested in the processing correlates of non-standardized IRs. They examined how the Dutch equivalents of negative state remarks such as (4) activate the concept of action despite the fact that, unlike imperatives or *Can you VP?* sentences, they contain no verbal phrase corresponding to the requested action.

(4) It is very hot here.

In their experiment with Dutch material, a picture was displayed on the computer screen, and then a spoken utterance was presented to the participants. For instance, for the request performed with (4), the corresponding 'non-request' utterance was (5).

(5) It is very nice here.

The participants were instructed to listen carefully and to decide whether the interlocutor wanted them to do something. In addition, on 15 per cent of the trials, they were prompted to indicate whether a request was performed or not. Van Ackeren et al. (2012) found that, even though negative state remarks such as (4) contain no lexical reference to action (the reference to action is implicit in the utterance), their comprehension activates cortical motor areas to a stronger extent than the comprehension of utterances lacking any implicit motor information such as (5). Furthermore, relative to the control statements such as (5), IRs such as (4) elicited more activation in the medial pre-frontal cortex and the temporo-parietal junction, which are taken to be 'theory of mind' areas. Van Ackeren et al.'s (2012) findings could be interpreted in terms of indirectness, assuming that extra activation of theory of mind areas is required to understand the indirect uses of sentences (see also the results of Bašnáková et al.'s (2011) experiments). These findings do not tell us whether negative state remarks used as IRs increase response times relative to direct requests or their use as direct statements. However, they indicate that these IRs induce extra cognitive processing, as measured by the activation of brain areas specifically implicated in the interpretation of indirectness.

In a different study, Tromp et al. (2016) proposed an original approach to the processing of negative state remarks by collecting measures of pupil size changes, a technique called pupillometry. Using van Ackeren et al.'s (2012) stimuli and a similar experimental design, they investigated whether processing negative state remarks either as IRs or as direct statements results in differences of pupil diameter. They found that negative state remarks were associated with larger pupil diameter when used as IRs, which supports the hypothesis that, relative to direct statements, IRs increase processing costs. However, as Egorova et al. (2014) point out, in van Ackeren et al.'s (2012) and in Tromp et al.'s (2016) studies, requests were compared to statements. It is therefore unclear to what extent the differences found in terms of brain activation reflect SA processing, the indirectness of these SAs, or perhaps both. In fact, there is, to the best of my knowledge, no evidence that directives are costlier to process than assertive SAs, such as statements, explanations or answers in general.

4.3 PROCESSING DIFFERENCES BETWEEN DIRECT AND INDIRECT SAs

Despite considerable theoretical debate about the phenomenon of IRs, there are very few experimental studies directly relevant to the processing differences between direct requests and IRs. A prominent reason for this relates to the conceptual issues underlying 'indirectness' and some degree of terminological confusion. Another reason is that an imperative and a construction used as an IR, such as *Can you VP?*, not only have pragmatic differences but also syntactic ones, which are difficult to control for in experimental settings. For example, in an imperative one can omit an explicit subject, and imperative sentences are always shorter than *Can you VP?* sentences.

A pioneering study is Munro's (1979) fieldwork experiment, which focused on IRs for answers (indirect questions). The contrast concerns indirect questions such as (6), or (7), and their 'direct' counterparts, such as (8).

(6) Could you tell me what time it is?

(7) Could you tell me the time?

(8) What time is it?

Assuming that responses to indirect requests for information can be taken as evidence for the availability of the direct meaning of an IR, Munro randomly selected passers-by who wore a watch, on a university campus, and asked them the time using (6)–(7) or (8). Half of the people prompted with (6)–(7) provided two-fold responses such as (9), responding both to the direct and the indirect meaning; the other half just said what time it was, as in (10).

(9) Oh sure, it's ten past four.

(10) It's ten past four.

By contrast, the participants presented with (8) systematically responded with (10).

Two-fold responses to the indirect questions show that, in some situations, people access both the direct and the indirect meanings of IR expressions. In particular, verbal responses such as (10) indicate, at least, that the literal meaning of ISA constructions play a role in the identification of the indirect meaning of these utterances.

Another relevant study is Baker and Bricker's (2010). These authors presented participants with essays including comments from an instructor. The participants were asked whether a correction was needed or not and instructed to carry on with the requested change if they answered 'yes' to the question asked. The comments consisted in praise and requests for changes. Three types of essays were used: one with imperative requests for changes such as (11), one with standardized IRs such as (12), and one with hedged IRs such as (13).

(11) Put a comma here.

(12) Could you put a comma here?

(13) You might want to put a comma here.

Despite the fact that the corrections were faster for the IRs – a somewhat surprising finding – the participants made more mistakes in their corrections when the instructions were IRs such as (12)–(13) in comparison with imperatives such as (11). Assuming that pragmatic ambiguity increases error rates, these results suggest that, in a situation where people are faced with written requests for change, some IR constructions, such as *Could you VP?* and *You might want to VP*, increase the interpreter's effort because these constructions need to be disambiguated.

A fairly similar approach has been proposed by Yin and Kuo (2013), who used the eye-tracking technique. They presented participants with written scenarios of professional interactions in Mandarin. Each scenario was followed by a short conversational exchange between a manager and an employee. The final utterance of the conversation was a remark made by the manager. Two versions of the conversations were developed, one in which the manager's remark was a DSA (14), and another one in which it was an ISA (15).[1]

---

[1] I thank Chun-Po Yin for sending me the original Mandarin sentences, which have then been glossed and translated into English by Kevin Henry to whom I am especially grateful.

4.3 Processing SAs: Direct versus Indirect

(14) 陳經理: 這次專案, 請 你 務必 在規定的時間內
Chen this please you absolutely in time
Director: project
完成 因為 專案的延後 會 造成
Execute because a delay in the COND cause
project
成本的增加
an increase in costs

'Director Chen: please make sure that this project be delivered truly in time, because any delay would cause an increase in the costs.'

(15) 陳經理: 這次專案, 我們 需要 找到 一些辦法,
Chen Director: this project, we need find some solutions,
以 能夠 準時交出 部分的產品
in order to be able to in time deliver part of the product

'Director Chen: we need to find some solutions for this project, in order to be able to deliver part of the production in time.'

The participants were asked to decide whether the manager performed a request and to indicate their confidence in their judgement. First, they less often interpreted the final remark as a request when it was realized as an IR, and they took more time to indicate that a request was performed by the manager when it was an IR. Second, the average fixation durations for a word were longer in the scenarios with IRs. Considering the longer response times for IRs, and assuming that longer fixation durations reflect extra processing costs involved in reading (e.g., Rayner & Pollatsek 1989; Rayner et al. 2006; Holmqvist et al. 2011: 377–83), we can conclude that the participants experienced more difficulty when interpreting the IRs in comparison with the imperative requests.

If we consider the results of Baker and Bricker's (2010) and Yin and Kuo's (2013) studies, IRs tend to be associated with higher error rates, which could be a corollary of higher processing load. But things are more complicated as far as response times are concerned. While Yin and Kuo found shorter response times for direct requests in Chinese, in Baker and Bricker's study no such difference was found for English utterances. Moreover, the exact nature of the task performed by the participants in these studies and the sort of contextual information available to them is very likely to have an impact on how direct and indirect requests are processed (cf. Gibbs 2014). What would therefore be interesting to see is whether any difference in response times would occur when more neutral contexts precede the target utterances, that is, when the 'request' meaning is not primed by the context. It should also be pointed out that, in these two approaches, utterance comprehension was not assessed from the perspective of an actual addressee, and this may have had an influence of the data collected: Yin and Kuo (2013) examined request comprehension from an observer's perspective, and the participants in Baker and Bricker's (2010) experiment were not the authors of the essays. Insofar as the interpretation made by a third party does not necessarily coincide with (and the cognitive processing thereof possibly differs from) that of the actual addressees, it remains unclear whether these authors' findings would be replicated in more naturalistic settings, with requests that are addressed to experimental participants.

4.4 ARE INDIRECT SPEECH ACTS NECESSARILY SECONDARY?

The available evidence I have discussed so far reveals processing correlates typically associated with ISAs. But, at this stage, it remains unclear whether retrieving the direct meaning of ISAs is always necessary to interpret these utterances correctly. A related issue is whether the activation of the direct meaning runs in parallel to or precedes the derivation of the indirect meaning.

Recall that, according to Grice's (1975) and Searle's (1975) approaches, deriving the direct meaning of ISAs should be the starting point of an inferential process leading to the recognition of the indirect meaning. That being said, what Grice (1975) actually proposed is a rational explanation of how the intended meaning could be arrived at by a third party, and not a psychological theory of utterance interpretation (see Bach 2006; Brisard 2011; Saul 2002). Likewise, Searle put forward a 'reconstruction of the steps necessary to derive the [indirect meaning] from the literal [i.e., direct meaning]', while pointing out that 'in normal circumstances, of course, no one would consciously go through the steps involved in this reasoning' (1975: 62–3).

According to the psychological model based on Grice's and Searle's theories, an ISA is necessarily *secondary*, that is, inferred on the basis of another, *primary* meaning that also logically precedes it. This sequential model of interpretation, which is the first model that has been tested in experimental literature on ISAs, is known as the *standard pragmatic model* (SPM). For instance, according to this model, an IR performed with *Can you VP?* is understood on the basis of an inference originating in the identification of the direct ability question meaning of the

4.4 Are Indirect Speech Acts Necessarily Secondary?

utterance. In other words, the derivation of this direct meaning is necessary to access the intended IR meaning of the utterance.

In an early attempt to test the SPM, Gibbs (1979) carried out a reading task including paraphrase judgements. He presented participants with stories followed by a target utterance such as (16) used either as an IR or as a direct question; in another condition, the target utterance was presented in isolation without the context story.

(16) Must you open the window?

After reading the target utterance, the participants were asked to decide whether another remark, such as (17)–(18), was a correct paraphrase of the utterance that had been just displayed.

(17) Need you open the window?

(18) Do not open the window.

When the target utterances were displayed without any preceding context, processing the 'direct question' paraphrases such as (17) took less time, which indicates that the direct meaning of these expressions was still available for interpretation. By contrast, when a context preceded the utterance, responses were faster for the IR paraphrases such as (18). When the targets followed a story, they took longer for the 'direct question' paraphrases than for the IR paraphrases. This shows that, provided an appropriate context precedes a construction typically used as an IR, it does not take longer to understand and to judge its paraphrase as (in)correct whether this construction is used as a DSA or as an IR. These results invalidate the SPM, according to which the IR uses, by definition secondary, of these expressions should have taken longer to comprehend than their direct uses. Other experiments, using different methodologies and/or different IR forms, confirmed this finding. For instance, Gibbs (1983) replicated these results for IRs using a grammatical acceptability task, and Gibbs (1986a) made similar findings in a paraphrase judgement task for sarcastic IRs such as *Sure is nice and warm here* meaning 'Please close the window'.

Gibbs concludes that an analysis of the direct meaning of IRs is not required to derive their request meaning. However, I believe that these response time (RT) data do not conclusively show this. Rather, they show that, even if there were an activation of the direct meaning of utterances used as IRs, such an activation *would not increase RTs*. Strictly speaking, the inference from RT differences to cognitive processing differences (i.e., as measured by higher brain activation) is unwarranted. Whether IRs entail additional processing, such as, for instance, extra brain activation, is an open question. Moreover, RTs are but one possible measure of processing. I will be discussing further issues concerning processing costs in general in Section 4.6.

The upshot of the experimental studies addressed so far is that a psychological model of ISA interpretation, such as the standard pragmatic model, is untenable. If an IR is secondary, longer RTs should be expected in comparison with the direct counterpart of the IR, rather than shorter (or equal) RTs. Available evidence makes it very likely that IRs need not always be secondary, but they do not enable us to conclude in which situations the direct meaning of IRs is also activated at some point during interpretation. We are now in a position to ask what features of the constructions used as ISAs make it more likely that the indirect meaning will be primary or, rather, secondary.

4.5 THREE LINGUISTIC FACTORS INFLUENCING THE PROCESSING OF ISAs

Three linguistic factors that have received some attention in experimental studies on ISAs are what I have been calling, following Clark (1979), the 'conventionality of means', the degree to which a construction is standardized for the performance of a type of ISA, and the degree of (indirect) illocutionary force salience. I will show that these three factors are expected to have a considerable influence on whether indirect meanings of utterances are primary or secondary, as well as on the cognitive processing of these utterances.

4.5.1 Conventionality of Means

One possible convention of means for the performance of indirect directives relies on the preparatory condition for this SA type: it amounts to asking a question about A's ability to do this action, as with the *Can you VP?* construction in (19).

(19) Could you tell me the price for a fifth of Jim Beam?

By contrast, this convention is not involved in the sentence in (20), which can nevertheless be used as a question about the price of a fifth of Jim Beam.

4.5 Linguistic Factors Influencing ISA Processing

(20) Does a fifth of Jim Beam cost £5?

On the basis of records of requests for information from local merchants in American English, Clark (1979) examined question–answer pairs and confirmed the intuition that constructions such as (19) make their indirect meaning more likely, and their direct meaning less likely, relative to constructions such as (20). From this finding, we can expect differences in cognitive processing associated with distinct conventions of means. However, as we will see, experimental evidence on this issue is scarce.

Some conventions of means, such as using an imperative, an obligation modal, or questioning A's ability to do some action, involve making a direct reference to A's future action. It seems plausible that, for such IRs, the explicit linguistic content of the utterance provides A with a cue for identifying which specific action he is requested to perform. This intuition was at the basis of Francik and Clark's (1985) obstacle hypothesis, which I have already mentioned in Chapter 2, according to which speakers formulate their requests, and, in particular, their requests for information, to deal with the greatest potential obstacle to the addressee's expected response. For instance, S would utter (21) if she believes that the greatest obstacle for A to provide the requested information is that he did not read the newspaper.

(21) Did you happen to read in the newspaper this morning what time the governor's lecture is today?

Following Francik and Clark, one can think of trying to identify a possible obstacle to A's compliance as a general convention of means for the performance of IRs. To validate their hypothesis, the authors combined a production task with appropriateness ratings for the requests produced. When the participants identified no specific obstacles to A's providing the desired information, they tended to produce requests that were quite straightforward, and not conditional on the presence of a specific obstacle, such as (22), but they also used questions such as (23), which refers to a very general obstacle to respond to a question, namely, not knowing the answer.

(22) What time is the governor's lecture?

(23) Do you know what time is the governor's lecture?

As for contexts in which specific obstacles were identified, Francik and Clark provide three main findings. First, speakers produced a request conditional on the absence or elimination of the obstacle; the more specific the obstacle, as in (21), the more specific the direct meaning of the utterance. Second, when the potential obstacle was hard to identify or very general, participants chose request forms that were more broadly applicable, such as *Can/Could you VP?*. Third, request forms that mention a given obstacle were preferred in the matching type of situations, that is, in situations where the obstacle they mentioned was most likely. For instance, (24) was preferred in the scenarios where A's willingness to tell the time was the greatest possible obstacle.

(24) Would you mind telling me the time?

In line with these findings, in her study of French verbal interactions in a bakery, Kerbrat-Orecchioni (2001) found that statements and questions about the availability of an item such as (25)–(26) were preferred when the customer could not see whether a desired item, for example, *une baguette* or a type of meringue, is included in the merchant's display (see also Kerbrat-Orecchioni 2004).

(25) Je voudrais savoir si vous avez des meringues au chocolat.
 'I'd like to know whether you have some chocolate meringues'.

(26) Vous avez des meringues au chocolat ?
 'Do you have any chocolate meringues?'

Interestingly, in these situations of daily life, French native speakers naturally referred to plausible obstacles preventing their addressees from satisfying their requests.

The idea behind the notion of a 'convention of means' is that the linguistic content of a particular construction makes it appropriate for the performance of a SA in a particular context. In line with this view, experimental studies have investigated the processing differences between appropriate and inappropriate ISA constructions. One such study is Gibbs's (1981), which examined how well the form of direct and indirect requests is retained in oral and written conversation. Gibbs's experiment consisted in a sentence recognition paradigm. Participants were presented with stories, five of which contained imperative requests such as (27), five of which contained standardized IRs such as (28), that were appropriate to the context, and the remaining five stories involved inappropriate standardized IRs, such

4.5 Linguistic Factors Influencing ISA Processing

as (29), which is not a natural way of ordering a hamburger in a fast-food outlet.

(27) Give me a hamburger.

(28) I'll have a hamburger.

(29) How about a hamburger?

Immediately after a distractor task, or forty-eight hours later, they did a multiple-choice recognition task in which they had to select the sentence that they had read or heard before. After no delay, participants recognized inappropriate IRs better relative to appropriate IRs, and inappropriate IRs were also recognized better than direct requests. In the forty-eight hour delay condition, again, inappropriate IRs were recognized better than appropriate IRs but, this time, only in the written condition. In both delays, participants chose appropriate IR distractors when they were initially presented with imperative requests, which indicates a bias toward remembering imperative requests not in their imperative form, but as IR expressions that are appropriate to the context of utterance. Gibbs's (1981) approach indicates that conversational memory for requests is only partly reconstructive. According to him, IRs that are not contextually appropriate are remembered better because more complex inferences are needed to understand them, an explanation that actually applies to any sort of utterance, whether indirect or not.

In a similar study, Gibbs (1987) reports that people remember better IRs that are inappropriate in the sense that speakers who performed these IRs did not deal with a possible obstacle to compliance (obstacle hypothesis). By contrast, in the absence of a conversational context, recognition rates did not differ for IRs specifying a plausible obstacle to compliance and IRs that did not specify such an obstacle. The results of this experiment also reveal that when the participants do not correctly recognize inappropriate IRs, they have a tendency to remember these IRs as being constructions that mention an obstacle, that is, appropriate IRs. This demonstrates that the memory advantage for inappropriate IRs is due to their under-specification in terms of possible obstacles to compliance.

Summing up, we saw that some conventions of means, such as questioning A's ability to do the action, mention very general obstacles to A's compliance, and make their indirect interpretation very likely. A safe bet is that for some conventions of means, the ISA constructions are more strongly associated with their indirect interpretation than for others. Another possible hypothesis is that some conventions of means increase the likelihood that the ISA will be primary rather than secondary. Another result, which is in line with the general finding that people have a better memory for what is socially unexpected or inappropriate, is that ISA constructions are remembered better when they do not fit the context in which they are uttered.

4.5.2 Degrees of Standardization

In addition to their convention of means, utterances used in the performance of ISAs vary as to the degree to which they are standardized for some SA type. In my definition, a high degree of standardization is the result of a diachronic process which has led to the sentence or expression having a 'preferred' indirect illocutionary force. This does not entail, however, that the construction can no longer be uttered with its direct illocutionary force. Consider, for instance, the pair in (30)–(31).

(30) Can you close the door?

(31) Is it possible to close the door?

The idea is that, even though they both refer to A's ability to perform the action requested, over time the form of (30) has come to be associated with an IR meaning to a stronger extent than that of (31); *Can you VP?* has developed a high degree of standardization qua IR performance. I therefore expect, from a cognitive perspective, the IR interpretation to be more easily accessible in (30) than in (31), and (31) to be more likely to convey a direct meaning. Degree of standardization and likelihood that the direct meaning is intended should correlate negatively. In fact, empirical support for this hypothesis was already provided by Clark (1979) in his study on telephone requests to merchants. He found, in his Experiment 3, that the literal, ability meaning of *Are you able to tell me ...?* was responded to 34% of the time by the merchants, while this figure dropped to 16% in the case of *Can you tell me ...?*, which has a higher degree of standardization qua IR. In addition, elliptical responses, that is, responses that do not make any reference to the literal ability meaning of the ISA construction, were less frequent for *Are you able to tell me ...?* (38%) than for its highly standardized counterpart (more than 50%).

Following the insights of Clark's (1979) experiments, the exploration in the French written corpus Frantext (*Base textuelle Frantext*) (2016),

4.5 Linguistic Factors Influencing ISA Processing

reported in Ruytenbeek et al. (2017), concerned the French equivalents of *Can you VP?* (i.e., *Pouvez-vous VP?*) and *Is it possible to VP?* (i.e., *Est-il possible de VP?*) in post-1900 French. Specifically, it shows that these two constructions are significantly different as to their degree of standardization qua IR. On the basis of the linguistic environment of the written utterances, Sophie Decaestecker and I classified the tokens of these two constructions into IRs, genuine questions and rhetorical questions. The IR uses of *Pouvez-vous VP?* illustrated in (32) were the most frequent (71%), followed by direct questions (25%) (see example 33) and rhetorical questions (4%) (example 34). By contrast, the most frequent uses of *Est-il possible de VP?* (including the conditional variant of this construction, *Serait-il possible de VP?*) were direct questions (70%), as in (35), followed by IR uses (16%) (example 36) and rhetorical questions (14%) (example 37).

(32) Pouvez-vous me donner quelques détails sur votre petit-fils, car vous êtes sa grand-mère, n'est-ce pas ? Et d'abord, quel âge a-t-il ?
'Can you give me some information about your grandson, as you are his grandmother, right? First of all, how old is he?'

(33) Pouvez-vous faire bouger cette photographie ?
'Can you cause this photograph to move?'

(34) Pouvez-vous imaginer une vie plus dénuée d'intérêt que celle d'un chef de gare ?
'Can you think of a life that is more deprived of interest than that of a train station manager?'

(35) Serait-il possible de les réconcilier ?
'Would it be possible to reconcile them?'

(36) Est-il possible de savoir ce que Number One vous a dit ?
'Is it possible to know what Number One told you?'

(37) La déportation, est-il possible de désirer cela ?
'Deportation, is it possible to desire that?'

Exploring authentic language corpora is a useful methodology that can be used to estimate the frequency of use of a construction with a particular SA meaning, and I believe that differences in frequency of use can be interpreted in terms of relative degrees of standardization. One obvious limitation of this sort of approach, however, is that the researcher may not always be certain as to how a specific instance of a construction was meant in its original context of utterance. This is why experimental studies are indispensable, as they complement findings based on corpus analyses.

In one such experimental approach, Holtgraves (1994) compared memory for the intended meaning of standardized IRs such as (38) and non-standardized IRs such as the negative state remark (39).

(38) Could you close the window?

(39) It's cold in here.

In his Experiment 1, participants were presented, on a computer screen, with scenarios describing an interaction between two people. Each scenario ended with a remark which consisted either in a standardized IR or in a negative state remark (non-standardized IR). After reading the target utterance, the participants pressed a key to indicate their comprehension, and they were asked whether a given sentence, for example, a request paraphrase, was an appropriate reformulation of the utterance. About five minutes later, they were re-presented with five different versions of the same scenario, and asked to identify which one they had previously read. Three results are worth commenting on here. First, it took the participants longer to make the paraphrase judgements for the negative state remarks in comparison with the standardized IRs. Second, request paraphrases were accepted more frequently for standardized IRs than for non-standardized IRs. Third, the negative state remarks were more often correctly recognized than the standardized IRs in the memory test. These results suggest that, relative to standardized IRs, negative state remarks, which are pragmatically more ambiguous, increase processing times.

There is a concern that, in Holtgraves's (1994) experiment, the utterances used as stimuli differed not only in their respective degrees of standardization, but also in terms of conventionality of means. In fact, Holtgraves systematically compared questions about A's ability/willingness to do the action (all of them being highly standardized) with negative state remarks (none of them being standardized) (1994: 1208). For instance, (38) is a question about A's ability to close the window, while (39) provides A with a reason to close the window, and these are two different conventions of means.

(38) Could you close the window? (repeated)

(39) It's cold in here. (repeated)

4.5 Linguistic Factors Influencing ISA Processing

To specifically test the effect of the degree of standardization on utterance interpretation, one should control for the conventionality of means and, accordingly, compare (38) with the less standardized (40), as they both express a question about the possibility that A close the window.

(40) Is it possible for you to close the window?

Therefore, one cannot determine whether the results of Holtgraves's (1994) study reflect differences in degrees of standardization or differences in the conventions of means.

Several studies concerning the processing of indirectness collected measures of how well the form and content of ISA constructions are remembered. For instance, Kemper's (1980) experiments are directly relevant to the study of standardization because they build on the idea that a higher degree of illocutionary force standardization gives rise to a better memory for the constructions used with that particular force. In Kemper's Experiment 2, participants were presented with constructions such as (41)–(42) occurring in isolation (neutral context), as a DSA in a scenario priming a direct interpretation, or as an IR in a scenario priming an indirect interpretation.

(41) Why are you just standing here?

(42) The leaves really should be racked.

Each speaker who produced a remark was referred to by her/his name. The participants performed a distractor task, after which they were asked to recall the remarks produced by each speaker. The results show that verbatim recall of the constructions was better for ISAs than for DSAs. This indicates that the recall of the exact form of these constructions is higher when they are used indirectly, which also confirms these constructions' high degree of standardization for the performance of IRs.

In Kemper's (1980) Experiment 3, participants were presented with either remarks used in DSAs or with remarks used to convey the indirect meaning of a request or an offer. Later, they were shown either the scenarios they had initially read or new scenarios. They were then asked to provide the appropriate concluding remark for each scenario. Verbatim recall of the remarks initially used indirectly was better than for the remarks initially used as DSAs. In addition, verbatim recall was better in the force-preserving condition relative to the force-changing condition. However, when the remarks were learnt in an 'indirect' context, no difference was found between force-preserving and force-changing conditions. All in all, the results of Kemper's (1980) experiments suggest that the form of a given construction is remembered better if this construction is used as an ISA rather than as a DSA. Nevertheless, this would be a hasty conclusion, as there remains the possibility that requests and offers are better remembered than assertions and requests for information qua SA types.

Assuming that a high degree of standardization is reflected in a high frequency of use in the performance of some SA, Holtgraves's (2008) experiments shed light on the relationship between standardization and ISA processing, showing that some expressions result in early activation of the SA representation corresponding to their preferred interpretation. Holtgraves studied a set of expressions having a preferred SA interpretation, such as the construction *Don't forget to VP* that can be considered highly standardized for the performance of reminders. In fact, it is hard to think of a context in which it would not be used as such. He created short conversational scenarios in which he manipulated the form of final remarks such as (43), which had the force of a reminder in the target condition; the corresponding remark in (44) did not have the meaning of a reminder in the control condition.

(43) Don't forget to go to your dentist appointment today.

(44) I'll bet you forgot to go to your dentist appointment today.

Note that the most obvious difference between (43) and (44) is that the former is an imperative sentence (addressed to a single person) and the latter a declarative with a first-person pronoun as grammatical subject of the verb *to bet*. Apart from *remind*, other SA verbs included *guess, ask, demand, apologize, deny, invite, offer*, to name only a few. These stimuli were used in two sorts of experiments: probe recognition tasks and lexical decision tasks (see also Holtgraves & Ashley 2001).

Holtgraves's probe recognition tasks consisted of written as well as auditory materials. Participants were asked to indicate, as quickly as possible, whether a probe word was literally present in the final remark of the scenario just displayed. In the target condition, the probe described the SA just performed, for instance *remind* for the utterance in (43). In the control condition, the probe was not an adequate description of the SA performed with the remark, as in (44). Saying that *remind* was not part of the preceding remark took the participants longer (and they made more mistakes) for (43) than for (44). This difference in RTs

4.5 Linguistic Factors Influencing ISA Processing

indicates that the actual illocutionary force of the remark interfered with the participants' positive answer to the question. In particular, one of Holtgraves's probe recognition tasks is worth commenting on here from a methodological perspective. This experiment consisted in a chat interaction where the participants, who were told that they would interact with another student, actually interacted with a computer program. The chat interaction was interfaced with a probe recognition task. This experiment was an attempt to examine how participants – instead of observers – understand the SAs performed with utterances. As in Holtgraves's other experiments, the participants took longer to verify the probe in the SA condition than in the control condition.

In the lexical decision experiments, participants were asked to decide whether a string of letters was a word of English or not. In one of these tasks, Holtgraves manipulated the interstimulus interval (ISI) between the presentation of the target remark and the presentation of the probe item. In the short delay condition, the remark-probe ISI was set to 250 ms, in the long delay condition, to 2000 ms. Stronger priming effects were found for the probes that described the SA performed by the remark, such as *reminder* for *Don't you forget to VP*. However, this effect only occurred in the short delay condition, which suggests that such a SA activation is not a conscious, time-consuming process.

Summing up, the results of Holtgraves's (2008) experiments demonstrate delayed decision times for the probes corresponding to the SA performed (probe recognition task), and shorter decision times in the short ISI condition for the probes corresponding to the SA performed (lexical decision task). According to Holtgraves, his results indicate that the activation of a SA representation is almost automatic. However, as he himself acknowledges, this conclusion should not be generalized beyond the sort of formulaic expressions he used in his experiments.

In fact, the general result that some remarks trigger stronger lexical activation for the words describing their illocutionary force points to a 'prototypicality effect' (Napoleon Katsos, personal communication). That is, higher lexical activation would be predicted for the words that describe the most prototypical uses of a construction (e.g., *request* for *Could you VP?*), and weaker activation for the words that describe the less prototypical uses of the construction (e.g., *question* for *Could you VP?*). For instance, there is a higher lexical activation for the word *remind* after reading the remark *Don't forget to VP* because the construction is typically used with the force of a reminder. However, one should not, on the basis of such a prototypicality effect, infer that SA representations are necessarily activated during utterance processing (not to mention that the concept of a SA itself is not unanimously agreed upon). It is therefore unclear whether the results of Holtgraves's experiments demonstrate, as he proposes, an automatic SA activation or, rather, a processing correlate of SA prototypicality. Furthermore, the differences in priming effects obtained by Holtgraves do not show that the SA representation of an utterance is *necessary* to its understanding. These differences could be just an epiphenomenon of utterance interpretation. On the basis of these results, assuming that a higher degree of standardization facilitates the recognition of the indirect meaning of an utterance, one would expect higher lexical activation for the target SA of 'request' when the SA performed by using a standardized *Can you VP?* constructions is an IR. Finally, similar priming effects are expected for direct, literal SA interpretations, if one considers that there is a prototypical association between the three major English sentence-types, namely, imperative, interrogative and declarative, and the SAs of request for action, request for information and assertion, respectively. Accordingly, in comparison with a declarative or an imperative, an interrogative sentence interpreted as a direct request for information should activate, at some point in the course of interpretation, SA verbs such as *question* and *ask*, which describe the SA of request for information.

We saw from Holtgraves's lexical decision task data that people understand SAs very quickly, because the priming effect for SA probes occurred only when the remark-probe ISI duration was set to 250 ms. Early SA recognition has been further demonstrated by Gísladóttir et al. (2012; 2015), who used a methodology similar to that of Coulson and Lovett's (2010) study. The results of Gísladóttir et al.'s ERP experiments reveal early processing differences between different SAs performed with one and the same remark, such as *I have a credit card*. After the question *How are you going to pay for the ticket?*, this remark consisted in a simple answer, following *I don't have any money for the ticket* it was a pre-offer, and after *I can lend you money for the ticket* it was a declination. Even though these findings do not enable comparisons between DSA and ISA realizations, they suggest that the indirectness of different SA types, such as refusals and pre-offers, can affect the processing correlates of these SAs.

4.5.3 Illocutionary Force Salience

Another – much less studied – variable that is expected to influence the processing and the primariness/secondariness of ISAs is the degree of illocutionary force salience. This is the view that constructions used as ISAs vary in terms of the extent to which they make their indirect illocutionary force linguistically explicit. In fact, I am not aware of any illocutionary force indicator having been investigated, with the

4.5 Linguistic Factors Influencing ISA Processing

exception of *please*, the directive force marker par excellence. To begin with, there is the well-known observation that the preverbal insertion of *please* is possible not only in imperatives such as (45), but also in interrogatives and declaratives such as (46)–(47) respectively (Bach & Harnish 1979; Sadock 1974).

(45) Please remove your car (it's in the staff parking part). (BYU–BNC)

(46) Could you please remove the image of my home from your site? (Internet)

(47) Hi, I would like you please to remove the facility for advertisers to enter 'Contract/Permanent' in this field. (Internet)

The presence of *please* in these utterances decreases their degree of pragmatic ambiguity. However, to the best of my knowledge, very little research has been devoted to the relationship between degrees of illocutionary force salience and the facilitation of indirect interpretations. An exception is Clark's (1979) pioneering study. In his study of telephone requests for information to local merchants, Clark showed with the pair of examples (19) and (48) that the use of *please* in *Could you VP?* increases the likelihood that the indirect directive meaning will be inferred by the interpreter and decreases the likelihood that the direct meaning of ability question will be inferred.

(19) Could you tell me the price for a fifth of Jim Beam? (repeated)

(48) Could you tell me the price for a fifth of Jim Beam, please?

Unfortunately, to date no study has been devoted to the facilitative effect of *please* on the processing of indirect directives. More generally, the influence of different degrees of illocutionary force salience on the recognition and processing of the indirect meaning of utterances remains under-researched.

Regardless of whether a particular ISA is primary or secondary, higher illocutionary force salience is expected to increase the likelihood of such an indirect interpretation and the rapidity of its recognition. Building on the view that emoticons and emojis can not only encode affective meaning (Dresner & Herring 2010) but also function as illocutionary force indicators (Thompson & Filik 2016), Holtgraves and Robinson (2020) investigated the influence of emojis on the disambiguation of pragmatically ambiguous remarks in computer-mediated communication (CMC), such as the indirect reply in (49b) in the context of the question in (49a).

(49) a   What did you think of my presentation?
      b   It's hard to give a good presentation.

The idea explored by these authors is that, in CMC, emojis enable writers to compensate for the lack of visual cues present in face-to-face communication. Thus conceived, emojis take the role of facial expressions and body language because they help clarify the intended meaning of utterances that could otherwise be misunderstood. In their experiment, participants read short conversations ending with a question followed by a reply, as in (49). The target stimuli also included requests for information, as in (50a), and IRs for help, as in (51a), which were responded to by irrelevant indirect replies implying, in (50b), a negative disclosure and, in (51b), a refusal to comply.

(50) a   How are you doing in chemistry?
      b   I watched the basketball game yesterday.

(51) a   Can you type my term paper for me?
      b   I think everyone should learn to cook.

In the replies including an emoji, it consisted in a grimacing face for opinions and refusals, and in a sad face for disclosures. After reading the short stories, the participants were presented with a paraphrase and had to indicate whether it corresponded to the intended meaning of the reply. Holtgraves and Robinson's (2020) results show that these paraphrases were more often endorsed, and the participants' paraphrase judgements were faster, when an emoji was included. These effects occurred both for disclosures and opinions, but not for the refusals to comply with the IRs. These findings are in line with previous research showing that the presence of emojis increases the likelihood that a remark will receive a sarcastic interpretation (Derks et al. 2008). More generally, they demonstrate the facilitative effect of a higher degree of illocutionary force salience, which can be contributed by emojis, on the likelihood and speed of ISA comprehension.

4.6 MEASURES OF COGNITIVE PROCESSING: SOME CLARIFICATION

As we have seen throughout this chapter, a common way to approach the processing costs of ISAs has been to compare literal and non-literal

4.6 Measures of Cognitive Processing: Clarification

(e.g., 'indirect') aspects of meaning in terms of response times – an approach mostly applied to the study of figurative language (Gibbs & Colston 2012: Chapter 3). Assuming, for instance, that imperative sentences and *Can you VP?* are alternative ways of performing requests, one can legitimately ask what it means for an IR to 'increase the processing costs' in comparison with a direct, imperative request. When asking this sort of question, one faces an important difficulty, namely the pervasive ambiguity in the use of expressions such as *processing/cognitive cost* and *cognitive effort* in contemporary experimental literature, even in the field of psychophysiology where these notions originate from (Pichora-Fuller et al. 2016).

Strictly speaking, mental effort is the 'deliberate allocation of mental resources to overcome obstacles in goal pursuit when carrying out a task' (Pichora-Fuller et al. 2016: 10S). But, in experimental linguistics, 'does cognitive effort refer to "extra time" or "more brain activity"…?' (Gibbs and Colston 2012: 126). Other practical issues relate to the operationalization of processing effort. For instance, should it be measured as differential brain activation or, in line with Pichora-Fuller et al.'s (2016) definition, inasmuch as effort can be defined as energy consumption, in joules? It remains far from clear which meanings scholars assign to these expressions.

We saw that response time patterns and brain activation patterns associated with the processing of negative state remarks vary according to the particular SA performed with these remarks. From that perspective, it is plausible that processing one and the same sentence, such as (52), for example, will elicit distinct brain activity depending on the SA that is performed by using this sentence.

(52) Open the box.

Depending on the situation, (52) could be taken as an offer, a permission, a request, a command, or advising, each of these SA interpretations in the opening of the sequence being associated, as Clark (1996: 213) rightly remarks, with a verbal response from the addressee that indicates his uptake of the utterance (closing): *No, thanks* for an offer, *Thanks* for a permission, *Okay* for a request, *Yes, sir* for a command and *What a good idea!* for advising. Whether these different interpretations would also give rise to differences in response times for the opening utterance is an open question. Unfortunately, SAs have not been investigated along these lines yet, and, as we have seen, very little evidence is directly relevant to the processing differences between different SA realizations, for example, direct versus indirect.

In most of the studies reviewed in this chapter, response times have been taken as a reliable indication of cognitive processing costs, and scholars often infer higher processing costs from longer response times. However, even though two linguistic stimuli do not entail differences in processing times, they may very well give rise to other processing differences. Another possible way to handle the 'costs' issue consists in collecting and comparing several psychophysiological measures during comprehension instead of just relying on response times data. The idea is that one should avoid interpreting the absence of differences in response times between a sentence used as a DSA or as an ISA as evidence for the absence of difference in terms of cognitive processing.

In line with this alternative view, the results of Hoeks et al.'s (2013) ERP study suggest that shorter response times and higher processing effort are not incompatible. These authors recorded ERPs such as P600 positivities, which are characterized by an increasing deflection starting around 500 ms after the stimulus that elicits it. This waveform is taken to reflect the construction or maintenance of a discourse representation (Brouwer et al. 2012). In Hoeks et al.'s (2013) experiment using Dutch data, participants were asked to read mini-dialogues and, on some occasions, to decide whether a probe word belongs to the same category as the items of a list (semantic probe task). Some of the utterances in the conversational scenarios consisted in questions used as IRs, such as (53):

(53) Could you please put out the garbage tomorrow?

(54) a No.
      b No, I'm sorry. I can't.

Larger P600 positivities were elicited for a response such as (54a) relative to the more prolix (54b); note that, because of the presence of the directive force marker *please* in the question, both responses can only be understood as a refusal, which dismisses a possible direct interpretation (i.e., ability question). This result indicates extra processing associated with laconic replies, for which it is more effortful to make sense of the answer. It would also be interesting to see whether P600 positivities are still larger for (54a) if *please* is not included in (53), as the mitigating effect contributed by *please* reinforces the inappropriateness of the laconic reply.

Building on the preceding discussion and on the critical review of experimental literature in this chapter, I propose that additional

4.6 Measures of Cognitive Processing: Clarification

studies are all the more welcome to evaluate the cognitive processing of utterance interpretation for at least two reasons.

First, a difference in cognitive processing should be assessed by collecting a combination of measures of brain activity and of RTs. Accordingly, brain activity could provide an indication of increased brain activation for ISAs even though no differences in RTs are found. To do this, psychophysiological measures of attention (e.g., of eye movements, of heart rate variability and of electrodermal activity) and neuroimaging techniques will be necessary to provide converging evidence about SA processing. One such approach would collect different types of data relative to cognitive processing, while keeping identical the stimuli used, as is common practice in experimental psychology.

Second, in the literature, ISA constructions have generally been compared with the direct interpretations of the same constructions. This makes sense, but few studies have directly investigated the differences between different realizations of one and the same SA. One understandable reason for this is that it is, in practice, very difficult to compare imperative and indirect requests *all other things being equal*. Obviously, the surface form of imperative sentences *VP!* is shorter than that of their corresponding *Can you VP?* counterparts, which also raises issues about the contribution of (covert) syntactic material to the ease of processing different constructions. Such differences, which are almost impossible to control for, make a direct comparative investigation of these two request forms very problematic. Also note that, in reading tasks, RTs should be shorter for imperatives relative to non-imperative sentences, not necessarily because directive force is typically associated with imperatives, but simply because imperatives take less time to read. However, the length of the sentences would no longer be a problem if one compares the interpretation of imperative requests and IRs at a given word in the sentence, such as the mention of the *red box* in (55)–(56).

(55) Put the red box on the table.

(56) Can you put the red box on the table?

From that perspective, it would be possible to test for processing differences between the imperative (55) and the IR (56) all other things being equal. Using the eye-tracking methodology, Ruytenbeek et al.'s (2017a) experiments addressed in Section 4.7 build on these methodological suggestions.

4.7 EYE-TRACKING EXPERIMENTS INTO THE INTERPRETATION OF ISAs

Past experiments concerning ISAs did not compare the processing of ISA constructions in contexts where they were pragmatically ambiguous between direct and indirect readings. Rather, they contrasted the interpretations of an ISA construction, for example *Can you VP?*, in a context where it could only be meant as a request versus in a context where it could only be meant as a question. For example, Coulson and Lovett (2010) and Tromp et al. (2016) investigated negative state remarks in their 'direct' and 'indirect' contexts. In contrast to them, Ruytenbeek et al.'s (2017a) experiments were designed in a way that French IR expressions, such as *Pouvez-vous VP ? (Can you VP?)* and *Est-il possible de VP ? (Is it possible to VP?)* could be appropriately interpreted, *in the same contexts*, both as *yes/no* questions and as IRs. In that respect, this design radically departs from previous studies.

This approach contains two eye-tracking experiments, one with IRs of the interrogative sentence-type, the other one with the declarative counterparts of these IRs. Both experiments involved the audio presentation of sentences with the display of coloured shapes in a grid and, just below, *yes* and *no* buttons (Figure 4.1; the shaded zone is the area of interest (AOI) for the eye-tracking measures).

For the sake of clarity, the French constructions will be referred to by their English translations. The sentences in Experiment 1 included imperatives, such as (57), *Can you VP?* interrogatives, such as (58), and *Is it possible to VP?* interrogatives, such as (59).

(57) Mettez le cercle rouge à gauche du rectangle jaune.
'Move the red circle to the left of the yellow rectangle.'

(58) Pouvez-vous mettre le cercle rouge à gauche du rectangle jaune ?
'Can you move the red circle to the left of the yellow rectangle?'

(59) Est-il possible de mettre le cercle rouge à gauche du rectangle jaune ?
'Is it possible to move the red circle to the left of the yellow rectangle?'

The participants were asked to respond to each spoken sentence either by answering (*yes/no*) or by displacing a shape. Thus only one response per item was allowed, and they automatically moved to the next item, after they had clicked on *yes/no* or moved a shape. This was to prevent them from assuming they always had to respond *both* to the direct and the indirect meaning of the utterance. To allow the

4.7 Eye-Tracking Experiments

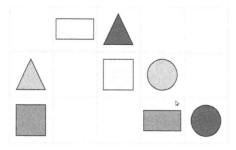

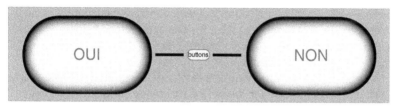

Figure 4.1 Grid with geometrical coloured shapes and response buttons

participants more flexibility in their responses, it would have been possible to add a special button for moving to the next item, but it could have interfered with the eye fixations on the *yes/no* and *true/false* buttons. Moving a coloured shape in the grid was possible only if the position was empty so that the object could be moved there.

For the interrogative sentences, there was an equal number of trials where the movement was possible and those where it was not (control items). Therefore, it was possible to respond to the sentence by moving the shape only for half of the target *Can you?* and *Is it possible?* stimuli. Control interrogatives such as (60), to which the only possible response was *yes* or *no*, were included to keep a balance between the number of *yes/no* and 'move in the grid' responses.

(60) Le carré bleu est-il à gauche du cercle vert ?
 'Is the blue square to the left of the green circle?'

In Experiment 2, *Can you VP?* and *Is it possible to VP?* were replaced by their declarative counterparts, that is, *You can VP* and *It is possible to VP*, and the *yes/no* buttons were replaced by *true/false* buttons. In these two experiments, eye movements, mouse clicks for the responses and RTs were recorded. The eye-tracking data consisted in the durations of the fixations on the AOI corresponding to the response buttons and the small area in between (Figure 4.1).

The results of these two eye-tracking experiments provide several insights into the processing of direct versus indirect request realizations, and they also raise a number of methodological issues.

First, the less standardized stimuli *Is it possible to VP?/It is possible to VP* were less often interpreted as IRs than *Can you VP?/You can VP*, the more standardized ones. However, the lower degree of standardization of *Is it possible to VP?/It is possible to VP* did not increase their processing times relative to the more standardized *Can you VP?/You can VP*. Ability interrogatives and declaratives with a low degree of standardization were, just like their more standardized counterparts, sometimes interpreted as IRs. This indicates that, for the expressions belonging to the same convention of means concerning the addressee's ability, an IR meaning remains accessible.

Second, in line with previous research, ability interrogatives/declaratives did not entail longer RTs when they were used as IRs. However, they increased RTs when they were interpreted as DSAs: *yes* responses in Experiment 1 and *true* responses in Experiment 2 took longer relative to the control interrogative and declarative stimuli. This suggests that the availability of an IR meaning interfered with the execution of *yes* and *true* responses. I interpreted these findings in terms of extra processing times for the direct readings caused by the 'competition' with another pragmatic interpretation more strongly associated with these constructions. In addition, the participants did not look at the *yes/no* or *true/false* buttons when they interpreted a stimulus as an IR. These eye-tracking data do not show extra processing activity entailed by indirectness, and they suggest that the IR interpretations of these ability sentences were primary rather than secondary. These results are incompatible with a processing model according to which the direct interpretation is accessed first, and, more generally, with any literalist model that predicts that inferring the IR meaning of an utterance also requires the activation of its direct meaning. Rather, these data should be accounted for by a model in which the relative ease of processing for different SA interpretations is determined by a complex of conventionality, degrees of standardization and degrees of illocutionary force salience.

Third, the relatively high frequency of the direct interpretation of ability interrogatives (about 65%) and of declaratives (70%) in these experiments is somewhat unexpected, because *Can you VP?* is a highly standardized request form. One possible reason why its direct interpretations outnumbered its indirect interpretations concerns the nature of the other experimental stimuli. For instance, in Experiment 1, the stimuli included *Can you VP?* and *Is it possible to VP?* utterances that could only be responded to with *no*, and questions about the position of geometrical shapes in the grid, such as (60).

(60) Le carré bleu est-il à gauche du cercle vert ? (repeated)
      'Is the blue square to the left of the green circle?'

It is possible that these stimuli biased the participants towards the direct interpretations of *Can you VP?*. That is, when an ability interrogative mentioned a shape displacement that could not be carried out, the only possible response was *no*. Likewise, participants may have developed a response strategy based on these impossible moves, associating utterances depicting possible moves with a *yes* response. Another reason that may explain the asymmetric distribution of direct versus indirect interpretations relates to politeness considerations. For instance, one may prefer to use an IR instead of a bare imperative because the former is contextually more appropriate, for example, in formal contexts. In the present experiments, however, participants were unlikely to develop any expectations about why some of the instructions were indirect. These instructions consisted in recorded utterances produced by a speaker who was unknown to the participants, whom they could not interact with, and to whom they had no reason for assigning any intention to be polite. From that perspective, despite the fact that *Can you VP?* is a highly standardized request form, it is actually surprising that IR interpretations were derived at all (in fact 35% of the time). Finally, the participants may have been more entitled to interpret *Can you VP?* as a direct question because it was cognitively easier to click on the *yes* button than to select and displace a geometrical shape in the grid: a *yes/no* response took them less time and decreased the risk of error caused by an incorrect displacement. Obviously, future replications of this experimental paradigm are necessary to determine which explanation is the most appropriate.

4.8 PROSODIC ASPECTS OF ISA COMPREHENSION

The fact that ISA constructions have (at least) two different possible SA interpretations entails that, sometimes, addressees will face difficulties when interpreting these expressions in context. One therefore expects that, in the case of spoken communication, speakers will try to avoid misunderstandings by exploiting prosodic features to clarify their illocutionary intent. Experimental evidence demonstrates the use of prosodic cues by speakers (Price et al. 1991) as well as the facilitative role of prosody in syntactic disambiguation (e.g., Beach 1991; Snedeker & Trueswell 2003). Previous research also indicates that prosody enables pragmatic disambiguation. For instance, intonational contours can be reliably used to interpret one-word utterances, such as *beer* and *bar*, in terms of the SAs of, for example, criticism, warning, suggestion and naming (Hellbernd & Sammler 2016). Concerning the relationship between prosody and SA interpretations, Ward (2019: 79–82) discusses intonational differences whether an utterance of, for example, (61) is meant as a request for information or as an invitation (offering one's guest a cup of tea).

(61)   Do you like tea?

While a flat prosodic contour is associated with the force of a request for information, the presence of a late increase in pitch (late pitch peak) would be expected in the case of an invitation. Wichmann (2004) also provides evidence for an association between a late pitch peak and imperatives, *Can you VP?*, and negative state remarks such as *It's cold in here* when they convey the force of a request.

The earlier findings reported in Nickerson and Chu-Carroll (1999) go in the same direction as Wichmann's (2004). They collected data about the intonational patterns of the utterance's nucleus (the accented syllable of the intonation unit), the maximal fundamental frequency (F0) at the final high boundary tone (a rise or fall in pitch), and the mean F0 of the unstressed vowel in the intonational phrase. In their experiment, they asked participants to read aloud parts of small dialogues including the utterance of an IR construction consisting in one of the following (the remainder of the dialogues were played by a recorded voice):

(62)   Can you move the couch?

(63)   Would you move the couch?

(64)   Would you be willing to move the couch?

In the DSA condition, the utterance had the meaning of a direct request for information; in the ISA condition, it was meant as a request for action. Nickerson and Chu-Carroll (1999) found that the majority of utterances were produced with an intonational contour typical of *yes/no* questions (an intonational contour consisting in a low plateau of F0

4.8 Prosodic Aspects of ISA Comprehension

followed by a rise in tone). However, these utterances were more likely to be requests when they had a low boundary tone: nineteen utterances with this intonational contour were IRs versus seven direct requests for information. In addition, while DSAs and ISAs were similar in terms of the mean F0 of the vowel carrying the nuclear pitch accent, they differed in the F0 values of their boundary tones.

Another experimental investigation that is closely related to Nickerson and Chu-Carroll (1999) is Trott et al.'s (2019). These authors asked whether speakers use prosodic information to differentiate direct and indirect meanings, and whether listeners use the same information to distinguish between these two sorts of interpretations. However, unlike Nickerson and Chu-Carroll (1999), they took into consideration not three but seven possible prosodic cues: mean F0, range F0 (maximum F0 minus minimum F0), duration, mean intensity, standard deviation of intensity and slope of F0. A further difference with these authors is that Trott et al. (2019) compared the role of prosody on the interpretation of both *Can you VP?* utterances and negative state remarks. To do this, they recorded native speakers uttering these two types of construction both with a direct question/statement meaning and with an IR meaning. Then the participants listened to pairs of utterances of one and the same construction, one as an IR and the other one as a direct request for information or a direct statement; their task was to identify which of the two was meant as a request for action. They were presented with a total of twelve pairs of utterances (six for *Can you VP?* and six for negative state remarks) spoken by five different speakers.

The first interesting result of Trott et al.'s (2019) study is that their participants were able to identify IRs above chance, and, for four out of five speakers, *Can you VP?* requests were easier to recognize than negative state remarks. Concerning the prosodic information conveyed by the speakers, mean intensity and standard deviation of intensity were the two most reliable cues for differentiating direct versus indirect uses of IR constructions. For both types of IR constructions, higher intensity and higher variations in intensity increased the likelihood of correct request interpretations. In the case of *Can you VP?*, utterances were less likely to be requests when they were longer, had more positive slopes of F0 and contained less variation in intensity. In contrast to *Can you VP?*, negative state remarks that took longer to pronounce were more likely to be requests.

Trott and colleagues (Trott et al. 2019) then investigated whether listeners actually use the speakers' prosodic cues to distinguish between direct and indirect interpretations. They found that participants'

Table 4.1 *Prosodic cues for the interpretation of IR constructions in English*

	Direct interpretation	Indirect request interpretation
Can you VP?	• Longer utterances (Trott et al. 2019) • More positive slopes of F0 (Trott et al. 2019) • Less variation in intensity (Trott et al. 2019)	• Higher intensity; higher variations in intensity (Trott et al. 2019) • Lower F0 at the boundary tone (Nickerson & Chu-Carroll 1999)
Negative state remarks	• Shorter utterances (Trott et al. 2019)	• Higher intensity; higher variations in intensity (Trott et al. 2019) • Late pitch peak (Wichmann 2004)

correct identifications of request utterances were predicted by F0 slope, mean F0, mean intensity and standard deviation of intensity. Mean intensity and mean F0 were useful for both types of IRs. Specifically, F0 slope and standard deviation of intensity predicted interpretation accuracy for *Can you VP?* stimuli. The findings of the studies discussed in this section are summarized in Table 4.1.

Even though the task designed by Trott et al. (2019) was not strictly speaking a SA classification task for individual utterances, its results provide important insights into the processing of pragmatically ambiguous constructions. They demonstrate that speakers produce reliable prosodic cues that enable interpreters to arrive at the intended meaning, and that interpreters effectively use these cues to disambiguate between alternative readings. However, to this day, very little is known about the exact circumstances under which speakers would use these cues, such as the social aspects of conversational interaction. It also remains to be seen whether these prosodic cues signal indirect interpretations or are simply contrastive markers that receive their SA interpretation in context. In addition, with the exception of Hellbernd and Sammler's (2016) work on one-word utterances, there is a lack of research into the intonational patterns specific to SA types. This is problematic, as the intonational patterns observed by Trott et al. (2019) are not necessarily specific to indirect communication nor to the SA of requesting, as distinct from the DSAs of questioning or stating.

That being said, in her empirical investigation of the prosody of *please*, Wichmann (2004) provides tentative evidence that requests modified by *please* performed with imperatives and *Can you VP?* have the same intonational contour. However, these patterns seem to be influenced by the position of *please* in the utterance and also by social considerations. I return to these social factors in the next chapter.

4.9 SUMMARY

The studies discussed in this chapter indicate that there is still much experimental research to be done on ISA processing, but they also provide key findings. Concerning the processing times associated with indirectness in directives, available evidence is not clear-cut: in some cases, IRs increase RTs, while in other contexts they do not take longer to process relative to their imperative and direct counterparts. This reminds us that indirectness does not constitute a homogeneous pragmatic category. A robust finding, however, is that understanding an IR does not systematically require the prior derivation of the direct meaning of the IR. In contrast to the absence of processing times differences, more recent experimental studies are helpful to document the brain activity and attentional correlates of indirectness, as measured by psychophysiological and neuroimaging techniques. I proposed that three linguistic variables determine to a large extent the processing of ISAs, and should be taken into account to determine whether an IR will be primary or secondary: conventionality of means, degree of standardization and degree of illocutionary force salience. However, the processing costs associated with different conventions of means and with different degrees of illocutionary force salience are still largely unexplored, and the notion of 'processing cost' itself required further clarification. Finally, we have seen that prosody provides reliable information that helps interpreters correctly interpret ambiguous spoken utterances such as ISAs.

4.10 DISCUSSION QUESTIONS

- We have seen that several online methodologies can be used to address ISA comprehension, and that most contemporary experimental approaches use online rather than offline methods. One could therefore argue that offline methodologies are outdated

and should be replaced altogether by online techniques. Do you totally agree? If not, can you think of some counterarguments to this view?
- Make a list of the different measures of processing that we have been discussing. Compare their respective benefits and drawbacks from the researcher's perspective.
- Building on the data discussed in this chapter and on the theoretical considerations of the previous chapters, what SA types other than directives should be more difficult to empirically investigate, and why so?

4.11 SUGGESTIONS FOR FURTHER READING

A whole body of experimental research devoted to figurative language interpretation, a topic closely related to indirectness, is critically reviewed by Gibbs and Colston (2012), who also discuss methodological issues related to the study of utterance interpretation.

Holtgraves and Bonnefon (2017) propose insightful discussions of contemporary online methods that are useful to study the relationship between linguistic (in)directness and (im)politeness.

5 Indirectness, Politeness and the Social Context

5.1 INTRODUCTION

Thus far, I have said little about the variety of reasons that speakers may have to resort to indirectness rather than performing their SAs in a straightforward, direct way. In this chapter, adopting a sociolinguistic perspective, I deal with the major reasons explaining the existence of indirect communication. In addition, I discuss in some detail the complex relationship between politeness and indirectness and how contextual variables, in particular interpersonal parameters, shape both the production of indirect utterances and their interpretation. Finally, I will present the results of ongoing research on Twitter complaints, showing that they are performed directly most of the time, but with different degrees of explicitness.

5.2 THE REASONS BEHIND INDIRECTNESS

A first category of reasons can be identified if we adopt the point of view of speakers, that is, an 'emic' perspective, a term borrowed from ethnolinguistic methodology. These are reasons that speakers can reflect upon, and which they can provide as justifications for the fact they expressed themselves indirectly; they can therefore be considered as giving rise to 'strategic' indirectness. This idea reflects the commonsensical view that speakers make rational choices when producing their utterances, one such decision being to use indirectness as an alternative to direct communication. There are several strategic reasons to the performance of an ISA as a preferred alternative to a DSA: being polite, avoiding committing oneself to the implied meaning (while attempting to get it across), and conveying multiple meanings at the same time.

5.2.1 Face-Threat and Politeness

The reason that first comes to mind when we talk about indirectness is politeness. Empirical investigations of speakers' choices between ISAs and DSAs are anchored in Brown and Levinson's (1987) politeness theory, where A's 'negative face' is defined in terms of A's freedom to do only what he wants to and his will that others do not impede his actions. For instance, a directive SA entails face-threat for A insofar as his negative face is threatened by S's telling him what he should do. For Brown and Levinson, if S wants to avoid the emotional costs associated with face-threat for A, while getting her message across, she resorts to ISAs. This view implies that indirectness is strategic by nature: it is a linguistic compensation for the estimated face-threat potential of a SA realization. In addition, for Brown and Levinson, unlike in Searle's (1969) SAT, (in)directness is a graded notion, according to which off-record utterances are more indirect (and more polite) than on-record indirect utterances. Unlike on-record indirectness, such as standardized ISAs, for which S's directive intent should be obvious to A, off-record indirectness is special because speakers, in using it, provide their addressees with an opportunity to display attentiveness by making offers instead of having to comply (or to refuse to comply) with their requests. As these requests can trigger helpful behaviour, they stimulate A's positive face: in making offers, the addressees of off-record IRs show that they pay attention to speakers' feelings and are able to anticipate their needs. This feature of off-record requests has been documented in languages such as Japanese (Fukushima 2000; 2015), Greek (Sifianou 1993) and English (Weizman 1989).

Brown and Levinson postulate a positive correlation between degrees of indirectness and degrees of face-threat. Accordingly, the higher the degree of face-threat in a situation, the more indirect an utterance should be; the lesser the face-threat, the more direct. In the case of directives, which primarily threaten A's negative face, speakers prefer ISA realizations over DSA realizations because the former enable the mitigation of the threats to A's negative face. Brown and Levinson's (1987) hypothesis that degrees of politeness correlate with degrees of indirectness has been challenged with data on requests in English and Hebrew (Blum-Kulka 1987), Nepali (Upadhyay 2003), Polish (Wierzbicka 1985) and Russian (Ogiermann 2009). First, the most indirect forms, that is, off-record utterances, are not necessarily the most polite, as in the case of extreme indirectness, often perceived as sarcastic (*overpolite* has a negative connotation, cf. Culpeper 2011: 100–103), and as impolite for the reason that it increases the costs of

5.2 The Reasons behind Indirectness

interpretation (Blum-Kulka 1987; for a discussion, see Manno 2002). Second, direct forms such as imperatives are acceptable under certain circumstances, for instance in routine coordination exchanges, as on a building site, or when urgency applies in the case of a fire alarm, which does not make DSAs particularly impolite. Third, as Sylvie's succession of directive utterances in (1) illustrates, an imperative is not necessarily the strongest, most persuasive request form, as it can be outranked by an IR expression such as *Voulez-vous VP ?* ('Will you VP?'). The use of an IR form after an unsuccessful imperative would be difficult to explain, as it is highly unlikely that Sylvie used *Voulez-vous VP !* in order to be more polite with Antoine. (The example (1) is taken from the 1971 French film *Jo*, directed by Jean Girault, in which Sylvie is played by Claude Gensac and Antoine by Louis De Funès.)

(1) Sylvie – Toitoine... Bon, c'est pas le moment, Toine. (Antoine is fainting) Bon, attends-moi là. Attends-moi là ! Veux-tu m'attendre là ? (Jo, 1971)

'Toitoine... Well, this is not the time, Toine. Well, wait here. Wait here! Will you wait here?'

For these reasons, I will not assume that indirectness necessarily entails politeness (see Freytag 2020 for additional arguments against this assumption). However, as a certain number of studies on linguistic (im)politeness in the footsteps of Brown and Levinson (1987) have endorsed this assumption, either explicitly or implicitly, whenever necessary I will reinterpret their findings to see what they tell us about the (in)directness of different SA realizations.

In a series of pioneering experiments, Clark and Schunk (1980) showed that politeness ratings for responses to IRs for information increased when a response to the direct meaning was present ('direct move'), such as *Yes, sure* following *Can you open the window?*. They also demonstrated that when participants were asked to make responses to IRs sound more polite, they inserted a direct move to the bare answer to the request for information, or they added another direct move, for example, *Yes, sure, I'll do that for you*. These results suggest that interpreters pay attention to the direct meaning of IRs (and to the direct moves included in their responses) because direct interpretations provide them with information about the (im)politeness of these utterances.

As Holtgraves (1992) puts it, speakers do not produce ISAs at random. Rather, they use them on purpose, one major such reason being an attempt to deal with face-threatening situations. The use of indirectness for politeness reasons is well illustrated by indirect replies to questions that are sensitive, as they elicit opinion disclosure, which can be either good or bad. I have already touched upon indirect replies such as (2b) in Chapter 4, where I considered experimental data pertaining to the role of illocutionary force salience on ISA interpretation.

(2) a What did you think of my presentation?
    b It's hard to give a good presentation.

When using (2b) as a reply to S's question about the quality of her presentation, A may imply a negative judgement while trying to be nice to the presenter, especially if the presentation was unsuccessful. But note that, when saying (2b), A may actually be complimenting S about her very good presentation, in the sense that, despite the difficulty inherent to conference presentations, he may have been impressed by the speaker's. As Holtgraves (1998) remarks, in the absence of any evidence for a face-threatening potential behind S's question, both interpretations are in theory possible. However, in the situation just described, the former interpretation is more likely, as face-threatening considerations are at stake: the difficulty of delivering a good presentation is presented as an excuse for the speaker's failure to do so.[1]

Holtgraves (1986; 1991) experimentally explored the relationship between indirectness and face-threat in the case of such IRs for opinion. In a way that is similar to (2a), an indirect question, (3) is an IR for information, with the meaning 'Do you like my new coat?'.

(3) Did you notice my new coat?

It is a question about a precondition (noticing the coat) that must obtain so that S can get across her implied request for information about whether A likes her new coat. Holtgraves calls this type of indirect requests for information 'conventional', as they involve a direct reference to the preconditions for the SA of requesting information (cf. conventionality of means). Another type of IR for information is the non-conventional IR in (4), which can be considered as more indirect than the one in (3), as it does not refer to a precondition to the question

---

[1] Note that the SA of asking a question is by definition always face-threatening, because S's requesting an answer from A restrains A's freedom of action. The sort of questions we are interested in here entail, in addition, a threat to S's positive face caused by a potentially negative judgement from her interlocutor A.

5.2 The Reasons behind Indirectness

about A's opinion about S's new coat – including an existential presupposition – but merely hints at the existence of the new coat.

(4) Did you know I went shopping?

As it is more indirect than (3), it is also more likely to give rise to misunderstandings and to A's failure to understand it as a request for opinion about S's new coat. Another difference between the two sorts of IRs for information is that the implied, indirect meaning is more difficult to deny in the case of (3) than it is for (4): in (4) the new coat is not even mentioned, so that A's attention is not oriented by S on her new coat, and it is easier for A to engage in a conversation about shopping habits instead of commenting on S's coat. A possible indirect and polite reply to the indirect utterances in (3)–(4) is (5), meaning 'I don't like the coat'.

(5) I think it takes so much effort to shop for clothes.

Holtgraves's hypothesis to explain the use of IRs for opinion, as well as the indirectness of the replies to them, is that the higher the face concerns for S and A, the more likely that S will privilege an indirect utterance. In addition, the facilitating effect of the face-threatening potential of a situation on the use of indirectness should be stronger for non-conventional IRs. The less ambiguous an utterance, the less likely it is that S attempted to mitigate the face-threatening act (FTA). Therefore, non-conventional IRs for information are more prone to the ambiguity of interpretation than conventional ones. Note, however, that in the case of excessive ambiguity A might not be able to identify the indirect meaning.

In his 1986 study, Holtgraves manipulated the variables of face-threat and (in)directness in short interactional scenarios ending with a request for opinion followed by a reply. For instance, (6a–b) was the direct version of the exchange, both the request for opinion and the reply being performed as DSAs. Face-threat was manipulated by changing the pronoun referring to the author of the presentation, for example, *I/your* in the face-threatening condition and *Fred/his* in the non face-threatening condition, as the target of the criticism was not present at the time of the conversation between S and A.

(6) a   What did you think of the presentation I/Fred gave to the board?
     b   I really didn't think your/his presentation was very good.

A conventional IR is (7), while (8) is a non-conventional one,

(7) Did you hear the presentation that I/Fred gave to the board the other morning?

(8) I/Fred gave my/his presentation to the board the other morning.

Both (9)–(10) are indirect replies: (9) is an evasive reply, and (10) is an irrelevant reply.

(9) I think we should have our board meetings on some day other than Monday.

(10) That latest stock market rally was sure a surprise.

Participants in this experiment read the conversational scenarios and, after that, they were asked about their perception of the politeness and likelihood of the requests for opinion and the replies. If indirectness is primarily motivated by face management, IRs and indirect replies should be perceived as more polite in the face-threatening situations than in the non-face-threatening situations. This prediction was only verified for the replies: indirect replies were perceived as more likely to occur in situations involving face-threat. In addition, evasive replies were considered to be more polite than direct replies in face-threatening situations. Evasive replies were more likely to be accepted, and were generally perceived as more polite, than irrelevant replies in these situations. In line with these findings, Holtgraves (1998) also demonstrates longer comprehension times and more hesitations to identify the intended meaning of indirect replies when face-threat is unlikely to be the reason for indirectness. It would be interesting to see whether empirical evidence from discourse completion task (DCT) data or corpora confirms these findings, that is, whether the use of indirect alternatives is guided by face-threat considerations.

As we will see in Section 5.3, the face-threat of a SA situation and its influence on the selection of SA strategies are, to a large extent, shaped by features of the interpersonal relationship between interlocutors, such as social status, familiarity and gender, to name only a few.

5.2.2 'Communication' without Commitment

We have seen that several types of SAs entail possible threats both to S's and A's positive face and negative face, which explains why they are often performed indirectly. However, in some cases, mitigating these

5.2 The Reasons behind Indirectness

SAs is not sufficient for S to save A's face, or to save her own face, because the costs associated with the SA are too high. Of course, she could refrain from performing the SA at all. But she can also try to avoid being committed to the very performance of the SA while indirectly attempting to get her message across. In other words, the indirectness of her utterance would enable her to deny the performance of the SA afterwards. Examples such as (4) and (7) constitute what Brown and Levinson call 'off-record indirectness', a phenomenon we already discussed at the end of Chapter 1.

(4) Did you know I went shopping? (repeated)

(7) Did you hear the presentation that I gave to the board the other morning? (repeated)

Strictly speaking, these cases do not constitute 'communication' in the sense of Grice (1957), because it is not possible to attribute to S 'a clear intention to communicate' (Brown & Levinson 1987: 211). The responsibility to assign a particular illocutionary meaning to the utterance is left to the interpreter. From a psychological perspective, in comparison with 'on record' ISAs such as (3) and (6a), 'off-record' ISAs also require more inferential work in order to be understood.

(3) Did you notice my new coat? (repeated)

(6) a What did you think of the presentation I gave to the board? (repeated)

Another obvious difference between on-record and off-record IRs for opinion is that it is perfectly acceptable to respond only to the direct, literal meaning of the latter while ignoring their indirect interpretation. By contrast, in responding *Yes, I did* to (3) and saying nothing more, A would not be conversationally cooperative.

Pinker et al. (2008) assume a game-theoretic perspective in which speakers are rational agents wanting to optimize the effects/costs ratio associated with their actions. According to their 'strategic speaker' model, off-record indirectness is used by speakers seeking to achieve their communicative goals while minimizing the emotional, social and legal costs that could be entailed by their SAs (see also Lee & Pinker 2010; Pinker 2011). The model thus allows an optimal balance between risk mitigation and payoff maximization. To illustrate, they take the example of a driver who is stopped by a police officer for driving too fast. The driver tries to escape the ticket, but, considering the possibility that the officer is cooperative (an honest policeman) or antagonistic (a dishonest policeman), she carefully phrases her bribe. Instead of saying (11), she opts for (12).

(11) If you let me go without a ticket, I'll pay you fifty dollars.

(12) So maybe the best thing would be to take care of it here.

It would be too risky to say (11) in case the officer is honest, because the driver would be arrested for bribery. In contrast, in using (12) the driver would play it safe with honest officers, while maintaining the possibility that dishonest ones would accept the bribe and let her free.

A consequence of this deniability of the implied meaning is that it allows the interlocutors to maintain their current relationship. For instance, to put it in Fiske's (1992) words, a sexual come-on would provoke a change in the type of relationship between S and A, moving from an 'authority' relationship or a 'communal relationship' of friendship to another, incompatible communal relationship: sexuality. In the event that S's attempt fails, that is, the invitation behind (13) is not responded to, both interlocutors would be better off than in the case of a direct proposal.

(13) Would you like to come up and see my etchings?

In (13), the form of the SA affords an out to the interlocutors: they can pretend that 'nothing happened' and avoid the awkward feeling caused by the explicit invitation for a sexual relationship – assuming it was declined, of course. Isaacs and Clark (1990) approach utterances such as (13) in terms of 'mutually recognized pretence' (see also Clark 1996: 378–83 for a discussion). They call the request for information in (13) an *ostensible* SA in the sense that both S and A are aware that the question in (13) is not meant seriously: S (a male speaker) has no genuine interest in knowing whether A (female addressee) wants to see his etchings. They point out that the primary goal of S's utterance, that is, here, of the sexual come-on, is off-record, which enables both interlocutors to save face. Another example they analyze is that of two people discussing their astrological signs, including whether they like taking risks, not because they have an interest in this topic, but because they have the off-record goal of challenging each other to prove that they deserve a chance at a relationship. Isaacs and Clark show, however, that, rather than being

5.2 The Reasons behind Indirectness

limited to the flirting or sexual come-on type, a variety of SAs involve mutually recognized pretence. For instance, (14) is an ostensible invitation made by Ross, in a situation where he is cancelling his date with Cathy to meet his friends instead (Isaacs & Clark 1990: 495).

(14) Ross: Cathy, Scott just called and told me that Brad and Dave and Rich and a lot of other guys from UCLA are going to be there tonight, so I guess we're going to go a night early. [He explains the plans for the night.] Do you want to come?
Cathy: That's all right. I'll pass.
Ross: Okay. (From the NBC TV series Friends)

Both Ross and Cathy know that it is highly unlikely that Cathy would be willing to join Ross and his friends, and that Ross seriously meant to invite her; it is therefore a case of mutually recognized pretence, which extends to Cathy's acceptance. This ostensible invitation makes it possible for Ross to avoid hurting Cathy's feelings in saying that he does not want her to join, while communicating, off-record, that he would have enjoyed being in Cathy's company and feels sorry for cancelling their date.

In some situations, however, deniability is no longer plausible in the eyes of the conversational participants, but it still makes sense from the perspective of a third party, for instance in the eventuality that the communicative exchange would be recorded and used as evidence in a legal context. In the case of the attempted bribe, for example, even if it was recorded by the police officer or heard by a bystander, the driver's off-record utterance could not be held against her in a courtroom.

In their comparison between Pinker et al.'s strategic speaker model and Brown and Levinson's (1987) theory, Soltys et al. (2014) highlight that the former approach centres on speakers who privilege indirectness first and foremost for their own sake, the form of their utterances being the output of a calculation of their personal risks. By contrast, Brown and Levinson's theory views off-record indirectness primarily as a strategy that is in the interest of addressees, who are provided with an 'out' and a compensation to face-threat (as in the case of on-record politeness strategies). However, I believe that, despite their differences, Pinker et al.'s and Brown and Levinson's views of off-record communication are not incompatible in the sense that speakers' avoidance of the costs for themselves generally goes hand in hand with the avoidance of similar costs for the addressee. This is not unexpected, given the mutual vulnerability of interlocutors' positive and negative face, and the fact that threatening A's face often entails a threat to S's own face. For instance, insulting A poses a threat to A's positive face, which results in S's loss of her positive face too, because being disrespectful reduces one's claim to seek approval.

5.2.3 Multiple Meanings, Immediacy and Intimacy

Another way to deal with the reasons for the existence of indirect communication is assuming the perspective of the researcher, that is, an 'etic' view (as compared with the 'emic' view discussed earlier). In contrast to the view that indirectness is inherently strategic, this is the idea that, in some situations, it is indirect communication that is expected, and directness that would be the marked, more cumbersome alternative. Accordingly, such cases of indirectness need not be the result of speakers' conscious decision-making processes. Against the view that ISAs arise from speakers' choices (Sections 5.2.1 and 5.2.2), empirical evidence suggests that the performance of an ISA is not always strategic (Terkourafi 2014). For instance, in the case of young children's directives such as (15)–(16), indirectness is the only option available.

(15) My nose is bleeding!

(16) Dad, I'm cold!

To compensate for the inability to identify the action that would help them satisfy their needs, children use negative state remarks to elicit assistance from adults (cf. Ervin-Tripp 1976).

A hallmark of ISAs is that both their direct and indirect interpretations can be intended. Remember that, in Searle (1975), ISAs always entail the performance of a DSA. In fact, in situations when there is a high degree of urgency for A to act, instead of spelling out the full meaning that S is intending to convey, she can produce a statement that alerts A to act in an appropriate way. As her SA is clearly performed in the benefit of A, he is likely to be grateful for S's caring, which prompts Soltys et al. (2014) to call this type of SA, as in (17), a 'directive-commissive':

(17) a You dropped your wallet. (Soltys et al. 2014: 48)
     b Thanks!

These situations give rise to indirect utterances, as these provide addressees with information upon which they can decide to act or not, without speakers assuming the full responsibility of deciding the course of action addressees will take.

5.3 Face Concerns and Social Variables

In other contexts, indirectness is the best option for conveying multiple meanings, as in (18), implying that A should not wait for S, that A need not make dinner for S, that S will miss her favourite TV show, etc. (Terkourafi 2014: 55–7).

(18) I have to work late tonight.

In such a case, S's utterance enables A to draw inferences in a direction ratified by S. Relying on mutual knowledge is a convenient way for S to highlight her intimacy with A, as this intimacy is precisely what is needed for this sort of indirectness to achieve its communicative effects (Terkourafi 2011). Because he is in a close relationship with S, A knows very well which tasks he is supposed to carry out when S has to work late. This sort of exchange typically takes place between members of a small social group, such as family or friends, and it reinforces their closeness and common ground, that is, their shared knowledge about how things are done. From a cognitive perspective, going indirect saves S time and effort, as she need not make a list of all the tasks that are entailed by her absence in the evening. It is the most straightforward way for her to get her message across. Interestingly, this phenomenon resembles young children's use of negative state remarks to elicit assistance from adults, which emphasizes, once again, its cognitive efficiency.

Summing up, it is by now clear that ISAs cannot be systematically regarded as more complex alternatives to DSAs, as in some situations ISAs can be less effortful to produce and, possibly, to process. That being said, viewing indirectness as a default mode of realization for some SAs is compatible with its use for other purposes, in the sense that the reasons behind indirectness are not mutually exclusive.

5.3 FACE CONCERNS AND SOCIAL VARIABLES

Our discussion of the motivations and affordances of indirectness revealed the crucial role of the interpersonal context in which communicative interactions occur. As Gibbs and Colston (2012) illustrate in the case of figurative language, a topic closely related to indirectness, many variables shape utterance interpretation, such as hierarchical status, social distance, formality and group size, to name only a few. An obvious example is (19): uttered by a high-status person, it is more likely to be understood as a request, but if it were produced by a lower status person, a more reasonable interpretation would be an invitation.

(19) Sit down.

These social variables have an influence on the ways people communicate with one another. For instance, if I were to ask one of my best friends to pass me the salt, he would not mind if I said (20), but the same expression would be inappropriate for addressing my hierarchical superior.

(20) Pass me the salt (please).

In addition, the very form of an utterance provides information about the speaker who produces it and about the interpersonal context where the utterance takes place. Upon hearing (21) at the workplace, one would probably assume that the speaker who said it is superior in status relative to her addressee.

(21) Bring me this file at once.

Thus the relationship between social variables and SA realizations is not unidirectional, but bi-directional. This is exactly the idea underlying Thomas Holtgraves's experimental research, which spans a period of more than thirty years, and addresses the relationship between the form of utterances and social variables in these two directions. His research has the merit of addressing the influence of the social context on both the interpretation and the production of utterances. It also explores the effects of face-threat considerations on these two facets of communication. This is an important and utterly relevant methodological decision, because, as Holtgraves puts it, the way people talk constitutes a highly distinctive feature of their personality. Indeed, language is a resource that is particularly useful for forming impressions of other people and for managing the impressions that individuals convey to one another. In the remainder of this chapter, I will follow Holtgraves, as it is more convenient for expository purposes to discuss these two aspects of language on a par than separately.

In Brown and Levinson's theory (1987), speakers who intend to perform FTAs must take into account three interpersonal variables: the perceived status relationship between S and A, the degree of imposition entailed by the SA in the culture, that is, the costs of the SA for A, and the social distance between S and A (e.g., a high social distance corresponding to a low degree of familiarity). As they are aware of this social information, speakers are expected to be strategic and careful when choosing the form of their SAs. The general idea here

5.3 Face Concerns and Social Variables

is that the social context of interaction encompasses many different variables, some of which have already been the target of empirical and/or experimental work, such as social status or power, degree of imposition and social distance, while other variables, such as affective distance and personality, deserve more attention. I will do justice to the available literature and address these three 'Brown and Levinsonian' variables first.

5.3.1 Status Asymmetries

For Brown and Levinson, higher addressee status entails a higher degree of face-threat. A higher degree of politeness – and, as they associate politeness with indirectness, of indirectness – is therefore expected when speakers address individuals who are hierarchically superior to them. More generally, S's social status, and, crucially, the extent to which it differs from A's status, is likely to affect the form of the SAs that will be performed by that speaker. In other words, assuming a particular speaker–addressee status relationship, some SA realizations (as well as some of the actions expected from A) will be more acceptable than others.

A first hypothesis concerning the effect of speaker–addressee relative status on the interpretation of ambiguous remarks is that, as higher status speakers have more options than lower status speakers (this is what it means to be 'higher' in status), they are more likely to be (successfully) indirect because they know that their addressees will tend to search for an indirect meaning (Thomas Holtgraves, personal communication). This also explains why they can afford a higher degree of directness without having to bear the social consequences of it, for example, being considered as impolite.

According to an alternative hypothesis, indirect interpretations of ambiguous utterances should be more frequent in the case of lower status speakers' utterances. For instance, pragmatically ambiguous utterances are more likely to be interpreted as ISAs when the speaker is lower (instead of higher) in status, because lower status individuals should be concerned with face-threat avoidance with respect to their superiors, resulting in the compensatory use of indirectness. Of course, this is no guarantee that the higher status addressee will actually act upon the indirect meaning. For example, the use of IR forms is preferred by lower status speakers who address higher status interlocutors even in emergency situations. This can lead to unfortunate misunderstandings, as in the case of the plane that crashed following a misunderstanding between the pilot and his lower status co-pilot, whose indirect utterances failed to warn the pilot about the danger of taking off in icy weather (Goguen & Linde 1983: 79–81; Linde 1988). The result was a tragic accident caused by ice buildup on the plane's wings. In that situation, the co-pilot might have succeeded in preventing the plane from taking off if he had expressed his concerns in a more straightforward way, setting aside politeness considerations related to status differences with the pilot.

Holtgraves's (1986) experiments, which I also discussed in Section 5.2.1, provide insights into the role of S's status on the perceived appropriateness of indirectness. In these experiments, status was manipulated, S either being higher (a president) or lower (another employee) in status relative to A. Direct requests for opinion such as (22a) were perceived as more polite when they were produced by higher status than by equal status individuals.

(22)   a   What do you think of my new dress? (Holtgraves 1986: 307)
       b   I don't think it looks very good on you. (Holtgraves 1986: 307)

Moreover, in face-threatening situations, an interaction was found between face-threat and the indirectness of a reply on assumed speaker status: in comparison with evasive and irrelevant (indirect) replies, direct replies such as (22b) were more frequently believed to have been made by higher status speakers. This result can be explained according to higher status individuals' smaller concern about face-threat: as they are less likely to be impacted by the face-threatening potential of a situation, they are also less likely to use linguistic indirectness as a compensation for the possible ensuing emotional costs for their addressees.

In the same vein, Holtgraves et al. (1989) investigated how information about S's status affects how interpreters remember conversational remarks. In Experiment 1, participants read conversational scenarios ending with an imperative request (23), an IR (24), or a mitigated IR (25).

(23) Tell them to hurry things up.

(24) You could ask them to hurry things up.

(25) Perhaps you could ask them to hurry things up.

S either was higher in status (a boss) or equal in status (a co-worker) relative to A. One half of the participants received information about S's status just before reading the scenario, the other half two days later.

5.3 Face Concerns and Social Variables

The results show that, when S was higher in status, participants recognized a smaller number of IRs that they had seen previously, and were more likely to incorrectly identify imperative requests as previously said by a speaker (even though they were not said by that speaker). In a similar experiment (Experiment 2), participants recalled, as accurately as possible, as many remarks as they could. In the higher status condition, more remarks were recalled as if they were imperative, and participants more often recalled the remarks as conveying directive illocutionary force (what the authors call 'assertiveness') in the higher status condition. The results of this second experiment were replicated in Experiment 3, where participants observed two people role play a conversation. To explain the finding that remarks are recalled as 'stronger' when S is higher in status, the authors propose that information about S's status plays a role in the encoding of interpretation. Observers believing that S is higher status would selectively encode 'strong' remarks because they are compatible with S's status. In contrast, observers believing that S is equal in status will tend to encode conversational remarks as weaker because these more indirect forms meet their expectations about lower status speakers. Similar findings were obtained by Holtgraves and Yang (1990) with data from American and Korean students. In their Experiment 3, participants were asked about their impression of S's status (and social distance) relative to that of A using a seven-point scale ranging from 'extremely low' to 'extremely high'. S was perceived as lowest in status when the request was a hint such as (26), and as highest in status when the request was performed with an imperative, as in (27).

(26) Hasn't the mail come by now?

(27) Go get the mail.

This is evidence that the form of the request influences the perception of S's relative status. In addition, in line with the thesis that utterances violating social norms should give rise to better memory, request forms that are unexpected given S's relative status are remembered better than those that are expected. For example, Kemper and Thissen (1981) asked their participants to rate the politeness and effectiveness of various request forms, ranging from imperatives (*Rake the leaves*) to questions including consultative devices (*Don't you think you could rake the leaves?*) and hedges (*I think the leaves really need to be raked*), before testing their verbatim memory for these requests. The more indirect the request, the better it was recalled when S was higher in status than

A; the more direct the request, the better it was recalled when S had a lower status than A.

In an experiment that I have already discussed in the previous chapter, Holtgraves (1994) manipulated S's status so as to investigate how information about social status can help infer the intended meaning of IRs. He used standardized IRs such as (28) and non-standardized IRs such as the negative state remark (29).

(28) Could you close the window?

(29) It's cold in here.

In Experiment 1, participants were presented, on a computer screen, with scenarios describing an interaction between two people. Each scenario was followed by an utterance produced by S, in which S was either equal (employee) or superior (manager/boss) to A (employee) in status; the utterance was either a standardized IR or a negative state remark. After reading the target utterance, the participants were asked to press a key to indicate that they had understood it. Then they were presented with a paraphrase and asked whether it was a correct interpretation of the remark they had just read. The data indicate that, while the standardized IRs took about the same time to understand in the higher status condition as in the equal status condition, the negative state remarks took longer to understand in the equal status condition. This result accords with the hypothesis that addressees will tend to search for an indirect meaning behind higher status speakers' utterances because the latter have more options. It seems to run against Brown and Levinson's (1987) prediction that negative state remarks are more polite than standardized IRs: if they were the most polite way of phrasing a request, negative state remarks should not take longer to comprehend when interlocutors are equal in status, because processing times are expected to increase not for appropriate, but for inappropriate utterances. By contrast, using similar scenarios, Holtgraves (1994) demonstrates, in another experiment, that negative state remarks are more likely, and easier, to be understood as directives if S is higher versus equal in status relative to A.

In contrast to Holtgraves's studies, to explore face-threat and the interpretation of IRs and indirect disagreements, Demeure et al. (2007) used a game as experimental setting. In this game, players interacted by exchanging cards and information, with the ultimate goal to control different areas of an imaginary city. Participants, acting as third parties, were asked about how they interpreted utterances produced

5.3 Face Concerns and Social Variables

by different players. Demeure et al. found a higher likelihood of the 'question' interpretation of ambiguous utterances such as *Do you have NP?* by addressees when these individuals were higher in status. A first explanation for this surprising result is based on speakers' reluctance to perform the SA of request at all. Even in the case of an indirect utterance, the face-threat associated with requesting something from a higher status person would be too high so that addressees would not understand these utterances as requests altogether. Another, perhaps more plausible explanation is that it is more common for lower status people to ask questions to higher status people, and more common for higher status people to tell their lower status addressees to do things. Therefore, the 'request for information' interpretation of IR utterances addressed to higher status individuals would be perceived as more likely from the participants' third-party perspective: lower status individuals are more entitled to ask their superiors about the availability of a certain item than to request that they give it to them. This second explanation was confirmed by Demeure et al.'s Experiment 2 (see Section 5.3.6 for a discussion of their other results).

5.3.1.1 Addressee Status in an Academic Setting

Relevant data pertaining to the effect of relative status on the use of indirectness comes from empirical studies of request production. Consisting mainly in DCT approaches, they have been criticized on the grounds that the data collected with this method are not representative of the participants' actual behaviours. This criticism is supported by substantial differences in the relative frequencies of different SA realizations whether the data are elicited or not (cf. Flöck 2016). A related problem, which concerns the corpus-based approaches to request production, is that they did not control for some possible sources of variability in the data. Such uncontrolled parameters include, to name only a few, demographic and sociolinguistic differences between speakers and addressees, differences in the content of the request, or in the course of action in which the performance of the request takes place. Unlike these approaches, in Ruytenbeek (2020), I used an original methodology that consisted in explicitly instructing French-speaking Belgian participants to perform an electronic request in an academic context. This experiment was presented as a situation test including background information to make the task more realistic. This enables a high control on the data because the content of the request is identical for all the participants, and the relative status of the addressee was explicitly stated in the instructions.

Scenarios in which a student requests the notes of a fellow student have frequently been used in previous research on the production of requests (Ogiermann 2009). In such scenarios, the relationship between the interlocutors is defined in terms of low social distance and equal hierarchical status, which suggests that potential threats to A's negative face are not an issue. By contrast, requesting something from a higher status person, such as a professor, is more likely to involve strategies to save A's negative face. In my production task experiment, I manipulated the status relationship between S and A, so that A was either equal in status (fellow student) or superior (Faculty Dean) to S. Concerning the influence of A's status on email communication, it has been shown that changes in the structure of the email reflect the knowledge that A is higher in status, in particular in the variety of expressions used in the opening and the closing of the messages (Bou-Franch 2011). In addition, using DCT, Saeli (2016) provides evidence for a significant influence of A's relative status on the form and structure of Persian requests. In his study, requests were addressed by graduate students to professors (higher status), peers (equal status) and undergraduate students (lower status). The requests to higher status people were more formal and longer – a cue that more politeness formulae and mitigating devices were included – than those addressed to lower status and equal status people.

In one of my experiments (Ruytenbeek 2020), I was interested in seeing whether more indirect forms, such as negative state remarks, occur more often when the addressee is higher in status, and more direct forms, such as standardized IRs, are more frequent when A is equal in status. The participants were asked to perform the following task: send an email to another person to ask that person for a contribution in the Linguistics student newspaper. Nothing in the instructions prevented the participants from including additional information in their email, as long as they complied with the task of requesting that A send her/his text to them. For half of the participants, A was the Faculty Dean, for the other half it was a female student, for the sake of realism, as the large majority of students at the Faculty are women. I agree that having a male recipient in the high status condition and a female recipient in the equal status condition is a debatable decision, as it introduces a confusion between status and gender. However, I believe that the impact of gender on politeness strategies and on the use of indirectness should be limited, as the highly salient status asymmetry and the low familiarity between email writers and recipients should minimize a possible effect of gender.

5.3 Face Concerns and Social Variables

In line with the coding scheme of Blum-Kulka and Olshtain's (1984) cross-cultural speech act realization project (CCSARP), I systematically distinguished the 'request head act' from the rest of the email. In the CCSARP, the 'head act' is the utterance by means of which a SA is communicated: it is distinct from the utterances, considered peripheral to the head act, which are used by the participants to ground their request, check whether the preconditions for their request SA obtain, and so on. A first result is that the relative frequencies of the request forms did not differ according to A's status. More than two-thirds of the requests were formulated with an interrogative about A's ability (and, very rarely, willingness) to perform the action. Imperatives and statements of obligation did not occur at all in the data. Non-standardized IRs, such as negative state remarks, reasons to act other than S's desire, and inquiries about A's performance of the expected action, were rare (6%). Of the 80 questions about preparatory conditions, 67 were highly standardized, such as (30)–(31).

(30) J'aimerais que vous me renvoyiez votre texte.
'I would like you to send me your text again.'

(31) Auriez-vous l'amabilité de m'envoyer votre texte ?
'Would you be so kind as to send me your text?'

Ability interrogatives with a low degree of standardization, such as (32), were more frequent when A was higher in status (14 out of 57) than when he was equal in status (6 out of 59).

(32) Serait[-]il possible que vous me l'envoy[i]ez dans les plus brefs délais ?
'Would it be possible for you to send it to me?'

However, probably due to the low frequencies of these request forms, this difference was not significant. Standardized IRs, such as *Could you VP?*, in the polite V-form as in (33) or in the T form (*Peux-tu...?*), tended to be more frequent when A was equal in status (37 occurrences) than when he was higher in status (30 occurrences), but the difference was not significant.

(33) Pourriez[-]vous me le faire transmettre le plus rapidement [possible ?]
'Could you have it forwarded to me in the shortest delay?'

However, in line with Brown and Levinson's (1987) approach, the participants increased the politeness of their message when they addressed a higher status person such as a Faculty Dean. For example, formal greetings were more frequent in the higher status condition, and *vous* was the only pronoun used for higher status addressees, while it was used in only 39 out of the 59 messages in the equal status condition. While the systematic use of V-forms of address for emails to the Faculty Dean cannot be interpreted in terms of more indirectness, it indicates a higher concern for A's status.

To sum up the findings presented in this section, information about the relative status of interlocutors has an influence both on the perception and on the production of ISAs. On the one hand, DSA realizations are taken by interpreters as evidence for the assumption that the speakers who produce them are higher in status in comparison with their addressees, while indirect realizations are characteristic of lower status speakers. On the other hand, there is partial evidence that more indirectness is to be expected in directive SAs addressed to higher status individuals, but the results of production tasks such as the one presented in Ruytenbeek (2020) do not confirm this hypothesis. While this indicates that indirectness is only one possible way to adapt one's communicative style to different addressees, it will also be necessary to explore the role of relative status on indirectness in other SA types than directives.

5.3.2 Degree of Imposition

Degree of imposition refers to Brown and Levinson's (1987) 'ranking of impositions' in the performance of FTAs. Impositions are defined as the costs, for A's negative and positive faces, that are associated with the performance of a SA as well as its immediate consequences. In their approach, the effects of the variables of relative status, social distance and degree of imposition on expected politeness are cumulative. Specifically, the higher the imposition for A entailed by the performance of some SA, the stronger the need to mitigate this threat to A's face.

Biesenbach-Lucas's (2007) investigation of the influence of the degree of imposition on the variety of request forms is based on a corpus of spontaneous emails sent by students to lecturers. In these emails, the status of and the social distance between the interlocutors were stable, while the degree of imposition associated with the request varied. Three sorts of requests constituted her corpus: requests for an appointment (low imposition), requests for feedback on a written work (moderate imposition) and requests for due date extensions (high imposition). This categorization is somewhat surprising, because the most considerable workload for the addressee corresponds to Biesenbach-Lucas's 'moderate imposition' condition. I also think that the author confused the

5.3 Face Concerns and Social Variables

costs for S, that is, the emotional costs resulting from the lecturer's refusal to extend the deadline, with the costs for A, the lecturer.

Following Blum-Kulka and Olshtain's (1984) CCSARP coding scheme, Biesenbach-Lucas analyzed a variety of request forms in terms of 'degrees of (in)directness': hints such as (34) are more indirect than questions about the preparatory conditions of the request, such as (35), which are in turn more indirect than want statements such as (36), or elliptic constructions such as (37). The following examples, provided by the author, illustrate a request for feedback on a written work.

(34) I'm having a very difficult time in figuring out how to put these lesson materials together.

(35) Would you mind taking a look and giving me some suggestions?

(36) I would like your suggestions.

(37) Any comments?

In her data, first, requests for feedback involved a large majority of direct strategies, but hints were more frequent than interrogatives about the preparatory conditions. The considerable number of direct requests for feedback is surprising, as these requests entailed the highest imposition on A's part. Second, requests for appointment involved as many direct strategies as interrogatives about the preparatory conditions, but no negative state remarks. Third, more than 50% of the requests for extension of due date were of the 'preparatory condition' type, and more than 30% were off-record, for instance negative state remarks. These results suggest that the degree of imposition has an influence on the likelihood that a request will be indirect, with standardized indirectness increasing in frequency when the imposition *for the speaker* is highest. The results for requests for feedback are not completely in line with Brown and Levinson's (1987) theory, as preparatory interrogatives (negative politeness), and not negative state remarks used as off-record ISAs, are the most frequent request strategy in the 'moderate imposition' condition.

In a similar vein, Chejnová (2014) studied a corpus of 260 email messages sent by university students in the Czech Republic. These messages contained a high imposition request for action and were addressed to a lecturer. The most frequent request forms were preparatory interrogatives such as (38)–(39), with 39.6%, followed by hedged performatives such as (40), with about 32%, and performatives such as (41), with 12%.

(38) Bylo by možné zapsat mě do kurzu?
'Would it be possible to enrol me in the course?'

(39) Mohla byste mě zapsat do kurzu?
'Could you enrol me in the course?'

(40) Chtěla bych vás poprosit o zapsání do kurzu.
'I would like to ask you to enrol me in the course.'

(41) Žádám vás o zapsání do kurzu.
'I am asking you to enrol me in the course.'

Imperatives (less than 2%) and direct requests for information (3.8%) were rare. In addition to the variety of request forms, Chejnová observed that the students often resorted to internal modifications, such as the conditional and lexical downgraders to mitigate the directive force of their messages. The results of this study reveal a majority of standardized IRs for high imposition requests. They also confirm that it is not only indirectness, but also the use of downgrading strategies that contributes to the degree of politeness of email directives (Savić 2018).

In the context of business communication, Freytag (2020) provides naturally occurring corpus data indicating that the degree of imposition of a request has an influence on the use of indirectness by email writers. For instance, in her corpus of British English emails, she finds that low imposition directives more often include imperatives than high imposition directives. Both in her British English and Peninsular Spanish corpora, preparatory interrogatives are more frequent when a request comes with a high imposition. She also shows that the frequency of IR forms changes depending on message purposes: interrogative sentences are used more often to request prices than, for instance, to request confirmation, and more than the half of the emails concerning price negotiation include preparatory interrogatives. These findings also indicate that degree of imposition and message purpose are not completely independent.

From an experimental perspective, Stewart et al. (2018) explored the processing correlates of direct versus indirect requests for bribery. Using two types of scenarios, they manipulated the degree of imposition associated with a driver's attempt to bribe a police officer in order to avoid paying a ticket. They considered that the higher the expectation that A should respond favourably to S's request, the higher the imposition of the request – a definition of imposition that is somewhat counter-intuitive, as requests are less likely to be successful if they entail high costs for addressees, in which cases the imposition would be low according to Stewart et al. (2018). In the high imposition scenarios, police officers were known to be dishonest, which made the driver's attempt to bribe them very likely to succeed. In the low imposition scenarios, police officers were described as honest people, unlikely to take the bribe, resulting in a smaller degree of imposition. Indirect attempts to bribe the officer (42) were contrasted with direct attempts (43).

(42) Perhaps there is another way we can solve this.

(43) I'll give you £20 and you could let me go.

Stewart and colleagues found that IRs for bribery were understood faster in situations where the imposition on the officer was high (dishonest officer). In contrast, the processing of direct utterances was not affected by the degree of imposition upon the officer.

5.3.3 Social Distance

In contrast to the variable of status, much less research has been devoted to the influence of social distance or 'degree of (un)familiarity' between interlocutors on the use of indirectness and its perceived appropriateness. As Holtgraves and Yang (1990: 246) insist, social distance should not be confused with the related notion of relationship affect. This confusion would explain divergent findings in the empirical literature. For instance, Blum-Kulka and Olshtain (1984), find that a high social distance goes together with more polite forms including standardized IRs and negative state remarks. Baxter's (1984) results support the hypothesis that a higher degree of indirectness corresponds to situations involving higher social distance. Another relevant study is Holtgraves's (1986) experimental work, which reveals that we are more likely to infer that two interlocutors are in a close relationship and like each other when a face-threatening request for information is answered with a direct reply; when the reply is irrelevant, the perceived liking and closeness are the lowest. By contrast, in Holtgraves and Yang's (1990) experiments, the most direct request forms give rise to the greatest perceived distance between interlocutors. Freytag (2020) also provides evidence that direct SA realizations are more likely to occur in high-distance than in low-distance situations, and that these strategies are generally combined with a higher use of downgraders when the distance between the email writer and the addressee is high.

Freytag's (2020) and Holtgraves and Yang's (1990) results are completely at odds with Brown and Levinson's (1987) politeness theory. In politeness theory, the degree of face-threat is proportional to social distance and, as a consequence, higher face-threat should give rise to a higher degree of politeness, hence to a higher degree of indirectness in interactions with unfamiliar people. These findings also confirm that the influence of the variables of status, imposition and distance on the use of indirectness is more complex than a positive correlation with additive effects.

5.3.4 Status, Imposition and Distance

As the respective influences of relative status, degree of imposition and distance on indirectness are not cumulative, it is useful to address studies that directly tap into their interactions. Holtgraves and Yang (1990), for example, manipulated these three variables in a discourse completion task consisting in a situation where an undergraduate student wanted to request something from another person. Three different versions of the scenario were created, corresponding to a low imposition request (ask for the time), a moderate imposition request (ask for a quarter to give a phone call) and a high imposition request (asking A to place a phone call for S). Concerning the manipulation of status, A could be lower (junior high school student), equal (undergraduate), or higher in status (professor) relative to the participant. Social distance, as indicated in the scenario, was low, moderate or high. American and Korean participants were asked to imagine being involved in different situations and to indicate how they would put their request into words. They also had to indicate, for the same scenarios, how they perceived the size of the request, the addressee's status and the closeness of their (virtual) relationship with the addressee. The politeness of their requests was assessed and coded by two bilingual speakers of American English and Korean. The authors followed Brown and Levinson's classical scheme, combined with insights from Blum-Kulka and Olshtain's (1984) CCSARP, and distinguished between address forms (formal, informal, absent), head act of request (bald on record, positive politeness, negative politeness, off-record strategy, or absence of request), and supporting moves (positive or negative politeness). An overall 0.75 inter-rater agreement between the two coders was achieved for this task. The major results can be summarized as follows: Higher speaker status was inferred for the most polite requests. The same finding applies to social distance between interlocutors and degree of

5.3 Face Concerns and Social Variables

imposition: high social distance and high imposition were associated with more polite request forms. In addition, an interaction was found between these variables. More precisely, when a request comes with a high degree of imposition, it is imposition, rather than relative status or distance, that primarily shapes its (im)politeness perception. Other research along the same lines points towards this sort of interaction (Blum-Kulka & Olshtain 1984; Holtgraves & Yang 1990; Lim & Bowers 1991). For instance, if the effect of status on the degree of indirectness increases, the effect of social distance is less noticeable, and vice versa.

5.3.5 Gender-Based Differences

Most of the available evidence concerning the role of gender on indirect communication comes from research on differences between the communicative style and sensitivity to (im)politeness considerations of women and men (e.g., Tannen 1990). For example, a gender-based difference in communicative style on online discussion forums is that men are more likely than women to contribute to spirals of verbal aggression (Herring 1994). This is exactly the pattern that would be expected if women orient more towards indirectness than men. Following this research, it makes sense to ask about gender-based asymmetries in the use and perception of indirect utterances. It is also important to explore this question, because stereotypical judgements about how women and men (should) behave in conversation are pervasive in our daily life. Are these stereotypes confirmed, and if so, to what extent?

In her pioneering research on gender differences in the use of indirectness, Lakoff (1973a: 56–7) considers a definition of indirectness in terms of S leaving up to A the decision as to whether or not act upon S's utterance. She proposes that women are more likely to use IRs with a negative polarity, as the former does not put on A the burden of a refusal to comply. Experimental evidence from Danish IRs, however, indicates that *Can't you VP?* requests such as (44) are more powerful than their affirmative counterparts such as (45) (Heinemann 2006).

(44) Ka' du ikk' tænde loftlyset? (Heinemann 2006: 1093)
    'Can't you turn on the overhead light?'

(45) Can you turn on the overhead light?

One therefore expects that negative polarity IRs would be perceived as less polite than positive polarity IRs. As Heinemann proposes, the reason for this difference is that negative interrogatives such as

Can't/couldn't you VP? convey the assumption that A is entitled to do the requested action and, in some situations, it may even implicate that A is a non-cooperative person.

In line with the demonstrated existence of gender-based differences in expressive (more strongly associated with women) and instrumental (more strongly associated with men) communication styles (Spence & Helmreich 1978), it has been suggested that women and men also differ in their use of politeness, with the expectation that women would be 'more polite' than men (Baxter 1984; Falbo & Peplau 1980). Even though Holtgraves and Yang (1990) (see Section 5.3.4) do not report on the results pertaining to the indirectness of the utterances produced, they say that their results about gender-based differences in the politeness of the utterances 'were essentially the same' as those for differences in the use of indirectness (1990: 249, fn. 2). They expected a gender-based asymmetry in ISA interpretation, and found an interaction between relative status and gender on the interpretation of indirect utterances. The effect of status was stronger for men's requests than for women's requests, that is, interlocutor status accounted for more variance in men's use of politeness in requests than it did for women. They also found a tendency of an interaction between distance and gender, as female participants were somewhat more likely to weight distance more heavily than were male participants. These findings are in line with the idea that men's instrumental communicative style is more oriented towards considerations of status, while women's communicative style is more concerned with the closeness of relationships (Tannen 1990). Women's higher degree of politeness enables them to 'take care of' the interpersonal relationship, especially when social distance is low.

Following the ideas developed by Lakoff (1973a), Crosby-Nyquist (1977) and Tannen (1981), Holtgraves (1991) proposed the hypothesis of a gender asymmetry in the interpretation and the production of ISAs. Accordingly, as female speakers are more indirect in their communicative style than male speakers, females are also more likely to derive indirect interpretations of IRs for opinion such as (3) and indirect replies such as (5).

(3) Did you notice my new coat? (repeated)

(5) I think it takes so much effort to shop for clothes. (repeated)

To test this hypothesis, he used short conversational scenarios involving face-threat and containing remarks varying in their degree of

5.3 Face Concerns and Social Variables

indirectness. While the results of his experiments confirmed the expected asymmetry of interpretation for indirect replies – that may not be surprising, as talking about shopping is typically a women's activity – no such difference was found for IRs for opinion. This may be due, as Holtgraves suggests, to the fact that indirect replies are more ambiguous than IRs for opinion, which makes gender-based differences less likely to emerge for the latter type of utterances. While this explanation is not implausible, it requires further experimental verification and clarification: in what sense are indirect replies more ambiguous than IRs for information? Another explanation I would suggest is not based on ambiguity, but on differences in face-threat associated with requests for information and replies, respectively. As indirect replies communicate negative evaluations, it is possible that women are more sensitive to the threats to A's positive face (negative opinion) than to the threats to his negative face (requests for opinion).

Another interesting study that reveals gender-based differences concerns the realization of apologies. Ogiermann's (2007) results indicate that women prefer to offer repair in an indirect way, as in (46), while men are more likely to make direct offers such as (47) when they apologize.

(46) Do you want me to buy you some new fish?

(47) I will buy you some new fish.

More precisely, in her study, women more often used illocutionary force markers such as *I'm sorry* and *I apologize* (405 times versus 317), and they were more likely to acknowledge their responsibility (116 times versus 70), in comparison with men. This can be explained by the facilitative effect of apologies on the maintenance of harmony in friendships, an aspect of social life that women are more sensitive to. Ogiermann does not report on the statistical significance of these tendencies, but the chi-square tests I carried out confirm that they both are significant ($\chi^2(1, N = 722) = 10.73$, $p = .001$ and $\chi^2(1, N = 186) = 11.38$, $p < .001$, respectively).

Gender-based differences in language use have also been explored within the field of simultaneous interpreting. Using a corpus consisting of original spoken French discourse and its Dutch and English translations, Magnifico and Defrancq (2017) demonstrate a higher use of hedges by female interpreters compared to male interpreters, but the difference was only significant in the Dutch data. In addition, in Dutch translations involving a FTA performed by the original speaker or an original utterance that was difficult to interpret, female interpreters' hedges included more additions than men's. Assuming a Brown and Levinsonian view on hedging as a form of indirect communication, these results indicate that French–Dutch translations carried out by women have a stronger orientation towards indirectness than those carried out by men. However, these results are contradicted by another study where the authors found a more frequent use of downtoners, such as for example, *it seems, maybe*, in male interpreters' translations of assertive SAs (Magnifico & Defrancq 2016). In (48), for example, the FTA is softened by the use of an epistemic marker of uncertainty (*it seems to me*).

(48) Now it seems to me that the source of inflation relates to the inaction of the finances.

It is nonetheless possible that the diverging results in these two studies is only apparent, in the sense that men would prefer direct SA strategies including downtoners, while women would prefer using indirect strategies and less often mitigating them with downtoners. Taken together, these findings suggest that gender-based differences in the use of indirectness are subtle and that experimental designs must be highly controlled for if they are used to investigate these effects. Furthermore, a number of studies report on an absence of differences in the use of indirectness by women and men. One of these is Briggs et al. (2017), which I will return to in Chapter 6, and which found a similar amount of indirect directives produced by women and men addressing robots. Likewise, in Freytag's (2020) corpus of business email directives, the gender of the writer had no impact on the choice of sentence-types, request strategies and mitigating devices. By contrast, she observed that direct requests (i.e., imperatives) were more frequent in same-gender emails. A possible explanation for this effect, which is compatible with some (but not all) findings about the role of social distance, is that social distance is lower in same-gender dyads, resulting in more directness in directive emails.

Finally, there is a clear link between gender and status: the variable of gender feeds into that of status, and vice-versa, especially in societies where men have more power than women. One should therefore be careful when discussing the respective effects of these two interrelated social parameters on indirect communication. In Baxter's (1984) experiment, for example, participants had to imagine themselves in different versions of the scenario in (49):

5.3 Face Concerns and Social Variables

(49) 'Imagine that you are involved in a group research project worth two-thirds of your course grade in a class where you very much want to get a high grade. Half of the grade on this project will be given to the group as a whole by the instructor, making the entire group dependent on the performance of each member. The other half of the project grade is to be determined separately for each individual by the group's designated leader, a member of the group designated by the instructor as the leader.

<u>You are your group's leader, thus you will determine half of each person's project grade.</u> In your view, all of the group members except one have done very well. This one member's work is of such poor quality that the group grade is in jeopardy, and you want to get this person to re-do his/her part of the project in the remaining time before the final project is due. <u>There are only three days remaining before the project is due, and the person will basically have to start over again, concentrating a term's worth of work into three days. It can be done, however, but only in a concerted, round-the-clock effort from the person. The person in question is someone you regard as a good friend.</u>' (Baxter 1984: 441–2)

As in Holtgraves's studies, the predictor variables were manipulated in the content of the vignettes presented to the participants. In the scenario given in (49), the participant is high in status (group's leader), the degree of urgency, and, therefore, of imposition is high (three days remaining before the due date), and the social distance is low (a good friend). The variables of social distance, relative status and the magnitude of the request were manipulated by modifying the information contained in the underlined sentences. The results of Baxter's experiment indicate that women and individuals in close relationships more often resort to linguistic politeness than men and individuals in more distant relationships. Her data also show that higher status speakers use politeness markers less often than less powerful speakers.

To conclude this discussion of the relationship between gender, (in)directness and (im)politeness, differences exist between the communicative styles typically associated with women and men. Women are more oriented towards indirectness than men, at least as far as the SAs of apologizing and requesting are concerned. By contrast, findings concerning indirectness in the performance of assertive SAs do not lend conclusive support to the gender-based asymmetry hypothesis. This suggests that the effects of gender on the use and interpretation of ISAs may be more complex than it seems at first, and additional research on this issue is therefore needed.

5.3.6 Individual Variables

In addition to the three social variables prioritized by Brown and Levinson (1987) and speaker's and addressee's gender, other interpersonal variables that have an influence on the use and perception of indirectness have been considered.

Culture, for instance, determines to some extent speakers' tendency to resort to indirect communication. As politeness and indirectness are, despite the absence of an absolute positive correlation between them, conceptually related, cultural differences in the use and interpretation of more or less indirect utterances are expected. In Holtgraves and Yang's (1990) study, Korean participants, who were compared to American English participants, considered that positive politeness requests such as (50) indicate greater closeness in comparison with negative politeness, as in (51), and off-record requests such as (52).

(50) You'll lend me a quarter, won't you? (Holtgraves & Yang 1990: 249)

(51) Could you lend me a quarter?

(52) I need to call my roommate so he can bring my paper and I don't have a quarter. (Holtgraves & Yang 1990: 249)

In addition, in a production task, these authors demonstrated that the politeness of Korean participants' requests varies more in function of the relative status variable than those produced by American participants. This result is in line with Hofstede's (1980) finding that Korean speakers weight interlocutors' relative status higher than American speakers do.

Another individual variable that is expected to shape the use of indirectness is addressee personality. In this regard, Demeure et al. (2007) tested the predictions of Brown and Levinson's (1987) theory and that of an alternative theory, the 'utilitarian relevance' approach. The latter theory is based on the relevance-theoretic idea that A assumes S to use the most relevant stimulus that is compatible with her personal preferences. With utilitarian relevance, Demeure et al. (2007) imply that it is S's goals and preferences that guide A's search for the correct intended interpretation, that is, the one that enables S to achieve her goals. These authors explored the role of face-threat, relative status, addressee personality and affective distance between the interlocutors on the interpretation of utterances with an indirect meaning. As I have already discussed the first two parameters, here I will focus on the variables of addressee personality and affective distance, which have,

5.3 Face Concerns and Social Variables

to date, rarely been investigated. In Demeure et al.'s Experiment 2, which consisted in a game involving protagonists trying to control different areas of a fictitious city, the players' teammates were described as having either a rigid or a flexible personality. Interested in interindividual differences in the interpretation of ambiguous utterances, the authors tested the influence of the state of mind of the teammate and his personality on third parties' interpretations of ambiguous utterances, that is, participants being presented with conversational exchanges between the protagonists. Specifically, they put forward the hypothesis that an IR expression such as (53) is more likely to be taken as a request when the teammate is irritable and likes to impose his point of view (rigid personality), in comparison with an teammate who is open-minded and has greater empathy.

(53) Avez-vous la carte de l'épicerie ?
      'Do you have the card of the grocery?'

They found that utterances such as (53) were more likely to be interpreted by third-party participants as requests when a teammate had a rigid personality. This result accords with Slugoski and Turnbull's (1988) study on the perception of face-threatening behaviour in function of social distance affectivity, which revealed that the perceived offensiveness of literal insults such as (54) increases as a function of disliking.

(54) Such a pity you haven't learned to paint yet, Sue. (Slugoski & Turnbull 1988: 109)

In their Experiment 4, Demeure et al. attempted to disentangle social distance from affective distance. While Brown and Levinson paid considerable attention to the former variable, without disentangling different conceptions of 'social distance', they said little on affectivity. Moreover, previous work on relative status and distance provides conflicting evidence concerning the effects of these variables on indirectness. In Demeure et al. (2007), the affective distance between S and A was manipulated: a low affective distance corresponds to a friendship relationship; a high affective distance to interlocutors who do not like each other. Their experimental stimuli consisted of indirect disagreements such as (55), in which the V-form of address already conveys some degree of affective and/or social distance towards A.

(55) J'ai peur de ne pas vous suivre.
      'I'm afraid I don't follow you.'

In line with Brown and Levinson's approach, an ambiguous utterance such as (55) was understood as a disagreement (and not as a request for clarification) in the case of a high affective distance between interlocutors. Thus, higher social distance increases face-threat, which results in a stronger need to compensate for the possible offence to A's positive face with indirectness.

5.4 EXPLICITNESS AND FACE-THREAT IN COMPLAINTS

Complaints provide an interesting case study of (in)directness. With Sofie Decock and Ilse Depraetere, I have investigated them from both an empirical and an experimental perspective. Here, I will only focus on two aspects of our research, namely, the relationship between (in)directness and explicitness in Twitter complaints and the impact of explicitness on the perception of face-threat in these complaints.

In Searle's (1975) SAT, (in)directness was a property of a SA, arising from a mismatch between a sentence-type and a SA type, instantiated in a particular utterance. Accordingly, (in)directness applies at the level of individual utterances, which entails that, while a single utterance can result in the performance of more than one SA at a time, as in the case of ISAs (the DSA and the ISA), the reverse is not true: a single SA cannot be performed by a combination of utterances. That being said, pace Searle, some SA types are best defined as a combination of individual utterances – some of which can give rise to the performance of SAs at the individual level too. Complaints, for example, often consist of an assertion (of the event that gave rise to S's complaining behaviour) combined with another assertion or expressive SA (S's subjective evaluation of the negative event) (Depraetere et al., 2021). This observation has led some researchers (e.g., Tanck 2002; Vásquez 2011) to put forward the concept of 'speech act sets' when they analyse such 'multi-component' SAs. For instance, according to Olshtain and Weinbach (1993), the 'SA set of complaint' includes a reproach, an expression of S's disapproval, an explicit complaint, and a warning or threat. In the same vein, Murphy and Neu (1996) propose that a complaint is made up of an explanation concerning the negative event that took place, a complaint utterance, a justification for why S is complaining, and a request for action. The problem with this analysis is that the approach in terms of SA sets seems redundant, as one of the SAs that it consists of itself is a complaint.

5.4 Explicitness and Face-Threat in Complaints

Unlike Murphy and Neu (1996) and Olshtain and Weinbach (1993), Decock and Depraetere (2018) do not make the circular claim that 'one component of a complaint is a complaint'. Rather, they define a complaint situation in terms of four constitutive components, which have been derived from House and Kasper's (1981) and Trosborg's (1995) work on complaints. Component A refers to a past or ongoing action/event that did not conform to S's expectations, the 'complainable'. Component B, 'speaker dissatisfaction', refers to S's disapproval of the complainable, which makes it clear that she is dissatisfied. Component C is the person or institution that S holds (at least partially) responsible for the negative consequences of the complainable. The fourth component, Component D, is S's wish for the complainable to be remedied.

Several classifications of complaint strategies that have been put forth in the literature involve an indirectness–directness continuum (e.g., House & Kasper 1981; Trosborg 1995), the lowest level being labelled as the most indirect, and the highest level as the most direct. According to this view, *direct* and *indirect* refer to the extremes of a scale. Following the insights provided by Brown and Levinson (1987), this scale has been applied to a wide range of SAs, such as requests. For instance, imperative requests are more direct than *Can you VP?* requests, which are in turn more direct than negative state remarks such as *It's cold in here*. This (in)directness scale has also been applied to different realizations of complaints, but the result is less convincing. For example, in House and Kasper (1981), a negative state remark such as (56), from a customer who is dissatisfied about her train journey, would be considered as less direct compared to for example, (57).

(56) The train was late.

(57) You [the railway company] are incompetent.

Unlike in the example of request (in)directness, it is less obvious that these two complaint realizations can be compared in terms of their degree of (in)directness. Even though they both can be considered as negative state remarks, because they express a different aspect of the situation that gave rise to the complaint, they do not have the same propositional content. This makes it difficult to assess their respective degree of (in)directness.

In Decock and Depraetere's approach, (56)–(57) can nonetheless be compared, not in their degree of (in)directness, but, rather, in their degree of explicitness, which they define in terms of the number of components that are linguistically realized (one, two, three or four components). The constitutive components of complaints can thus give rise to one-utterance or multiple-utterance complaints. The complaint can be more or less explicit depending on the number of components that are linguistically realized. Four-component complaints are the most explicit ones; single-component complaints are the least explicit ones.[2] We have seen that the binary or graded notion of (in)directness cannot satisfactorily be applied to a complaint as a whole. I believe, however, that (in)directness can be operationalized at the level of the individual constitutive components of complaints. In particular, components A and D can be linguistically expressed with different degrees of (in)directness. Component A (complainable) can be realized, for instance, with an assertion (*The train is delayed*), or by means of a presupposition (*Why are we not informed about the train delay?*), and component D, the wish for compensation or solution, by means of a variety of request forms.

The first aim of our research on complaints was to apply the taxonomy outlined in Decock and Depraetere (2018) to a corpus of authentic complaints and to examine how complaints are (para)linguistically realized in this sample (Depraetere et al., 2021). To this end, we compiled a corpus of one hundred French-language Twitter complaint interactions on the Twitter pages of the SNCF (French National Railway company) and one hundred on the SNCB/NMBS (Belgian National Railway company). This means that in all cases, including those threads with an opening customer tweet in which the complaint is left implicit, it was clear from the interaction that the customer initiated the Twitter conversation because something was wrong, she was dissatisfied about the situation and she held the railway company accountable for the situation. We coded the opening complaint tweets in terms of the number and types of constitutive components that were linguistically expressed, that is, component A (complainable), component B (customer dissatisfaction), component C (person or institution responsible for the complainable) and component D (wish for the complainable to be remedied). Once we had identified the components

---

[2] In fact, Decock & Depraetere (2018) make a distinction between 'implicit' and 'explicit' complaints. For them, a complaint is implicit if none of the constitutive components is linguistically realized, in which case the complaint is, in principle, cancellable. For instance, if someone is dissatisfied about her train journey, she might say *next time I'll stay home*, in which case the complaint is implicated. I will consider that their 'purely implicit' complaints can be situated on the same scale of explicitness as complaints for which one or more components are linguistically realized, i.e., that they are even less explicit than one-component complaints.

5.4 Explicitness and Face-Threat in Complaints

Table 5.1 *Frequency of one-, two-, three-, four-component combinations*

	SNCF (100)	SNCB (100)	Relative frequency (%)
One component	3	11	7
Two components	20	41	30.5
Three components	51	35	43
Four components	26	11	18.5

realized in the opening complaint tweets, we examined the different formal realizations of these constitutive components.

Concerning the explicitness of Twitter complaints, we found that the complaints were more explicit in the SNCF sample than in the SNCB sample, in the sense that there was a higher number of components linguistically expressed in the SNCF tweets (see Table 5.1). Our quantitative analysis was based on chi-square tests (with $p < .05$ as statistical significance level). In the table below, the figures in bold (i.e., the figures for one, two and four components) point to the statistically significant differences.

The most frequent type of complaints (43%) included three constitutive components. Complaints in the SNCF sample were more explicit in the sense that complaints with a higher number of components being linguistically realized were more frequent. The question here is whether the differences found in terms of pragmalinguistic patterns can be explained by intercultural differences, are the result of differentiated response policies, or a combination of both. In the light of Tobback's (2014) findings that the Belgian French debating style is quite close to the French communicative style, how customer service employees respond to complaints (response strategy/policy) is most likely to be the main factor explaining the differences between the Twitter complaints in these two linguistic communities.

In their reassessment of (in)directness in complaints, Decock and Depraetere (2018) make – unlike previous studies on (in)directness in complaints – a clear distinction between the degree of linguistic (in)directness, which refers to the researcher's assessment of how a particular SA is linguistically realized, and the degree of perceived face-threat, which refers to interpreters' and addressees' affective evaluations of SAs. This distinction parallels that between the levels of illocutionary meaning and perlocutionary effects, respectively. Our second aim was therefore to test the effect of degrees of explicitness (as assessed by the researchers) on the perception of face-threat in complaints. We used the results of our corpus approach to design the experiments presented in Ruytenbeek et al. (in press). Our investigation was inspired by the observation that consumers frequently voice negative feedback to organizations on online public platforms. Against this background, it is important to know how customer complaints are perceived, because these perceptions are likely to influence both customer service employees' responses to these complaints and potential customers' purchase decisions. We manipulated the explicitness of complaints in terms of the number of constitutive components that were linguistically expressed. The aim of one of our experiments was to explore how the number and the nature of these constitutive components determine complaint perception.

In this experiment, we asked participants to indicate how they perceived Twitter complaints along different dimensions related to face-threat, using Likert scales representing these dimensions. Following Brown and Levinson (1987), we first expected that a higher degree of explicitness would cause the complaints to be perceived as more face-threatening, and therefore less polite, resulting in higher scores on the scales of perceived strength, dissatisfaction and impoliteness. Indeed, Brown and Levinson postulate a positive correlation between directness (and, arguably, explicitness) and face-threat across a variety of contexts (but see, e.g., Culpeper 2011: 100–103; Ogiermann 2009; Wierzbicka 1985, who discuss exceptions to this tendency): the more direct the SA (or the combination of SAs), the more face-threatening it is. Accordingly, the more explicit a complaint, the more face-threat, and explicitness in complaints should also positively correlate with their perceived strength. Second, building on the negativity bias according to which negative information weighs more on our perceptions (of complaints) than neutral or positive information (see, e.g., Liebrecht et al. 2019 for recent empirical evidence, and Jing-Schmidt 2007 for a review), component B (customer dissatisfaction about the complainable) should play a crucial role with regard to perceived dissatisfaction, of course, but also with respect to perceived strength and (im)politeness.

We predicted that participants' judgements on the scales of perceived customer dissatisfaction and complaint strength should be stronger for more explicit complaints, that is, complaints containing three or four components in comparison with less explicit ones with only one or two components. However, assuming a negativity bias, we also predicted that the presence/absence of component B would

5.4 Explicitness and Face-Threat in Complaints

moderate the effect of explicitness on complaint perception: the judgements for complaints including component B should be stronger than those for complaints where B is absent, regardless of the degree of explicitness, that is, the number of components (para)linguistically realized. We also expected more explicit complaints to be perceived as more rude and as implying stronger dissatisfaction than less explicit ones. Finally, we predicted that the judgements on the scales of complaint strength, customer dissatisfaction and impoliteness, should positively correlate.

The stimuli used in this experiment were directly based on our corpus study (Depraetere et al., 2021). For example, (58) is an experimental stimulus based on an original complaint tweet (no longer retrievable on Twitter), with a specification of the components expressed.

(58) A/R Paris Grenoble dans la journée. 20 min de retard à l'aller. Pour l'instant, déjà 50 au retour. Ça sent la belle journée ça, @SNCF!! A quand le respect des horaires?

'Return trip Paris Grenoble today. 20 minutes' delay on outward journey. For the moment, already 50 on the way back. Looks like it'll be a nice day, @SNCF!! When will the timetables be observed?'

While the original tweet only contained component A (the train is delayed), component B (the use of exclamation marks and the sarcastic comment *Looks like it'll be a nice day*) and component C (@SNCF used as a vocative), the stimulus in (58) also includes component D, that is, an invitation to observe the timetables.

A Latin square design was used, based on eight original Twitter complaints from the SNCF sample. The form of these complaints was manipulated to make them match the complaint component combinations attested in our corpus. Eighty native speakers from France and Belgium were recruited on Prolific. The experiment took the form of a short questionnaire available online, which was designed using Psytoolkit (Stoet 2010, 2017) and presented to the participants on Prolific. For each complaint tweet, the participants had to answer a question we used to verify that they understood the tweets as complaints ('How certain is it that the traveller is complaining?'), and three questions about the face-threatening aspects of the complaint, namely, 'How strong is the traveller's complaint?', 'How polite is the traveller's message?' and 'How dissatisfied is the traveller?'. Four different seven-point Likert scales were used to elicit the participants' responses to these questions, with labels at the left and right ends of the scales that corresponded to the notion under investigation. We assumed that these scales reflected different degrees of certainty, strength, (im)politeness and dissatisfaction, thus presenting these as graded notions. The labels at the left end of the scales were, respectively, 'not at all certain/very weak/very rude/not at all dissatisfied' (1) and those at the right end of the scale were 'completely certain/very strong/very polite/very dissatisfied' (7). The data generated by this experiment are available on the Open Science Framework (https://osf.io/qu6jd).

The results of this experiment confirmed our predictions about the effects of explicitness and the negativity bias on complaint perception. Generally speaking, when the complaints were more explicit, that is, they included a larger number of components, they were perceived as stronger, as expressing higher customer dissatisfaction and as less polite than complaints with fewer components. Specifically, these judgements were stronger when the complaints included component B. By contrast, we did not find evidence for a similar effect of components C and D on complaint perception. We can therefore conclude that it is not only the degree of explicitness, but also the nature of the constitutive components present in a complaint that shape complaint perception. A remaining question, which we are currently exploring, concerns the influence of different, that is, more or less (in)direct realizations of components A, B, C and D, and the interaction of different realizations of these components, on the perception of complaints.

The small corpus of Twitter complaints that we analyzed and used in our experiment shows that, unlike the other SA types explored in this chapter, Twitter complaints addressed to railway companies do not have implicitness (or indirectness, as, at the level of their individual components, complaints often contain direct assertions about and negative evaluations of the complainable) as their preferred mode of realization. This is somewhat surprising, as the SA of complaining is intrinsically face-threatening, but this can be explained by, first, the fact that these complaints are addressed to institutions, not to individuals, and, second, the primary function of a complaint as a means to exert some degree of pressure towards the company so that they improve customer satisfaction and/or offer dissatisfied customers a compensation. From that perspective, there is no advantage in trying to make one's complaints less explicit, because implicit complaints would be less likely to result in a solution for the customer. However, whether this reasoning also applies at the level of the (in)directness of the individual components of complaints remains an open question.

5.5 SUMMARY

In this chapter, we have seen that different variables, most of which concern the interpersonal context of utterance, influence how speakers phrase their SAs, and also how these SAs are understood. In addition, experimental evidence reveals that the form of SAs provides information about the interlocutors. Another important finding is that the effects of these variables are not necessarily additive, and that they give rise to complex interactions. While available research largely focused on the three variables central to Brown and Levinson's (1987) theory, that is, relative status, distance and degree of imposition, a few scholars have been interested in other interpersonal parameters, such as affective distance, addressee personality, and speaker and addressee gender, and also cultural differences in the perception of indirectness. However, to date, experimental evidence concerning the role that these variables play in ISA interpretation is too scarce to enable us to draw generalizations. Moreover, two main research gaps can be identified: the over-reliance of these studies on indirect directives as a case study for indirectness in general, and the lack of investigation of other variables that may impact the use and interpretation of ISAs. Finally, I addressed Twitter complaints, which are best thought of as a combination of different components of a situation that can be linguistically realized, at the individual level, with various degrees of (in)directness and, at the macro level, with different degrees of explicitness depending on the number of components expressed. Experimental evidence indicates that the more explicit the complaint, the more face-threatening and the less polite it is perceived. Even though complaint explicitness is distinct from the (in)directness of individual components of complaints, this finding confirms Brown and Levinson's hypothesis of a positive correlation between degree of explicitness and degree of perceived face-threat.

5.6 DISCUSSION QUESTIONS

- Data bearing on the use and perception of indirect utterances come, on the one hand, from empirical studies and corpus data, and, on the other hand, from experimental research. In your opinion, which type of data will provide the most reliable results, and why?
- Experimental studies on ISA interpretation have revealed interaction effects between several interpersonal variables. Would it

also be possible to explore such interactions with corpus data? What obstacles would such an approach face?
- Can you think of contextual parameters (social or non-social) other than those discussed in this chapter? Considering different SAs (promises, invitations, compliments, etc.), how would you expect each of these parameters to influence speakers' use of indirectness, and the likelihood that an indirect meaning is inferred?

5.7 SUGGESTIONS FOR FURTHER READING

On sociocultural approaches to indirect communication (broadly defined): Hendry and Watson (2001); Grainger and Mills (2016).

Although its focus lies on impoliteness, Culpeper's monograph provides insightful discussions about the (in)appropriateness of indirectness, especially when it is excessively high: Culpeper (2011).

6 Computational and Artificial Intelligence Approaches to Indirectness

6.1 INTRODUCTION

In Chapter 4 and Chapter 5, I distinguished between different types of indirectness, taking into account the semantic meaning and other relevant properties of the linguistic expressions used as ISAs: conventionality of means, degree of standardization and degree of illocutionary force salience. I have also presented the results of a large variety of experimental and empirical studies on ISAs, bearing on both their comprehension and their production, in particular their relationship with politeness and the social contexts of conversational interaction. However, two key questions remain. First, how can we model the inferential processes leading to the recognition of the intended (indirect) meaning of an utterance, and what does experimental evidence tell us about these processes? And, second, could such models be integrated into natural language understanding systems to improve our routine interactions with computer programs and robots? Instead of entering the technical details underlying the computational and formalistic aspects of these approaches, I will be interested in their relevance and viability with respect to the recent experimental findings concerning the processing and social dynamics of indirectness.

6.2 COMPUTATIONAL MODELS OF ISA INTERPRETATION

Since the late seventies – even before any psychological evidence about ISA comprehension was available – artificial intelligence (AI) specialists started elaborating computational models able to solve the pragmatic ambiguities that characterize ISAs. Unsurprisingly, with the boom of digital communication and automatization over the last couple of years, scholars' interest has increased, in particular within the field of human–robot interactions (HRI). Inferential models of ISA interpretation have been proposed, the first by Searle (1975), including the possibility that some inferential steps are bypassed, but their implementation in natural language processing (NLP) systems was not straightforward.

6.2.1 Plan-Based Approaches

One possible way to deal with the interpretation of ISA expressions is to use the 'plan-based model' introduced by Perrault and Allen (1980) and Allen and Perrault (1980). This approach, also called 'inferential', assumes a Gricean view of communication based on intention recognition, and it adopts SAT's definition of SA types in terms of perlocutionary intentions. These authors take it that ISA comprehension is a matter of intention recognition that enables the interpreter to identify S's goals or 'plans' behind her utterance. On the basis of examples of requests for information in train stations, such as (1a), they put forth a small number of rules that interpreters can use to make sense of indirect utterances.

(1) a Do you know when the Windsor train leaves? (Allen & Perrault 1980: 169)
    b Yes, at 3.15.

In order to be able to answer (1a) with (1b), a NLP system must infer S's plan behind the literal meaning of (1a), that is, S's goal of knowing whether the system knows the Windsor train's departure time. The 'know-positive rule' specifies that, if an agent wants to know whether a proposition is true, then it is possible that it wants to achieve a goal requiring the truth of that proposition. Applying this 'know-positive rule', the system identifies the goal that 'S knows the train's departure time'. This step enables the system to perform the action of informing the customer about the departure time ('precondition-action rule'), and this informative act achieves the customer's goal of knowing the departure time. The customer's goals inferred from the direct and indirect interpretations of her utterance are considered by the system as obstacles that it is designed to overcome. It is thus capable of responding both to the direct and indirect meanings of ISA expressions, although, as we will see later, not necessarily to assign both to a particular utterance at the same time. These interpretation rules have been tested by having a computer program implementing them simulate an information clerk at a railway station. They are able to account for a variety of pragmatically ambiguous expressions.

Despite its empirical coverage, this approach has a major drawback: it does not differentiate between distinct expressions that have the same semantic meaning, such as (2)–(3)–(4). Even though their direct

6.2 Computational Models of ISA Interpretation

meaning is that of a question about A's ability to do some action, the higher degree of standardization for the performance of IRs that is associated with the *Can you VP?* construction in (2) makes it more likely to be used as an ISA in comparison with the other two expressions.

(2) Can you tell me when the Windsor train leaves?

(3) Is it possible for you to tell me when the Windsor train leaves?

(4) Are you able to tell me when the Windsor train leaves?

In addition, the psychological plausibility of the plan-based model is difficult to assess. In the footsteps of Morgan (1978), who introduced the notion of a 'short-circuited implicature', Allen and Perrault (1980) acknowledge that, in practice, human interpreters may bypass some of the inferential steps they propose, but they view such a reduction in the size of the inference as less likely to occur in the case of expressions with a lower degree of standardization.

6.2.2 Specific Interpretation Rules

An alternative approach to the plan-based model has been developed by Lehnert (1978) in QUALM, a computer program designed for answering questions from customers. It is based on a larger number of rules than the plan-based model, which makes it less economical, but more efficient than its 'rival' as its rules are more specific. For example, a rule concerns interrogatives about the availability of a particular item of the 'Do you have NP?' type, as in (5).

(5) Do you have a piece of paper?

This interrogative could be interpreted as a question to verify whether A possesses the object mentioned in the NP. However, the rule says, if the object has a small size and is inexpensive, it will count as a request that A give the object to S. Although I am not entirely sure that the physical size is a reliable criterion – small relative to what? and a piece of paper is light, but it is not something that we would normally regard as small, yet (5) can easily be understood as a request – I agree with Lehnert that it makes sense to take into account the financial costs associated with the item and, perhaps, a combination of size and weight.

One limitation of QUALM is that, despite its high specificity, it has to contain a very large amount of rules, as ISAs can be performed using a variety of constructions. It is also unlikely that, however representative of the reality of indirectness the system would be, its rules would exhaust the space of possibilities, as many different constructions can be meant as ISAs, such as negative state remarks, which a robot equipped with QUALM would not be able to successfully disambiguate. Furthermore, this system cannot capture generalizations about recurring patterns, such as, for example the observation that IRs can be performed by using different instantiations of the abstract construction 'modal verb (+ negation) + 2nd person pronoun + VP?', as in (6).

(6) Will/can/shouldn't you bring me a piece of paper?

Instead, it associates a different interpretation rule to each different modal construction that can be used as an IR.

6.2.3 Hybrid Approaches

Halfway between the plan-based model and the specific interpretation rules approach, hybrid approaches combine their respective benefits. One example is Schulenburg and Pazzani's (1989) explanation-based model implemented in the computer program 'Sally'. They propose a system, called Sally, that interprets indirect utterances by learning a rule based on the first ISA it encounters. For the next ISA it has to interpret, this rule becomes a simplified rule that enables it to deal with similar examples of indirect utterances. For instance, a rule specifies that a person should give another person an object if it is of little value (thus not necessarily small) and there is a cordial relationship between the interlocutors. Example (7) is an utterance that can be interpreted as an IR according to this rule.

(7) Do you have some gum?

The advantage of such a model is its cognitive plausibility: in proposing that a computer program reduces the size of its interpretative rules over the course of 'ISA encounters', it is reminiscent of Morgan's (1978) short-circuited implicature. It inherits, however, the shortcoming of the plan-based model because it does not differentiate between ISA expressions having a similar semantic meaning, such as *can* and *be able to*, and, as a consequence, it is as likely to interpret an utterance of *Are you able to VP?* as it is in the case of *Can you VP?*.

A more recent hybrid approach has been developed by Briggs and Scheutz (2013), who propose that, in case a given utterance does not fit

6.2 Computational Models of ISA Interpretation

the specific interpretation rules approach, a more expensive procedure will be used (an 'inferential' or plan-based approach). As it has a strong connection with HRI, I will discuss it in more detail in Section 6.3.

6.2.4 Indirect Directives and Reasons to Act

The approaches we have discovered so far did not attempt to make strong generalizations accounting for the variety of expressions with a potential indirect use, or at least they have failed in that regard. Unlike these models, Longin (2006) proposed an extension of Champagne-Lavau et al.'s (2002) classification of IR forms. His new typology goes beyond Searle's (1975) category of constructions expressing reasons for A to do the action requested by S (in a similar vein, Brown & Levinson (1987: 128–9) mention giving reasons as an indirect strategy). The idea developed by Champagne and colleagues is that a given utterance is a potential IR if: (a) it is a question about – or a statement of – a felicity condition for the performance of directives; (b) it mentions reasons for A to act (or the existence of such reasons); or (c) it refers to the preconditions for the planning of the requested action. There are several types of reasons to act, some of which are commonly used in IRs: deontic reasons (8), reasons related to necessity (9) and those that are to A's benefit (10).

(8) You should drive more slowly. (adapted from Longin 2006)

(9) Do you have to drive that fast? (adapted from Longin 2006)

(10) You'd better mind your fuel tank.

Longin proposes that virtually any expression used as an IR makes, in some respect, reference to a 'reason to act'. His major improvement to Champagne et al.'s classification is his distinction in terms of the realization mode of the IR – a declarative sentence or a polar interrogative – of four types of arguments: existence of reasons (11), content of reasons (8), inexistence of reasons (12), and part of reasons (13).

(11) I have good reasons to ask you to drive more slowly.

(12) There's no reason why you shouldn't drive more slowly. (adapted from Longin 2006)

(13) You're driving at 60mph [where the limit is 40mph]. (adapted from Longin 2006)

Only the first two categories were present in Champagne-Lavau et al.'s (2002) typology. These arguments have as possible scope the action itself, a related action, or a request (not) to do the action. The combination of realization modes, arguments and scopes gives rise to sixty-four different IR realizations that a NLP system should be able to recognize. Explicit performatives such as (14), and even metapragmatic references to the SA of requesting, as in (15), fit Longin's generalization, as someone's telling someone else to do something can be considered as a reason for A to carry out the requested action.

(14) I am telling you to open the window.

(15) How many times did I tell you to open the window?

Longin's approach is particularly useful for computational models designed to help NLP systems to identify the indirect meaning of utterances: a search for the content or the existence of reasons would then lead to the identification of the intended IR meaning of the expression. However, a serious issue with this approach is that it overgeneralizes. That is, the subcategory of 'parts of reasons' includes any possible information that is conceptually related to a reason for A to do some action. As a consequence, it would be a very complex task for a NLP system to decide when the content of a particular utterance is 'part of a reason'. In addition, Longin does not explain why imperatives, which are prototypically used to request action from others, are excluded from his approach. As they do not convey statements, I fail to see how they could be taken as expressing (part of) reasons for A to carry out some action, but Longin does not address this issue.

6.3 INDIRECTNESS IN HUMAN-ROBOT INTERACTIONS

From the perspective of human cognition, computational systems able to process indirectness are not highly relevant. After all, utterance interpretation is a task we carry out as a routine, most of the time automatically. A more useful application of these computational models is robots. Unlike humans, robots do not acquire their language skills over the course of the years and their exposure to a variety of linguistic stimuli and their responses. Still, if we want them to interact with us in our daily life, should they not learn how to infer the indirect meaning of utterances? A inability to understand ISAs can result in

6.3 Indirectness in Human–Robot Interactions

communication failure, which must be avoided if we want our robots to be pragmatically competent. The conversation in (16) is very indicative in this respect (Briggs et al. 2017: 71).

(16) Robot – Hello, my name is Waiterbot. I am taking care of you today. Please tell me what drink I should bring you.
Subject – Uh, I'd like a water.
Robot – That is nice. Please tell me what drink I should bring you.
Subject – Uh could I have a water?
Robot – You could order that. Please tell me what drink I should bring you.
Subject – Um I would like to have a glass of water please.
Robot – That is interesting. Please tell me what drink I should bring you.
Subject – Uh, I need a water.
Robot – Okay. Please tell me what drink I should bring you.
Subject – Um could I have a water?
Robot – You could order that. Please tell me what drink I should bring you.
Subject – Water.

In this dialogue, it is obvious that the robot is unable to go beyond the literal meaning of the IR expressions used by the participant, *I'd like NP*, *Could I have NP?* and *I would like to have NP*. This is illustrated by the robot's replies *Okay* and *That's nice*, which would be appropriate if the participant's utterances were statements. In addition, the robot's reply *You could order that* corresponds to the literal interpretation of *Could I have a water?* as a possibility question. Concerning the participant's behaviour, the conversation is quite effortful in the sense that she is trying to identify, by trial-and-error, the (only) request forms that the waiterbot is able to act upon. She addresses the robot, from the onset, with her repertoire of 'polite' request forms, as she would normally do in interactions with other humans, treating the robot as if it were a person whereas its verbal responses reveal the gap between human and human-like. Even though the sample of the dialogue in (16) does not conclusively show this, Briggs et al. explain that the user eventually succeeds in her attempt at getting some water from the robot when she uses the simple NP *water*. This is far from being an easy, straightforward way of interacting with a robot. Another aspect that makes the participant's task complicated is that she faces uncertainty regarding what form is contextually appropriate or whether any special formula is expected from her, as when she adds *please* to her IR, either to make it more polite (directive force mitigation) or to specify that it is a request (directive illocutionary force indicating device). Other examples of participant–robot exchanges indicate that *My order is NP* would also have been successful with this kind of robot and, as soon as the participant recognizes that the robot understands these forms, she systematically re-uses these patterns for her other requests. This repetitiveness and lack of naturalness is not a proper characterization of our daily conversations, and robots should be able to do better.

6.3.1 Do People Use Indirectness with Robots?

At first glance, it is not obvious why robots should be pragmatically competent with ISAs. Even if some robots are human-like, they are not exactly humans, so one should not jump to the conclusion that we actually speak to them as we do with one another.

In fact, somewhat surprisingly, recent experimental evidence indicates that we often use indirect utterances when communicating with robots. For instance, the participants in Williams et al.'s (2018) study produced IRs in the context of a social interaction in a restaurant, where their orders as customers were taken care of by a 'waiterbot', a virtual waiter, as in dialogue (16) (see also Briggs et al. 2017). More surprisingly, ISAs were also quite common in a situation where social norms were lacking, such as the 'tower toppling scenario' described in Briggs and Scheutz (2014) and used as an experimental setting by Briggs et al. (2017). In that simple task, participants had to tell the robot to knock over coloured towers, and they did so with indirect formulations 28 per cent of the time. These results suggest that people bring their social norms, for instance about contextually appropriate ways to say things, in their interactions with robots. However, additional research shows that imperative requests to robots in tower toppling scenarios are not perceived as less appropriate than IRs (Williams et al. 2018). This might indicate that the participants' social norms are weakened in these contexts, in the sense that more direct forms are considered to be more acceptable with robots, where it would not necessarily be the case with humans. Another possible explanation is that the contextual appropriateness of DSA realizations increases in situations with a strong orientation towards efficiency.

Briggs et al.'s (2017) results concerning the human tendency to use ISAs with robots were replicated by Williams et al. (2018). They also demonstrate that indirectness is more common in contexts that include expectations about compliance with social norms, according to which IR forms are most appropriate. Moreover, in a questionnaire administered to participants, these authors confirmed that robots capable of

6.3 Indirectness in Human–Robot Interactions

understanding ISAs are considered to be easier to interact with than with the 'literal' robots lacking that ability. More precisely, robots' failure to interpret ISAs and, as a result, to act appropriately upon these ambiguous utterances affects in a negative way how they are perceived by the people who interact with them. Most participants who interacted with a 'literal' robot explained that they would phrase their requests in a more direct manner if they had to interact again with the robot. However, even if they had to do so, they would still feel it somewhat unnatural and even impolite. These results are particularly insightful in the current era of automatization and digitalization, where AI applications, such as vocal assistants, only work with very direct spoken commands. For instance, users' instructions will be responded to if they consist in imperative requests for action (*Call [person name]*, *Send a message to [person name]*, *Take me to [place]*, *Wake me up at [time]*), direct requests for information (*Where is [place]?*), and even noun phrases (*Length of [movie name]*) and, for example, in French, infinitive commands. As available evidence suggests that users do not feel comfortable being 'impolite' with their vocal assistants, it is surprising that nowadays the only successful request forms are the most direct ones.

Insofar as humans have a strong tendency to talk to robots as they would with other humans, a certain number of indirect utterances are expected in human–robot interactions, even in situations that do not call for 'polite' indirectness. It is therefore necessary that robots be able to deal with ISAs in an appropriate manner in order to satisfy users' needs. A failure to understand indirectness would dramatically increase the number of mistakes made by robots, and make them less likeable. The first challenge, then, is to make robots human-like when it comes to the disambiguation of ISA expressions, so that their interpretations and the ensuing responses be contextually appropriate. The second challenge consists in having a robots use indirectness when it is required to do so, as specified, for instance, by the peculiarities of the interpersonal relationship between the robot and its addressee. This is also relevant from the perspective of language learning in online environments, as in the case of non-native users interacting with virtual agents.

6.3.2 How to Make a Robot Disambiguate ISA Utterances

Several computational models have been developed to enable computer programs to satisfactorily respond to ISAs.

6.3.2.1 *One or Two Speech Acts?*

Wilske and Kruijff (2006) propose that, if a robot is uncertain as to how it should interpret ISA expressions such as (17)–(18), using its knowledge of linguistic meaning and the current situation of utterance, it can ask S to clarify the intended meaning of her utterance.

(17) Could you bring me a cup of tea?

(18) I would like to have a cup of tea.

In Wilske and Kruijff's model, a 'situation' refers to the robot's ability, readiness and willingness to fulfill S's request, and there are three modes corresponding to the human–robot interaction. In the 'servant' mode, the robot explicitly offers its services to the person, which makes it very likely that constructions such as (17)–(18) will be meant as requests. In the 'non-servant' mode, it is not ready to serve, because it is, for instance, busy with another task or lacks appropriate knowledge to fulfill the user's request. In that case, it will provide a justification for its refusal, for example, (19), and will respond only to the literal meaning of statements such as (18) with (20). A default mode covers other possible cases.

(19) Sorry, I do not know where the kitchen is.

(20) I see.

Wilske and Kruijff propose a heuristic for the robot's decision process. First, it has to determine on the basis of its knowledge about ISA expressions, whether or not the utterance has a possible IR meaning. If it is not the case, it will only address its literal meaning. Second, if the expression used by S is classified as an ISA expression, and the action is not feasible from the robot's perspective, it will reject the request and apologize for its non-compliance. Third, if the utterance concerns an action that is feasible, the robot will check whether or not it is pragmatically ambiguous. Fourth, if it is not ambiguous, it will interpret it as an IR and carry out the requested action, but if the ambiguity remains, it will ask for clarification and, depending on S's explanation, either reject it or act upon it. The robot's requests for clarification will also enable it to deal appropriately with future utterances in directly adopting the correct interpretations.

The content of Wilske and Kruijff's (2006) heuristic, however, has a major shortcoming: it simplifies the actual mechanics of ISAs. It looks as if a pragmatically ambiguous utterance either is an DSA or is a ISA, but the picture is more complex. HRI approaches to indirectness – and thus human-like robots – should be capable of dealing with situations

6.3 Indirectness in Human–Robot Interactions

where both the direct and the indirect interpretations of an ISA expression are intended by S. Briggs et al. (2017) make an important step in that direction. They propose a model taking into account the possibility of multiple interpretations being conveyed by a single utterance at the same time. This is important not only because there are cases where an utterance communicates both a DSA and an ISA, but it is sometimes necessary to respond to the direct meaning of an ISA, if only for the sake of politeness. Unlike Hinkelman and Allen (1989) and Allen et al. (2001), for instance, Briggs et al. (2017) do not assume that NLP systems are under an obligation to respond to the direct meaning of an ISA expression. This is a sound decision because, in some situations, it would be irrelevant to respond to the DSA. Instead, they take into account not only formal features of the utterances, such as the directive illocutionary force indicator *please*, but also previous uses of an ISA expression, for example, *Can you VP?*, for which it is already known that the robot is able to do the expected action. They therefore introduce rules that are not dependent on S's beliefs, but on the beliefs that a robot assigns to S. The corpus data that they report on exclusively contain utterances concerning the preparatory and sincerity conditions for the performance of directives, complemented by, to use Longin's terminology, 'parts of reasons' such as bare NPs (e.g., *water*). However, the interpretation mechanisms they suggest are also able to handle other request forms, such as negative state remarks.

6.3.2.2 Social Status Asymmetries

The idea that indirectness depends heavily on the context of utterance is a common thread of this book. It is also a concern of computational approaches to ISA comprehension. Moreover, as humans have a strong tendency to treat robots as if they were humans, it is not surprising that the social appropriateness of ISAs also caught the attention of HRI scholars. In particular, whether or not an ISA is appropriate is determined, to a large extent, by the social norms and obligations of the conversational participants. This aspect of human–robot communication has been demonstrated by Lee and Makatchev (2010), who explored human utterances addressed to 'Roboceptionist', a receptionist robot, on a university campus. For instance, half of the participants used greetings before formulating their requests, and these participants were more likely than 'non-greeting participants' to include polite behaviour in their interaction with Roboceptionist. These 'polite' elements include saying goodbye, thanking the robot, apologizing and using *please* in a request.

One social norm that influences the appropriateness of indirectness is the status relationship between interlocutors. In Chapter 5, we saw, for instance, that direct requests are more acceptable in downward than in upward status relationships, while the opposite pattern holds for standardized IRs. Thus a proper knowledge of the interlocutors' social roles is necessary to the production of appropriate utterances. In the same vein, Briggs and Scheutz (2013) attempt to account for the effect of asymmetric status on the form of SAs performed by robots in HRI. In order to model social roles, they refer to Perrault and Allen's (1980) 'cause-to-want' action, which enables an agent to make another agent's goals its own. In their computational model, they replace this 'cause-to-want' action by 'obligation modelling actions'. This allows them to differentiate the cases where S is superior in status to A from those where interlocutors are equal in status. They propose that the degree of obligation for the robot to act upon S's utterance varies according to the type of status relationship that holds between S and the robot. The examples they consider involve a robot attempting to get one of its human co-workers to help it clean the floor. If the robot and its co-worker are equal in status, the robot can report a third party's directive, for instance Alice's, who is the hierarchical superior of the robot's co-worker. In that case, an obligation modelling action of the type 'Alice puts the co-worker under an obligation to clean the floor' can be triggered. To get the co-worker to act, the robot will then produce a contextually appropriate statement such as (21), which will be interpreted as an IR.

(21) Alice wants the floor cleaned.

When there is a supervisory relationship between the interlocutors and the robot is superior to the co-worker, two sorts of situations are identified: those where there is an expectation of politeness, and those lacking that expectation. In the former situations, the obligation modelling action cannot apply, and a polar interrogative such as (22) will be preferred over the direct request (23) acceptable in situations with no politeness expectations.

(22) Can you clean the floor?

(23) Clean the floor.

What I find a little surprising, however, is that Briggs and Scheutz do not discuss a situation where the robot is lower in status in comparison with a human protagonist (here, Alice), because robots are, in general,

6.3 Indirectness in Human–Robot Interactions

hierarchically inferior to human agents; after all, humans design robots in the first place to assist them in their tasks. In these situations, I would assume that the robot's utterances will have to comply with politeness expectations.

6.3.2.3 Representing Robots' Uncertainty

We have seen that, in some situations, robots may face uncertainty when dealing with pragmatically ambiguous utterances, such as ISA expressions. Sometimes, the indirect interpretation of an ISA is not its correct, intended meaning. For example, depending on whether or not the interlocutors are aware of some piece of cake being available, (24) can be taken by A as a request to bring S some cake.

(24) I'd love some cake.

In the default mode conceived by Wilske and Kruijff (2006), the robot asks its interlocutor, S, to clarify how she intended her utterance to be understood. Asking for clarification will probably be useful in some contexts, where S's intentions cannot be ascertained for sure by the robot in the absence of any evidence supporting a direct or indirect interpretation. One example of 'social uncertainty' is that of a speaker who has to interact with a robot, but does not know whether her own status is equal to or higher than the robot's. Asking this question will come with extra cost when it is obvious from the context that the DSA is irrelevant. An illustration concerns pre-requests that remove possible obstacles to A's compliance (Francik and Clark 1985): in the dialogue (25), the first question–answer pair strongly increases the likelihood that (25c) is a request, and this is something that a robot should be able to take into account.

(25) a   Do you have any enchiladas? (Gibbs 1986b)
      b   Sure, we have enchiladas with potatoes, cheese and beans.
      c   Can you give me one with cheese?

Williams et al.'s (2014) computational model of ISA interpretation includes a representation of a robot's uncertainty with respect to the intended meaning of an ISA utterance. Here, the robot ascribes a level of confidence in each interpretation. The key features of this model are: uncertainty, adaptation and belief modelling. Uncertainty refers to the idea that it is impossible for an agent to have knowledge about all the possible contexts where the indirect interpretation of an ISA utterance applies. Therefore, each context will be used to assign a certain level of confidence in the indirect interpretation, and the 'adaptative robot' will use feedback from its interlocutors to update its beliefs. In fact, as S's beliefs can diverge from the robot's, and it is the former that reliably predict S's intended meaning, the interlocutor's beliefs are more important than the robot's capacities and obligations.

Williams et al.'s (2014) model is reminiscent of Clark's (1979) pioneering study, where he examined the form of (indirect) requests for information addressed to local merchants and their replies. For Clark (1979), when a merchant is faced with a question such as (26), he computes estimates to determine whether S intended her utterance as a DSA (ability question) and/or as an ISA (IR for the price).

(26) Could you tell me the price for a fifth of Jim Beam?

According to him, whether people interpret the direct illocutionary meaning and/or the indirect illocutionary meaning of an utterance depends on their relying on different sources of information, including the 'conventions of means'. For instance, he showed that sentences such as (26) make their indirect meaning more likely, and their direct meaning less likely, relative to sentences such as (27).

(27) Does a fifth of Jim Beam cost £5?

An approach such as the one proposed by Williams et al. (2014) is more than welcome, as in previous work a robot's beliefs were binary, that is, its interlocutor either had or had not a particular belief. In real life, however, beliefs are best conceived of in terms of relative degrees of (un)certainty, some goals being more likely to be attributed to an agent than others. This model, however, also has some limitations. For instance, it would be interesting to extend their algorithm so that new, non-conventional ISA expressions can be dealt with.

6.3.2.4 *Monitoring Interlocutors' Belief States*

As in Williams et al.'s (2014) approach, taking into account the interlocutor's beliefs is central to Trott and Bergen's (2017) model. In contrast to most of the computational literature on ISAs with a high degree of standardization, such as preparatory interrogatives and want declaratives, which mention the requested action or part of it, these authors concentrate on less standardized IRs. If a robot is able to keep track of the different belief states of interlocutors, including its own beliefs about its interlocutor's goals, then it should be able to correctly disambiguate negative state remarks such as (28).

6.3 Indirectness in Human–Robot Interactions 195

(28) It's cold in here.

Trott and Bergen address the challenge of enumerating the disambiguating contexts for these expressions: for instance, the likelihood that (28) is an IR is different whether it is uttered in a room or outside during a winter walk. They propose that robots track and represent their interlocutors' beliefs, and that they use their model of the world to infer the intended meaning of utterances. Accordingly, the robot's own beliefs are not sufficient to interpret pragmatically ambiguous utterances correctly (and they can sometimes be misleading). For example, if S is unaware of the fact that the heating is broken, she could say (28) to get the robot to turn on the heating. The robot will use S's incorrect belief – incompatible with its own world knowledge – to understand (28) as a request, while disregarding its own knowledge that the heating is broken. The robot's best interpretation will therefore be selected on the basis of what it believes its interlocutor believes, and divergent beliefs will not result in misinterpretation. This means that the robot would carry out another action to increase the room's temperature, and one that is possible in the particular situation. If a negative state remark is not interpreted as a request but as a genuine complaint, it will be responded to with an offer of sympathy.

The likelihood of an indirect interpretation also increases if the robot believes that S considers herself as capable of or obliged to fulfill S's request and the request has not already been fulfilled (cf. Searle's preparatory conditions for directives). I suggest that other features of the interpersonal relationship between S and the robot, which I have addressed in some detail in Chapter 5, such as their relative status, and whether S is familiar with human–robot interactions more generally, and with a specific robot in particular, play a similar role. For example, if S believes that the robot is responsible for the heating of the house, and the robot is aware of S's belief, an IR interpretation of S's ambiguous utterance should be more likely than a direct interpretation.

Experimental evidence for Trott and Bergen's (2017) model comes from studies on contextual expectations facilitating ISA interpretations and supporting the mutual knowledge hypothesis, such as those carried out by Gibbs (1979; 1983; 1986a) and discussed in Chapter 4. Now, a drawback of this approach is that an agent needs to maintain extensive world knowledge, in particular the information that is relevant to utterance interpretation. But this is precisely what theory of mind is about. As we saw in Chapter 5, theory-of-mind brain areas are involved in the processing of negative state remarks only when these remarks are understood as IRs (van Ackeren et al. 2012). Another advantage of this model is that it is not specific to indirectness, but applies to any sort of SA realization and is also relevant for the resolution of lexical ambiguities.

6.4 SUMMARY

This chapter centred on computational models of ISA interpretation, with special reference to human–robot interactions. I distinguished between two types of approaches, namely the general inferential rules of the plan-based model and the specific interpretation rules of the idiomatic approach, with, in-between, models building on the idea that the complex inferential route appropriate for dealing with more creative forms of indirectness could be short-circuited when applied to ISAs with a high degree of standardization. These computational models have been used to enable computer programs and robots to deal with difficulties inherent to indirectness, such as the combination of DSA and ISA interpretations for a single utterance and the need to ask a speaker to clarify her illocutionary intent. In addition, solutions have been proposed to reflect the fact that interpreters face some degree of uncertainty when processing pragmatically ambiguous utterances: the most efficient models involve artificial agents' representing and monitoring their interlocutors' beliefs. As the likelihood of an ISA interpretation largely depends on the interpersonal context of an utterance, these models also help robots use social information about the conversational participants, so that they both appropriately respond to users' indirectness and themselves produce ISAs in the right contexts. Despite users' reluctance to use a high level of directness with robots, given the nuances and complexities inherent in the diversity of ISAs, the contemporary vocal assistants' restriction to direct, unambiguous utterances is easily understandable.

One challenge that remains to be addressed properly concerns an agent's previous exposure to different and possibly incompatible interpretations of ambiguous ISA utterances. Furthermore, interindividual differences in the use and the interpretation of ISA constructions deserves more attention. Bayesian pragmatics, a recent development of the field, provides an interesting approach. It takes into account the information, already available to a model before being exposed to new data, to compute estimates for ISA interpretations. Bayesian models of utterance interpretation have been proposed by HRI scholars such as Williams et al. (2014). In Bayesian inference terms, one could formulate (and, hopefully, answer by experimental manipulation) questions such as the following: What is the probability for an ISA expression to be intended as an ISA, given a previous request SA? What is the probability that an ambiguous utterance is meant as a request, given S's higher status relative to A? And, conversely, what is the probability that S is higher in status relative to A given S's utterance being a direct request, or an indirect question? To the best of my knowledge, no experimental study exploring the role of interpersonal factors on indirect interpretations has been carried out assuming a Bayesian modelling of ISA inference. Despite these recent developments, however, robots and NLP systems are still far from being able to handle the whole variety of ISAs, especially when the propositional content of the utterance is very different from that of the ISA. This task is made even more complicated when it comes to the attribution of desires and intentions to agents that display very few cues about their own mental states.

6.5 DISCUSSION QUESTIONS

- Consider some obvious differences between humans and robots, related, for instance, to the emotional reactions and the paralinguistic features associated with utterance production. Which of these differences would you say should be improved in robots, along with indirectness?
- Available experimental research on ISAs in HRI involves neurotypical participants, but robots play a key role for older and disabled individuals, as they help these people overcome physical obstacles in their daily life. Why do you think it would be useful for users with a disability to communicate more freely, for example, to formulate their SAs using whatever linguistic constructions they feel comfortable with, when addressing robots?

6.6 SUGGESTIONS FOR FURTHER READING

For an excellent overview of computational approaches to pragmatics in general: Jurafsky, Dan. 2006. Pragmatics and computational linguistics. In L.R. Horn and G. Ward, eds., *The Handbook of Pragmatics*. https://doi.org/10.1002/9780470756959.ch26.

The performance of different SA types by robots is a very interesting issue. A promising direction for further research on indirectness in HRI is discussed in this experimental study of the delivery of bad news and feedback: Fischer, Kerstin and Alicja Depka Prondzinska. 2020. Experimental contrastive pragmatics using robots. *Contrastive Pragmatics* 1 (1): 82–107.

Conclusion

The goal of this book was threefold: describe the theoretical complexity of ISAs, explain how people manage to interpret them correctly and understand why speakers resort to them.

The starting point of research on ISAs is the traditional speech act theoretic definition of indirectness, according to which there is a one-to-one correspondence between the three major English sentence-types and the three macro SA categories. Declarative, interrogative and imperative sentences are associated with assertions, requests for information and requests for action, respectively. When the SA accomplished with an utterance matches the SA type predicted by its sentence-type, it is a direct and literal SA, otherwise it is indirect and non-literal. One literalist model of utterance interpretation is the standard pragmatic model (SPM), which has been discarded as untenable by psycholinguistic experiments comparing response times for direct and indirect interpretations of ambiguous utterances. This model has been regarded as an experimental test case for literalism. However, one should not jump to the conclusion that other literalist models are not worth testing, or that literalism per se should be abandoned. Yet, to date, there has been little discussion of experimental evidence relevant to the validity of literalist approaches.

Several definitions of indirectness have been proposed since Searle's (1975) article on ISAs, where indirectness was conceived of as a binary feature of SAs. Instead of adding to the already long list of distinctions available, I have tried to clarify them in order to achieve an adequate and complete description of the phenomenon of indirectness. For instance, another binary distinction between 'conventionalized' and 'non-conventionalized' ISAs is often taken for granted in the literature. I did not endorse it, because it confuses between conventionality of means and standardization. Rather, I proposed that three linguistic parameters influence the processing of ISA constructions: the categorical criterion of conventionality of means, and the graded criteria of standardization and illocutionary force salience. I critically surveyed experimental data in the light of these three criteria, which enabled me to demonstrate their empirical validity. In an attempt to tease apart (in)directness and primariness/secondariness, I discussed the results of eye-tracking experiments where I collected two distinct measures of processing, namely, response times and eye fixation durations. These experiments show that ability interrogatives/declaratives take longer to process when they are interpreted as DSAs, and that their IR interpretations are primary. More experimental studies focusing on these three criteria need to be carried out, because the nature of the linguistic constructions used as stimuli are likely to influence how indirectness is perceived and responded to.

Saying that ISA production and comprehension are shaped by context is a truism. In a broad sense, the notion of 'context of utterance' encompasses all the assumptions against which communication takes place, such as the interlocutors' beliefs, intentions and desires, for example about the speaker–addressee relationship. It also includes features of experimental designs such as the nature of the task and the wording of the instructions. By manipulating different aspects of the design, the likelihood of an IR interpretation can be increased or decreased according to the experimenter's desiderata. This is especially useful for addressing the cognitive processes associated with different linguistic constructions. However, previous experiments on ISA comprehension have generated different results whether it is the direct or the indirect reading of pragmatically ambiguous utterances that is facilitated by the preceding context. I therefore suggest that future experiments should privilege contexts that are not biased either towards the direct or the indirect interpretations of ISA utterances, so that we can verify which ISA constructions participants regard as ambiguous. We also saw that, while indirectness applies to the micro, utterance level of communication, the notion of implicitness is more adequate to account for the realizations of complaints, which are best operationalized in terms of 'SA sets'.

When I turned to the reasons why speakers resort to indirectness instead of opting for direct communication, I considered three distinct, but not necessarily incompatible, motivations: face-threat avoidance, economy of means for speakers – multiple meanings can be conveyed using a single utterance – and possible deniability of the intended meaning vis-à-vis the addressee or a third party. Unlike face-threat minimization, the communication of 'politeness effects' that would be absent in DSAs is unlikely to be a valid motivation of indirectness, and it was disconfirmed by data from production tasks. In fact, the polite evaluations associated with different types of indirect communication are the output of a complex of linguistic features and contextual elements, and it does not do justice to the heterogeneity of indirectness to reduce it to an 'indirect=polite' equation.

More generally, the research discussed in this monograph demonstrates that the status of indirectness with respect to its direct alternative(s) should be rethought. There is no reason, on the basis of the empirical data available, to view ISAs as a conscious, marked departure from DSAs, which would be 'default'. Whether directness or indirectness is 'marked' depends on the context of interaction. I also believe that ISAs should be more often investigated from a cross-cultural and intercultural perspective. As the content of the present monograph shows, the majority of theories of indirectness, in particular in relation to politeness, assume an Anglo-Saxon point of view that does not necessarily match the link between the sentence-types and the range of SAs available in any language. The idea of moving away from the Anglo-Saxon focus lies behind much of the empirical research in intercultural pragmatics, but this approach should be adopted more systematically when it comes to experimental studies. I expect that some of the results obtained so far will differ across cultures, but, at the same time, the general framework I have proposed can easily be applied to languages other than English, as the few examples from French, Czech and Chinese have illustrated.

Another topic that has been largely under-researched in linguistic pragmatics concerns inter-individual differences in the processing of ISAs. Whether an interpretation is inferred – and the processing costs of this interpretation – can be influenced by a variety of parameters according to which people differ. Such variables are relative social status, social distance, affective distance, imposition and gender. They have been addressed to some extent, but their complex interactions, and how they feed into one another, have not been thoroughly established. Moreover, interpersonal parameters, such as age and education, for example, remain open to investigation (see Gibbs & Colston 2012: 260–326 on other relevant variables). These variables should be controlled for, of course, but their impact on the processes and products of utterance comprehension deserves more attention (Gibbs 2014). This also applies to human–robot interactions, because humans have a tendency to use ISAs when addressing robots, and they expect robots to do the same. These social considerations should therefore be taken into account when designing intelligent NLP systems such as human-like robots and vocal assistants. In particular, focusing on personality traits, such as introvert versus extravert, adaptability, patience, self-presentation and cognitive skills (attention, working memory capacity, speed of information processing, etc.) is a promising direction for the coming research on the use and interpretation of indirectness. I believe that, in order to meet these empirical challenges, psychophysiological and neuroimaging methods will be most appropriate.

This book might have given you the impression that it raised more issues than it solved. This is somewhat justified: much more research needs to be carried out before we will properly understand the multiple facets of indirectness.

Glossary

area of interest (eye-tracking): Selected portion of a visual stimulus, for example of a text displayed on a computer screen.
assertion: Type of speech act that consists in presenting some information about the world as being true.
availability condition: Condition according to which speakers of a language are aware, first, of the distinction between primary and secondary meanings, and, second, of the inference from the primary to the secondary meaning.
cognitive effect: The cognitive effects of an utterance (or of any stimulus) are the changes brought about by the utterance on an individual's mental representations.
cognitive linguistics: Cognitive linguistics encompasses a range of theories that are especially interested in the relationship between language, mind and body. They developed as a departure from generative linguistics, in that they seek to explain language use and understanding in terms of general principles of human cognition.
common ground: The common ground of conversational participants is the set of assumptions mutually shared by the participants.
computational linguistics: Branch of linguistics that is concerned with the modelling of natural language using IT and statistical methods.
cortical motor areas: Areas of the motor cortex. The motor cortex is primarily involved in the control, planning and execution of deliberate body movements.
declarative: The declarative sentence-type is typically used for making statements. In English, it is characterized by non-inverted word order.
default interpretation: The interpretation of an utterance is default if it is automatically derived by the interpreter, without the need of a conscious inference.
deniability: Possibility of denying one's intention to communicate a particular interpretation.
direct move: Verbal response to the direct meaning of an ISA utterance.
directive: Type of speech act that consists in trying to get the addressee to carry out some action.
discourse completion task (DCT): Method of data collection consisting in a questionnaire prompting the participant to produce a series of spoken or written utterances.

Glossary

event-related potential (ERP): Non-invasive psychophysiological technique consisting in measuring electrical brain activity as a response to a stimulus.

eye-tracking: Non-invasive psychophysiological technique consisting in measuring eye movements and the durations of eye fixations of a particular area as a response to a stimulus.

face (negative): The negative face of an invididual refers to their claim to be free to do only what they want to and their will that others do not impede their actions.

face (positive): The positive face of an individual refers to their want to be approved of by others.

face-threat: Threat that a particular utterance constitutes for the face of conversational participants.

felicity condition: Condition that has to be fulfilled for the successful performance of a given speech act to take place.

force dynamics: Cognitive semantic theory that describes the force interactions between conceptual entities.

game theory: Game theory studies how the interacting choices of agents give rise to outcomes with respect to these agents' preferences.

generative linguistics: Generative linguistics is a theoretical framework that defines a language by specifying a set of rules by which all (and only) the possible sentences of that language can be generated.

head act: Main utterance by means of which a particular speech act is communicated.

hedge: Linguistic device that enables a speaker to minimize her committment with respect to the communicated content of her utterance.

idealized cognitive model (ICM): Mental structure of conceptual representation that is constituted by an ontology and a structure.

illocutionary act: Social action that is accomplished in producing a written or spoken utterance. It should not be confused with the causal effect of an utterance (see 'perlocutionary act').

illocutionary force indicating device (IFID): Morpho-syntactic features of a sentence that specify the illocutionary meaning it has as an utterance.

metonymic illocutionary scenario: Cognitive linguistic construal according to which an utterance 'stands for' an indirect SA scenario, as it makes a reference to a constitutive component of that scenario.

illocutionary verb: Verb that names a type of illocutionary act.

imperative: Sentence-type typically used in the performance of directives or in good wishes. In English, its grammatical subject is optional and it is usually uttered with a flat intonation.

implicature: Implicature refers either to the act of implicitly communicating something, or the content of that act.

imposition: In Brown and Levinson's (1987) politeness theory, imposition refers to the costs, for the speaker and the addressee, that are associated with the performance of a speech act; it also includes the immediate consequences of the speech act.

inquisitive semantics (IS): Theoretical framework according to which the meaning of an interrogative or declarative sentence resides in the changes it can cause in the interlocutors' informational states.
interrogative: Sentence-type typically used for asking questions. In English, it is characterized by inverted word order and/or rising intonation.
late positive component (LPC): A LPC is a positive-going event-related potential component characterized by a peak 600 ms after the onset of the stimulus that elicits it.
literal: A speech act is literal if the utterance by means of which it is performed has the meaning corresponding to its sentence-type.
literalism: Thesis that the speech act performed with an utterance is determined by the sentence-type.
locutionary act: Utterance of a meaningful sentence.
logical form: The logical form of an utterance is the formal representation of the structure that specifies its logical role and properties.
mitigation: In Brown and Levinson's (1987) politeness theory and in the Cross-Cultural Speech Act Realization Project (CCSARP) framework, mitigation is a linguistic modification of an utterance that reduces its face-threatening impact.
negative state remark: Utterance of a declarative sentence that describes a negative state of affairs.
non-literal: A speech act is non-literal if the utterance by means of which it is performed departs from the meaning corresponding to its sentence-type.
non-natural meaning: According to Grice's (1957) definition of non-natural meaning, a speaker uttering a sentence to mean that p must have three intentions: the intention (i1) to provoke an effect on her addressee's mental states, the intention (i2) that he recognize her i1 intention, and the intention (i3) that the satisfaction of i2 be the cause and the reason for the satisfaction of i1.
obstacle hypothesis: Hypothesis that speakers formulate their requests for information to deal with the greatest potential obstacle to the addressee's compliance.
off-record: Way of performing a speech act that provides the speaker with deniability with respect to the performance and content of her speech act.
on-record: Way of performing a speech act that results in the speaker being committed to the performance and content of her speech act.
parenthetical qualifier: Addition to an utterance that motivates the performance of a particular speech act with that utterance.
partition theory: Theory of interrogative sentences, according to which an interrogative denotes a function that partitions the logical space of possibilities, each block within the partition standing for one possible answer to the interrogative.
performative: A performative utterance consists in a sentence with a main verb in the first person singular, in the simple present indicative active. When uttered in the appropriate circumstances, it constitutes the performance of the speech act it describes.

Glossary

perlocutionary act: A perlocutionary act refers to the triggering of perlocutionary effects.

perlocutionary effect: Causal effect that can, but need not, be achieved by virtue of the performance of an illocutionary act.

power: In Brown and Levinson's (1987) politeness theory, the degree to which an individual has the legitimacy to impose their own plan or face to others.

preparatory condition: State of affairs that has to hold for the successful performance of a given speech act to take place.

presupposition: Phenomenon by which a speaker conveys information that she takes as uncontroversial, and distinct from the content of her speech act.

proposition: Semantic content of an utterance or belief.

prototypical: A particular speech act is prototypical if it is a highly representative member of its speech act category.

pupillometry: Psychophysiological method that collects measures of changes in pupil size as a response to a stimulus.

quantifier: Type of determiner that contributes information about quantity (for example, *some*, *all*, *a few*, *many*).

recipient: The recipient of a written utterance, for example an email, is the individual who receives the written message. The term 'recipient' also refers to the individual who happens to hear/read an utterance without being its unique addressee, as in the case of advertising.

redress/redressive action: Use of politeness strategies to compensate for the face-threat entailed by the performance of a speech act.

relevance theory (RT): Sperber and Wilson's (1995) relevance theory conceives of human cognition as geared towards the minimization of processing costs and the maximization of cognitive effects. The addressee of an utterance expects that the information the speaker intends to convey will have a substantial cognitive effect that should offset additional interpretative effort.

segmented discourse representation theory (SDRT): Theory of discourse interpretation that combines dynamic semantics and artificial intelligence approaches.

social distance: Degree of (un)familiarity between interlocutors.

speech act: See 'illocutionary act'.

speech act theory: Searle's (1969) speech act theory posits that 'speech acts' are the fundamental units of communication. It is considered as an elaboration on Austin (1962)'s work on performative utterances.

tag question: Type of interrogative structure that transforms a declarative or imperative utterance into a interrogative. For example, in *It's cold in here, isn't it?* the tag question *isn't it?* changes the declarative utterance into a confirmation question.

third party: A third party is different from a participant in a spoken or written exchange. It refers to a person who might overhear (or read) what is communicated by conversational participants.

References

Abbeduto, Leonard, Laurie Furman and Betty Davies. 1989. Identifying speech acts from contextual and linguistic information. *Language and Speech* 32 (3): 189–203.
Allen, James F., Dona Byron, Myroslava Dzikovska, George Ferguson, Lucian Galescu and Amanda Stent. 2001. Toward conversational human-computer interaction. *AI Magazine* 22 (4): 27–37.
Allen, James F. and Raymond Perrault. 1980. Analyzing intention in utterances. *Artificial Intelligence* 15 (3): 143–78.
Aloni, Maria, Alastair Butler and Paul Dekker, eds. 2007. *Questions in Dynamic Semantics*. Amsterdam: Elsevier.
Asher, Nicholas and Alex Lascarides. 2001. Indirect speech acts. *Synthese* 128: 183–228.
Austin, John L. 1962. *How to Do Things with Words*. Oxford: Clarendon Press.
Bach, Kent. 1998. Standardization revisited. In Asa Kasher, ed., *Pragmatics: Critical Assessment*. London: Routledge, 712–22.
  2006. The top 10 misconceptions about implicature. In Betty J. Birner and Gregory Ward, eds., *Drawing the Boundaries of Meaning: Neo-Gricean Studies in Pragmatics and Semantics in Honor of Laurence R. Horn*. Amsterdam: John Benjamins, 21–30.
Bach, Kent and Robert M. Harnish. 1979. *Linguistic Communication and Speech Acts*. Cambridge, MA: MIT Press.
Baker, Wendy and Rachel H. Bricker. 2010. The effects of direct and indirect speech acts on native English and ESL speakers' perception of teacher written feedback. *System* 38: 75–84.
Barker, Stephen. 2004. *Renewing Meaning: A Speech-Act Theoretic Approach*. Oxford: Oxford University Press.
Base textuelle FRANTEXT. 2016. Online corpus. ATILF – CNRS and Université de Lorraine. www.frantext.fr, last accessed 14/11/2020.
Bašnáková, Jana, Kirsten Weber, Karl Magnus Petersson, Peter Hagoort and Jos J. A. van Berkum. 2011. Understanding speaker meaning: neural correlates of pragmatic inferencing in discourse comprehension. Poster presented at the Neurobiology of Language Conference, March 2011, Annapolis.

Baxter, Leslie A. 1984. An investigation of compliance-gaining as politeness. *Human Communication Research* 10 (3): 427–56.
Beach, Cheryl M. 1991. The interpretation of prosodic patterns at points of syntactic structure ambiguity: evidence for cue trading relations. *Journal of Memory and Language* 30 (6): 644–63.
Biesenbach-Lucas, Sigrun. 2007. Students writing emails to faculty: an examination of e-politeness among native and non-native speakers of English. *Language Learning and Technology* 11: 59–81.
Blum-Kulka, Shoshana. 1987. Indirectness and politeness in requests: same or different? *Journal of Pragmatics* 11 (2): 131–46.
Blum-Kulka, Shoshana and Elite Olshtain. 1984. Requests and apologies: a cross cultural study of speech act realization patterns (CCSARP). *Applied Linguistics* 5 (3): 196–213.
Blum-Kulka, Shoshana, Juliane House and Gabriele Kasper, eds. 1989. *Cross-Cultural Pragmatics: Requests and Apologies*. Norwood, NJ: Ablex.
Boisvert, Daniel and Kirk Ludwig. 2006. Semantics for nondeclaratives. In Barry C. Smith and Ernest Lepore, eds.,*The Oxford Handbook of the Philosophy of Language*. Oxford: Oxford University Press, 864–92.
Bolinger, Dwight. 1977. *Meaning and Form*. London: Longman.
Bou-Franch, Patricia. 2011. Openings and closings in Spanish e-mail conversations. *Journal of Pragmatics* 43 (6): 1772–85.
Briggs, Gordon and Matthias Scheutz. 2013. A hybrid architectural approach to understanding and appropriately generating indirect speech acts. Proceedings of the Twenth-Seventh AAAI Conference on Artificial Intelligence. Bellevue, WA, 1213–19.
  2014. How robots can affect human behavior: investigating the effects of robotic displays of protest and distress. *International Journal of Social Robotics* 6: 343–55.
Briggs, Gordon, Tom Williams and Matthias Scheutz. 2017. Enabling robots to understand indirect speech acts in task-based interactions. *Journal of Human-Robot Interaction* 6 (1): 64–94.
Brisard, Frank. 2011. H. P. Grice. In Marina Sbisá, ed., *Philosophical Perspectives for Pragmatics*. Amsterdam: Benjamins, 104–24.
Broadbent, Marianne and Ellen Kitzis. 2005. *The New CIO Leader: Setting the Agenda and Delivering Results*. Harvard Business School Press.
Brouwer, Harm, Hartmut Fitz and John Hoeks. 2012. Getting real about semantic illusions: rethinking the functional role of the P600 in language comprehension. *Brain Research* 1446:127–43.
Brown, Penelope and Stephen Levinson. 1987. *Politeness: Some Universals in Language Usage*. Cambridge and New York: Cambridge University Press.
Carston, Robyn. 2002. *Thoughts and Utterances: The Pragmatics of Explicit Communication*. Oxford: Blackwell.
Champagne-Lavau, Maud, Andreas Herzig, Jean-Luc Nespoulous and Jacques Virbel. 2002. Formalisation pluridisciplinaire de l'inférence d'actes de langage non littéraux. *Information, Interaction, Intelligence*: 197–225.

Chejnová, Pavla. 2014. Expressing politeness in the institutional e-mail communications of university students in the Czech Republic. *Journal of Pragmatics* 60: 175–92.
Chomsky, Noam. 1957. *Syntactic Structures*. The Hague and Paris: Mouton de Gruyter.
Ciardelli, Ivano, Jeroen Groenendijk and Floris Roelofsen. 2013. Inquisitive semantics: a new notion of meaning. *Language and Linguistics Compass* 7 (9): 459–76.
  2015. On the semantics and logic of declaratives and interrogatives. *Synthese* 192 (6): 1689–1728.
Clark, Billy. 1993. Relevance and pseudo-imperatives. *Linguistics and Philosophy* 16 (1): 79–121.
  2013. *Relevance Theory*. Cambridge: Cambridge University Press.
Clark, Herbert H. 1979. Responding to indirect speech acts. *Cognitive Psychology* 11: 430–77.
  1996. *Using Language*. Cambridge: Cambridge University Press.
Clark, Herbert H. and Dale H. Schunk. 1980. Polite responses to polite requests. *Cognition* 8: 111–43.
Coates, Jennifer. 1983. *The Semantics of the Modal Auxiliaries*. London: Croom Helm.
Coleman, Linda and Paul Kay. 1981. Prototype semantics: the English word 'lie'. *Language* 57 (1): 26–44.
Coulson, Seana and Christopher Lovett. 2010. Comprehension of non-conventional indirect requests: an event-related brain potential study. *Italian Journal of Linguistics* 22 (1): 107–24.
Crosby, Faye and Linda Nyquist. 1977. The female register: an empirical study of Lakoff's hypothesis. *Language in Society* 6 (3): 313–22.
Culpeper, Jonathan. 2011. *Impoliteness: Using Language to Cause Offence*. Cambridge: Cambridge University Press.
Davies, Eirlys E. 1986. *The English Imperative*. London: Croom Helm.
Davies, Mark. 2004. *BYU–BNC*. Online corpus, based on the British National Corpus from Oxford University Press. http://corpus.byu.edu/bnc/, last accessed 14/11/2020.
  2008. *The Corpus of Contemporary American English (COCA)*: 520 million words, 1990–present. http://corpus.byu.edu/coca/, last accessed 14/11/2020.
Davis, Wayne. 1998. *Implicature*. Cambridge: Cambridge University Press.
Decock, Sofie and Ilse Depraetere. 2018. (In)directness and complaints: a reassessment. *Journal of Pragmatics* 132: 33–46.
Demeure, Virginie, Jean-François Bonnefon and Éric Raufaste. 2007. Rôle de la face et de l'utilité dans l'interprétation d'énoncés ambigus question/requête et incompréhension/désaccord. Actes des 4e Journées Francophones Modèles Formels de l'Interaction (MFI 07), Paris, 30 May–1 June.
Depraetere, Ilse, Sofie Decock and Nicolas Ruytenbeek. 2021. Linguistic (in) directness in Twitter complaints: a contrastive analysis of railway complaint interactions. *Journal of Pragmatics* 171: 215–33.

Derks Daantje, Arjan E. R. Bos and Jasper von Grumbkow. 2008. Emoticons in computer-mediated communication: social motives and social context. *CyberPsychology and Behavior* 11 (1): 99–101.
Dresner Eli and Susan C. Herring. 2010. Functions of the non-verbal in CMC: emoticons and illocutionary force. *Communication Theory* 20: 249–68.
Dryer, Matthew S. 2013. Polar questions. In Matthew S. Dryer and Martin Haspelmath, eds., *The World Atlas of Language Structures Online*. Leipzig: Max Planck Institute for Evolutionary Anthropology. http://wals.info/chapter/116, last accessed 14/11/2020.
Egorova, Natalia, Friedemann Pulvermüller and Yury Shtyrov. 2014. Neural dynamics of speech act comprehension: an MEG study of naming and requesting. *Brain Topography* 27 (3): 375–92.
Enfield, Nick J. 2014. Human agency and the infrastructure for requests. In Paul Drew and Elizabeth Couper-Kuhlen, eds., *Requesting in Social Interaction*. Amsterdam and Philadelphia: John Benjamins, 35–53.
Ervin-Tripp, Susan. 1976. Is Sybil there? The structure of some American English directives. *Language in Society* 5(1): 25–66.
Escandell-Vidal, Victoria. 1998. Politeness: a relevant issue for relevance theory. *Revista Alicantina de Estudios Ingleses* 11: 45–57.
  2004. Norms and principles: putting social and cognitive pragmatics together. In Rosina Márquez-Reiter and María E. Placencia, eds., *Current Trends in the Pragmatics of Spanish*. Amsterdam: Benjamins, 347–71.
Falbo, Toni and Leticia A. Peplau. 1980. Power strategies in intimate relationships. *Journal of Personality and Social Psychology* 38: 618–28.
Fiengo, Robert. 2007. *Asking Questions: Using Meaningful Structures to Imply Ignorance*. Oxford: Oxford University Press.
Fiske, Alan P., 1992. The four elementary forms of sociality: framework for a unified theory of social relations. *Psychological Review* 99: 689–723.
Flöck, Ilka. 2016. *Requests in American and British English: A Contrastive Multi-method Analysis*. Amsterdam: John Benjamins.
Francik, Ellen P. and Herbert H. Clark. 1985. How to make requests that overcome obstacles to compliance. *Journal of Memory and Language* 24: 560–68.
Fraser, Bruce. 1974. An examination of the performative analysis. *Papers in Linguistics* 7: 1–40.
Freytag, Vera. 2020. *Exploring Politeness in Business Emails: A Mixed-Methods Analysis*. Bristol: Multilingual Matters.
Fukushima, Saeko. 2000. *Requests and Culture: Politeness in British English and Japanese*. Bern: Peter Lang.
  2015. In search of another understanding of politeness: from the perspective of attentiveness. *Journal of Politeness Research* 11 (2): 261–87.
Furmaniak, Grégory. 2010. A frame-based approach to modality: the case of obligation. *Belgian Journal of Linguistics* 24 (1): 17–35.

García Carpintero, Manuel. 2013. Explicit performatives revisited. *Journal of Pragmatics* 49 (1): 1–17.
Gazdar, Gerald. 1979. *Pragmatics: Implicature, Presupposition and Logical Form.* New York: Academic Press.
Gibbs, Raymond W. 1979. Contextual effects in understanding indirect requests. *Discourse Processes* 2: 1–10.
  1981. Memory for requests in conversation. *Journal of Verbal Learning and Verbal Behavior* 20: 630–40.
  1983. Do people always process the literal meanings of indirect requests? *Journal of Experimental Psychology: Learning, Memory and Cognition* 9 (3): 524–33.
  1986a. On the psycholinguistics of sarcasm. *Journal of Experimental Psychology* 15 (1): 3–15.
  1986b. What makes some indirect speech acts conventional? *Journal of Memory and Language* 25 (2): 181–96.
  1987. Memory for requests in conversation revisited. *The American Journal of Psychology* 100 (2): 179–91.
  2014. Is a general theory of utterance interpretation really possible? Insights from the study of figurative language. *Belgian Journal of Linguistics* 28: 19–44.
Gibbs, Raymond W. and Herbert Colston. 2012. *Interpreting Figurative Language.* New York: Cambridge University Press.
Giora, Rachel. 2002. Literal versus figurative language: different or equal? *Journal of Pragmatics* 34: 487–506.
  2003. *On Our Mind: Salience, Context and Figurative Language.* New York: Oxford University Press.
Gísladóttir, Rosa S., Dorothee J. Chwilla, Herbert Schriefers and Stephen C. Levinson. 2012. Speech act recognition in conversation: experimental evidence. In Naomi Miyake, David Peebles and Richard P. Cooper, eds., *Proceedings of the 34th Annual Meeting of the Cognitive Science Society.* Austin, TX: Cognitive Science Society, 1596–1601.
Gísladóttir, Rosa S., Dorothee J. Chwilla and Stephen C. Levinson. 2015. Conversation electrified: ERP correlates of speech act recognition in underspecified utterances. *PLoS ONE* 10 (3): e0120068.
Glynn, Dylan. 2006. Concept delimitation and pragmatic implicature. Issues for the study of metonymy. In Krzysztof Kosecki, ed., *Perspectives on Metonymy.* Frankfurt am Main: Peter Lang, 157–74.
Goffman, Erving. 1955. On face-work: an analysis of ritual elements in social interaction. *Psychiatry: Journal for the Study of Interpersonal Processes* 18: 213–31.
  1967. *Interaction Ritual: Essays in Face-to-Face Behavior.* Chicago, IL: Aldine Publishing Company.
Goguen, Joseph and Charlotte Linde. 1983. *Linguistic Methodology for the Analysis of Aviation Accidents.* Technical report, structural semantics. NASA Contractor Report 3741, Ames Research Center.

Grainger, Karen and Sara Mills. 2016. *Directness and Indirectness across Cultures*. Basingstoke: Palgrave Macmillan.
Grice, H. Paul. 1957. Meaning. *Philosophical Review* 66: 377–88.
  1975. Logic and conversation. In Peter Cole and Jerry L. Morgan, eds., *Syntax and Semantics, Vol. 3: Speech Acts*. New York: Academic Press, 41–58.
Groefsema, Marjolein. 1992. 'Can you pass the salt?' A short-circuited implicature? *UCL Working Papers in Linguistics* 3: 213–40.
Groenendijk, Jeroen. 2007. The logic of interrogation. In Maria Aloni, Alastair Butler and Paul Dekker, eds., *Questions in Dynamic Semantics*. Oxford and Amsterdam: Elsevier, 43–62.
Groenendijk, Jeroen and Martin Stokhof. 1984. Studies on the semantics of questions and the pragmatics of answers. Unpublished PhD dissertation, Universiteit van Amsterdam.
  1997. Questions. In Johan van Benthem and Alice ter Meulen, eds., *Handbook of Logic and Language*. Amsterdam: Elsevier, 1055–1124.
Gunlogson, Christine. 2002. Declarative questions. In Brendan Jackson, ed., *Proceedings of Semantics and Linguistic Theory 12*. Ithaca: CLC Publications, 124–43.
Hamblin, Charles Leonard. 1972. Quandaries and the logic of rules. *Journal of Philosophical Logic* 1: 74–85.
  1987. *Imperatives*. Oxford: Blackwell.
Han, Chung-Hye. 1998. The structure and interpretation of imperatives: mood and force in universal grammar. Unpublished PhD dissertation, University of Pennsylvania.
  2002. Interpreting interrogatives as rhetorical questions. *Lingua* 112: 201–29.
Haugh, Michael. 2015. *Im/Politeness Implicatures*. Berlin: Mouton de Gruyter.
Heinemann, Tine. 2006. 'Will you or can't you?' Displaying entitlement in interrogative requests. *Journal of Pragmatics* 38 (7): 1081–1104.
Hellbernd, Nele and Daniela Sammler. 2016. Prosody conveys speaker's intentions: acoustic cues for speech perception. *Journal of Memory and Language* 88: 70–86.
Hendry, Jay and Bill Watson, eds. 2001. *An Anthropology of Indirect Communication*. London: Routledge.
Herring, Susan C. 1994. Politeness in computer culture: why women thank and men flame. Cultural Performances: Proceedings of the Third Berkeley Women and Language Conference, 278–94. Berkeley Women and Language Group.
Hickey, Leo. 1992. Politeness apart: why choose indirect speech acts? *Lingua e Stile* 27 (1): 77–87.
Hinkelman, Elizabeth A. and James F. Allen. 1989. Two constraints on speech act ambiguity. *Proceedings of the 27th Annual Meeting of Association for Computational Linguistics*, 212–219.
Hobbs, Jerry R. 1990. *Literature and Cognition*. Stanford, CA: CSLI.

Hoeks, John C. J., Lotte Schoot, Ryan C. Taylor and Harm Brouwer. 2013. Did you just say 'NO' to me? An ERP study on politeness in dialogue. Poster presented at XPRAG, September 2013, Utrecht.

Hofstede, Geert. 1980. *Culture's Consequences: International Differences in Work-Related Values*. Beverly Hills, CA: Sage.

Holmqvist, Kenneth, Marcus Nyström, Richard Andersson, Richard Dewhurst, Halszka Jarodzka and Joost van de Weijer. 2011. *Eye Tracking: A Comprehensive Guide to Methods and Measures*. Oxford: Oxford University Press.

Holtgraves, Thomas R. 1986. Language structure in social interaction: perceptions of direct and indirect speech acts and interactants who use them. *Journal of Personality and Social Psychology* 51 (2): 305–14.

  1991. Interpreting questions and replies: effects of face-threat, question form and gender. *Social Psychology Quarterly* 54 (1): 15–24.

  1992. The linguistic realization of face management: implications for language production and comprehension, person perception and cross-cultural communication. *Social Psychology Quarterly* 55 (2): 141–59.

  1994. Communication in context: effects of the speaker status on the comprehension of indirect requests. *Journal of Experimental Psychology: Learning, Memory and Cognition* 20 (5): 1205–18.

  1998. Interpreting indirect replies. *Cognitive Psychology* 37: 1–27.

  2008. Automatic intention recognition in conversation processing. *Journal of Memory and Language* 58 (3): 627–45.

Holtgraves, Thomas R. and Aaron Ashley. 2001. Comprehending illocutionary force. *Memory and Cognition* 29: 83–90.

Holtgraves, Thomas R. and Caleb Robinson. 2020. Emoji can facilitate recognition of conveyed indirect meaning. *PLoS ONE* 15(4): e0232361.

Holtgraves, Thomas R. and Jean-François Bonnefon. 2017. Experimental approaches to linguistic (im)politeness. In Jonathan Culpeper, Michael Haugh and Daniel Kadar, eds., *Palgrave Handbook of Linguistic (Im)Politeness*. London: Palgrave Macmillan.

Holtgraves, Thomas and Joong-Nam Yang. 1990. Interpersonal underpinnings of request strategies: general principles and differences due to culture and gender. *Journal of Personality and Social Psychology* 59 (4): 719–29.

Holtgraves, Thomas, T. Srull and D. Socall, 1989. Conversation memory: the effects of speaker status on memory for the assertiveness of conversation remarks. *Journal of Personality and Social Psychology* 56: 149–60.

House, Juliane and Gabriele Kasper. 1981. Politeness markers in English and German. In Florian Coulmas, ed., *Conversational Routine: Explorations in Standardized Communication Situations and Prepatterned Speech*. New York: Mouton de Gruyter, 157–85.

Isaacs, Ellen A. and Herbert H. Clark. 1990. Ostensible invitations. *Language in Society* 19 (4): 493–509.

Isac, Daniela. 2015. *The Morphosyntax of Imperatives*. Oxford: Oxford University Press.
Jary, Mark. 1998a. Is Relevance Theory social? *Revista Alicantina de Estudios Ingleses* 11: 157–69.
  1998b. Relevance Theory and the communication of politeness. *Journal of Pragmatics* 30: 1–19.
  2007. Are explicit performatives assertions? *Linguistics and Philosophy* 30: 207–34.
Jary, Mark and Mikhail Kissine. 2014. *Imperatives*. Cambridge: Cambridge University Press.
Jing-Schmidt, Zhuo. 2007. Negativity bias in language: a cognitive-affective model of emotive intensifiers. *Cognitive Linguistics* 18 (3): 417–43.
Johnson, Mark. 1987. *The Body in the Mind*. Chicago: University of Chicago Press.
Jurafsky, Dan. 2006. Pragmatics and computational linguistics. In L.R. Horn and G. Ward, eds., *The Handbook of Pragmatics*. https://doi.org/10.1002/9780470756959.ch26.
Katz, Jerrold J. and Paul Postal. 1964. *An Integrated Theory of Linguistic Descriptions*. Cambridge, MA: MIT Press.
Kemper, Susan. 1980. Memory for the form and force of declaratives and interrogatives. *Memory and Cognition* 8 (4): 367–71.
Kemper, Susan and David Thissen. 1981. Memory for the dimensions of requests. *Journal of Verbal Learning and Verbal Behavior* 20 (5): 552–63.
Kerbrat-Orecchioni, Catherine. 2001. 'Je voudrais un p'tit bifteck': la politesse à la française en site commercial. *Les Carnets du CEDISCOR* 7: 105–18.
  2004. Politeness in France: how to buy bread politely. In Leo Hickey and Miranda Stewart, eds., *Politeness in Europe*. Clevedon: Multilingual Matters, 29–44.
Kissine, Mikhail. 2008. Locutionary, illocutionary, perlocutionary. *Language and Linguistics Compass* 2 (6): 1189–1202.
  2013. *From Utterances to Speech Acts*. Cambridge: Cambridge University Press.
Kratzer, Angelika, 1977. What 'must' and 'can' must and can mean. *Linguistics and Philosophy* 1 (3): 337–55.
  1991. Modality. In Arnim von Stechow and Dieter Wunderlich, eds., *Semantics: An International Handbook of Contemporary Research*. Berlin: Walter de Gruyter, 639–50.
Lakoff, George. 1987. *Women, Fire and Dangerous Things: What Categories Reveal About the Mind*. University of Chicago Press.
Lakoff, Robin T. 1973a. Language and woman's place. *Language in Society* 2: 45–80.
  1973b. The logic of politeness; or minding your P's and Q's. In C. Corum, T C. Smith-Stark and A. Weiser, eds., *Proceedings of the Ninth Regional Meeting of the Chicago Linguistic Society*, 292–305.
Langacker, Ronald W. 2008. *Cognitive Grammar: A Basic Introduction*. New York: Oxford University Press.
Lee, James J. and Steven Pinker. 2010. Rationales for indirect speech: the theory of the strategic speaker. *Psychological Review* 117 (3): 785–807.

Lee, Min Kyung and Maxim Makatchev. 2010. How do people talk with a robot? An analysis of human-robot dialogues in the real world. Proceedings of the 27th International Conference: Extended Abstracts on Human Factors in Computing Systems, *CHI' 2009*, April 2009.
Leech, Geoffrey. 1983. *Principles of Pragmatics*. London: Routledge.
Lehnert, Wendy G. 1978. *The Process of Question Answering : A Computer Simulation of Cognition*. Hillsdale, NJ: Erlbaum.
Lepore, Ernie and Matthew Stone. 2015. *Imagination and Convention: Distinguishing Grammar and Inference in Language*. Oxford: Oxford University Press.
Levinson, Stephen. 1983. *Pragmatics*. Cambridge: Cambridge University Press.
  2012. Interrogative intimations: on a possible social economics of interrogatives. In Jan P. de Ruiter, ed., *Questions: Formal, Functional and Interactional Perspectives*. Cambridge: Cambridge University Press, 11–32.
Liebrecht, Christine, Lettica Hustinx and Margot van Mulken. 2019. The relative power of negativity: the influence of language intensity on perceived strength. *Journal of Language and Social Psychology* 38 (2): 170–93.
Lim, Tae-Seop and John W. Bowers. 1991. Facework solidarity, approbation and tact. *Human Communication Research* 17 (3): 415–50.
Linde, Charlotte. 1988. The quantitative study of communicative success: politeness and accidents in aviation discourse. *Language in Society* 17 (3): 375–99.
Longin, Dominique. 2006. Des raisons qu'ont certains actes à être indirects. *Psychologie de l'Interaction* 21–22: 237–58.
Magnifico, Cédric and Bart Defrancq. 2016. Impoliteness in interpreting: a question of gender? *Translation and Interpreting* 8 (2): 26–45.
  2017. Hedges in conference interpreting: the role of gender. *Interpreting* 19 (1): 21–46.
Manno, Giuseppe. 2002. La politesse et l'indirection: un essai de synthèse. *Langage & Société* 100 (2): 5–47.
Mastop, Rosja. 2005. What can you do? Imperative mood in semantic theory. Unpublished PhD dissertation, Universiteit van Amsterdam.
  2011. Imperatives as semantic primitives. *Linguistics and Philosophy* 34: 305–40.
McGinn, Colin. 1977. Charity, interpretation and belief. *Journal of Philosophy* 74: 521–35.
Merritt, Marilyn. 1976. On questions following questions in service encounters. *Language in Society* 5 (3): 315–57.
Morgan, Jerry L. 1978. Two types of convention in indirect speech acts. In Peter Cole, ed., *Syntax and Semantics*, Vol. 9 of *Pragmatics*. New York: Academic Press, 261–80.
Munro, Allen. 1979. Indirect speech acts are not strictly conventional. *Linguistic Inquiry* 10 (2): 353–56.

Murphy, B. and J. Neu. 1996. My grade's too low: the speech act set of complaining. In S. M. Gass and J. Neu, eds., *Speech Acts across Cultures*. Berlin: Mouton de Gruyter, 191–216.
Neale, Stephen. 1992. Paul Grice and the philosophy of language. *Linguistics and Philosophy* 15: 509–59.
Nickerson, Jill S. and Jennifer Chu-Carroll. 1999. Acoustic-prosodic disambiguation of direct and indirect speech acts. *Proceedings of the 14th International Congress of Phonetic Sciences, San Francisco*. International Phonetic Association, 1309–12.
Ninan, Dilip. 2005. Two puzzles about deontic necessity. *MIT Working Papers in Linguistics* 51: 149–78.
Ogiermann, Eva. 2007. Gender-based differences in English apology realizations. In *Cross-Cultural Pragmatics and Interlanguage English*, 127–42. München: Lincom Europe.
  2009. Politeness and in-directness across cultures: a comparison of English, German, Polish and Russian requests. *Journal of Politeness Research* 5: 189–216.
Olshtain, Elite and Liora Weinbach. 1993. Interlanguage features of the speech act of complaining. In Gabriele Kasper and Shoshana Blum-Kulka, eds., *Interlanguage Pragmatics*. New York and Oxford: Oxford University Press, 108–22.
Pagin, Peter. 2004. Is assertion social? *Journal of Pragmatics* 36: 833–59.
Palmer, Frank R. 1986. *Mood and Modality*. Cambridge: Cambridge University Press.
Panther, Klaus-Uwe and Linda Thornburg. 1998. A cognitive approach to inferencing in conversation. *Journal of Pragmatics* 30: 755–69.
  2004. The role of conceptual metonymy in meaning construction. *Metaphorik.de* 6: 91–116.
  2005. Motivation and convention in some speech act constructions: a cognitive-linguistic approach. In Sophia Marmaridou, Kiki Nikiforidou and Eleni Antonopoulou, eds., *Reviewing Linguistic Thought: Converging Trends for the 21st Century*. Berlin: Mouton de Gruyter, 53–76.
Papafragou, Anna. 2007. *Modality: Issues in the Semantics-Pragmatics Interface*. Bingley: Emerald.
Pérez Hernández, Lorena. 2013. Illocutionary constructions: (multiple source)-in-target metonymies, illocutionary ICMs and specification links. *Language and Communication* 33: 128–49.
Pérez Hernández, Lorena and Francisco José Ruiz de Mendoza. 2002. Grounding, semantic motivation and conceptual interaction in indirect directive speech acts. *Journal of Pragmatics* 35: 259–84.
Perrault, Raymond C. and James F. Allen. 1980. A plan-based analysis of indirect speech acts. *Computational Linguistics* 6: 167–82.
Pichora-Fuller, M. Kathleen, Sophia E. Kramer, Mark E. Eckert et al. 2016. Hearing impairment and cognitive energy: the framework for understanding effortful listening (FUEL). *Ear and Hearing* 37: 5S–27S.

Pinker, Steven. 2011. Indirect speech, politeness, deniability and relationship negotiation: comment on Marina Terkourafi's 'The Puzzle of Indirect Speech'. *Journal of Pragmatics* 43: 2866–68.

Pinker, Steven, Martin A. Nowak and James J. Lee. 2008. The logic of indirect speech. *PNAS* 105 (3): 833–38.

Portner, Paul. 2004. The semantics of imperatives within a theory of clause types. In Kazuha Watanabe and Robert B. Young, eds., *Proceedings of Semantics and Linguistic Theory 14*. Ithaca, NY: CLC Publications, 235–52.

  2007. Imperatives and modals. *Natural Language Semantics* 15: 351–83.

  2009. *Modality*. Oxford: Oxford University Press.

Price Patti J., Mari Ostendorf, Stefanie Shattuck-Hufnagel and Cynthia Fong. 1991. The use of prosody in syntactic disambiguation. *Journal of the Acoustical Society of America* 90: 2956–70.

Rayner, Keith and Alexander Pollatsek, 1989. *The Psychology of Reading*. Hillsdale, NJ: Lawrence Erlbaum.

Rayner, Keith, Kathryn Chace, Timothy J. Slattery and Jane Ashby. 2006. Eye movements as reflections of comprehension processes in reading. *Scientific Studies of Reading* 10: 241–55.

Recanati, François. 1980. Some remarks on explicit performatives, indirect speech acts, locutionary meaning and truth-value. In John R. Searle, Ferenc Kiefer and Manfred Bierwisch, eds., *Texts and Studies in Linguistics and Philosophy, Vol. 10: Speech Act Theory and Pragmatics*. Dordrecht: D. Reidel Publishing Company, 205–20.

  1987. *Meaning and Force: The Pragmatics of Performative Utterances*. Cambridge: Cambridge University Press.

  2004. *Literal Meaning*. Cambridge: Cambridge University Press.

Rosch, Eleanor. 1973. Natural categories. *Cognitive Psychology* 4 (3): 328–50.

Rosch, Eleanor and Carolyn B. Mervis. 1975. Family resemblances: studies in the internal structure of categories. *Cognitive Psychology* 7 (4): 573–605.

Ross, John R. 1970. On declarative sentences. In Roderick A. Jacobs and Peter S. Rosenbaum, eds., *Readings in English Transformational Grammar*. Waltham, MA: Ginn and Co., 222–72.

Ruytenbeek, Nicolas. 2017a. The comprehension of indirect requests: previous work and future directions. In Ilse Depraetere and Raphael Salkie, eds., *Semantics and Pragmatics: Drawing a Line*. Amsterdam: Springer.

  2017b. The mechanics of indirectness: a case study of directives. Unpublished PhD dissertation, Université libre de Bruxelles, Brussels.

  2019a. Current issues in the ontology and form of directive speech acts: a critical assessment of recent cognitive linguistic approaches. *International Review of Pragmatics* 11 (2): 200–221.

  2019b. Lexical and morpho-syntactic modification of student requests: an empirical contribution to the study of im/politeness in French e-mail speech acts. *Lexique* 24: 29–47.

2020. Do indirect requests communicate politeness? An experimental study of conventionalized indirect requests in French email communication. *Journal of Politeness Research* 16 (1): 111–42.

Ruytenbeek, Nicolas, Ekaterina Ostashchenko and Mikhail Kissine. 2017. Indirect request processing, sentence-types and illocutionary forces. *Journal of Pragmatics* 119: 46–62.

Ruytenbeek, Nicolas, Sofie Decock and Ilse Depraetere. (in press). What makes a complaint (im)polite? Experiments into (in)directness and perceived face-threat in Twitter complaints. *Journal of Politeness Research*.

Sacks, Harvey. 1992. *Harvey Sacks: Lectures on Conversation*, Vol. 1, edited by Gail Jefferson. Oxford: Blackwell.

Sadock, Jerrold M. 1974. *Toward a Linguistic Theory of Speech Acts*. New York: Academic Press.

Sadock, Jerrold M. and Arnold M. Zwicky. 1985. Speech act distinctions in syntax. In Timothy Shopen, ed., *Language Typology and Syntactic Description, Vol. 1: Clause Structure*. Cambridge: Cambridge University Press, 155–96.

Saeli, Hooman. 2016. Persian favor asking in formal and informal academic contexts: the impact of gender and academic status. *Pragmatics* 26 (2): 315–44.

Saul, Jennifer M. 2002. What is said and psychological reality: Grice's project and relevance theorists' criticisms. *Linguistics and Philosophy* 25: 347–72.

Savić, Mila. 2018. Lecturer perceptions of im/politeness and in/appropriateness in student e-mail requests: a Norwegian perspective. *Journal of Pragmatics* 124: 52–72.

Schegloff, Emanuel A. 1980. Preliminaries to preliminaries: 'Can I ask you a question?' *Sociological Inquiry* 50 (3–4): 104–52.

Schiffer, Stephen. 1972. *Meaning*. Oxford: Oxford University Press.

Schulenburg, David and Michael. J. Pazzani. 1989. *Explanation-Based Learning of Indirect Speech Act Interpretation Rules*. Technical report, Irvine Computational Intelligence Project, University of California, Irvine, CA, USA.

Searle, John. R. 1969. *Speech Acts: An Essay in the Philosophy of Language*. Cambridge: Cambridge University Press.

  1975. Indirect speech acts. In Peter Cole and Jerry L. Morgan, eds., *Syntax and Semantics, Vol. 3: Speech Acts*. New York: Academic Press, 59–82.

  1979. *Expression and Meaning: Studies in the Theory of Speech Acts*. Cambridge: Cambridge University Press.

Searle, John R. and Daniel Vanderveken. 1985. *Foundations of Illocutionary Logic*. Cambridge: Cambridge University Press.

Shapiro, Amy M. and Gregory Murphy. 1993. Can you answer a question for me? Processing indirect speech acts. *Journal of Memory and Language* 32 (2): 211–29.

Sifianou, Maria. 1993. Off-record indirectness and the notion of imposition. *Multilingua* 12 (1): 69–79.

Slugoski, Ben R. and William Turnbull. 1988. Cruel to be kind and kind to be cruel: sarcasm, banter and social relations. *Journal of Language and Social Psychology* 7 (2): 101–21.

Snedeker, Jesse and John Trueswell. 2003. Using prosody to avoid ambiguity: effects of speaker awareness and referential context. *Journal of Memory and Language* 48 (1): 103–30.

Soltys, Jessica, Marina Terkourafi and Napoleon Katsos. 2014. Disentangling politeness theory and the strategic speaker approach: theoretical considerations and empirical predictions. *Intercultural Pragmatics* 11 (1): 31–56.

Spence, Janet T. and Robert L. Helmreich. 1978. *Masculinity and Femininity: Their Psychological Dimensions, Correlates and Antecedents*. Austin, TX: University of Texas Press.

Sperber, Dan and Deirdre Wilson. 1995. *Relevance: Communication and Cognition*, 2nd ed. Oxford: Blackwell.

Stewart, Andrew, Elizabeth Le-luan, Jeffrey Wood, Bo Yao and Matthew Haigh. 2018. Comprehension of indirect requests is influenced by their degree of imposition. *Discourse Processes* 55 (2): 187–96.

Stoet, Geert. 2010. PsyToolkit: a software package for programming psychological experiments using Linux. *Behavior Research Methods* 42 (4), 1096–1104.

  2017. PsyToolkit: a novel web-based method for running online questionnaires and reaction-time experiments. *Teaching of Psychology* 44 (1), 24–31.

Sweetser, Eve E., 1990. *From Etymology to Pragmatics: Metaphorical and Cultural Aspects of Semantic Structure*. Cambridge: Cambridge University Press.

Takahashi, Hidemitsu. 2012. *A Cognitive Linguistic Analysis of the English Imperative: With Special Reference to Japanese Imperatives*. Amsterdam: John Benjamins.

Talmy, Leonard. 2000. *Toward a Cognitive Semantics, Vol. 1: Concept Structuring Systems*. Cambridge, MA: MIT Press.

Tanck, Sharyl. 2002. Speech act sets of refusal and complaint: a comparison of native and non-native English speakers' production. *Studies in Second Language Acquisition* 13 (1): 65–81.

Tannen, Deborah. 1981. Indirectness in discourse: ethnicity as conversational style. *Discourse Processes* 4 (3): 221–38.

  1990. *You Just Don't Understand: Women and Men in Conversation*. New York: Morrow.

Terkourafi, Marina. 2003. Generalized and particularized implicatures of linguistic politeness. In Peter Kühnlein, Hannes Rieser and Henk Zeevat, eds., *Perspectives on Dialogue in the New Millennium*. Amsterdam and Philadelphia: John Benjamins, 149–64.

  2008. Toward a unified theory of politeness, impoliteness and rudeness. In Derek Bousfield and Miriam A. Locher, eds., *Impoliteness in Language: Studies on Its Interplay with Power in Theory and Practice, Language, Power and Social Process*. Berlin: Mouton de Gruyter, 45–74.

2011. The puzzle of indirect speech. *Journal of Pragmatics* 43: 2861–65.

2014. The importance of being indirect. *Belgian Journal of Linguistics* 28: 45–70.

2015. Conventionalization: a new agenda for im/politeness research. *Journal of Pragmatics* 86: 11–18.

Terkourafi, Marina and Aline Villavicencio 2003. Toward a formalization of speech act functions of questions in conversation. In Raffaella Bernardi and Michael Moortgat, eds., *Questions and Answers: Theoretical and Applied Perspectives*. Utrecht: Utrecht Institute of Linguistics OTS, 108–119.

Thompson Dominik and Ruth Filik. 2016. Sarcasm in written communication: emoticons are efficient markers of intention. *Journal of Computer Mediated Communication* 21 (2): 105–20.

Tobback, Els. 2014. A chacun son tour : analyse comparative des styles conversationnels des néerlandophones et des francophones de Belgique dans des débats télévisés. *Canadian Journal of Linguistics/Revue canadienne de linguistique* 59 (3): 373–93.

Traugott, Elizabeth C. 1988. Pragmatic strengthening and grammaticalization. *Proceedings of the Fourteenth Annual Meeting of the Berkeley Linguistics Society*, 406–16.

Traugott, Elizabeth C. and Richard B. Dasher. 2005. *Regularity in Semantic Change*. Cambridge: Cambridge University Press.

Tromp, Johanne, Peter Hagoort and Antje S. Meyer. 2016. Pupillometry reveals increased pupil size during indirect request comprehension. *Quarterly Journal of Experimental Psychology* 69: 1093–1108.

Trosborg, Anna. 1995. Interlanguage pragmatics: requests, complaints and apologies. *Studies in Anthropological Linguistics* 7. Berlin and New York: Mouton de Gruyter.

Trott, Sean T. and Benjamin Bergen. 2017. A theoretical model of indirect request comprehension. *AAAI Fall Symposium Series*.

Trott, Sean T., Stefanie Reed, Victor Ferreira and Benjamin Bergen. 2019. Prosodic cues signal the intent of potential indirect requests. *Proceedings of the 41st Annual Meeting of the Cognitive Science Society*.

Upadhyay, Shiv R. 2003. Nepali requestive acts: linguistic indirectness and politeness reconsidered. *Journal of Pragmatics* 35 (10–11): 1651–77.

van Ackeren, Markus J., Daniel Casasanto, Harold Bekkering, Peter Hagoort and Shirley-Ann Rueschemeyer. 2012. Pragmatics in action: indirect requests engage theory of mind areas and the cortical motor network. *Journal of Cognitive Neuroscience* 24 (11): 2237–47.

van Tiel, Bob. 2020. Prototype effects in speech act concepts. https://osf.io/9h3j4/, last accessed 14/11/2020.

Vanderveken, Daniel. 1990. *Meaning and Speech Acts*, Vol. 1. Cambridge: Cambridge University Press.

Vásquez, Camilla. 2011. Complaints online: the case of TripAdvisor. *Journal of Pragmatics* 43: 1707–17.

Vega Moreno, Rosa E. 2007. *Creativity and Convention: The Pragmatics of Everyday Figurative Speech*. Amsterda and Philadelphia: John Benjamins.

Ward, Nigel G. 2019. *Prosodic Patterns in English Conversation*. Cambridge: Cambridge University Press.

Weizman, Elda. 1989. Requestive hints. In Shoshana Blum-Kulka, Juliane House and Gabriele Kasper. eds., *Cross-Cultural Pragmatics: Requests and Apologies*. Norwood, NJ: Ablex, 71–95.

Wichmann, Anne. 2004. The intonation of please-requests: a corpus-based study. *Journal of Pragmatics* 36: 1521–49.

Wierzbicka, Anna. 1985. Different cultures, different languages, different speech acts. *Journal of Pragmatics* 9: 145–78.

Williams, Tom, Daria Thames, Julia Novakoff and Matthias Scheutz. 2018. 'Thank you for sharing that interesting fact!' Effects of capability and context on indirect speech act use in task-based human-robot dialogue. HRI '18: Proceedings of the 2018 ACM/IEEE International Conference on Human-Robot Interaction, 298–306.

Williams, Tom, Rafael C. Núñez, Gordon Briggs, Matthias Scheutz, Kamal Premaratne and Manohar N. Murthi. 2014. A Dempster-Shafer theoretic approach to understanding indirect speech acts. In Ana Bazzan and Karim Pichara, eds., *Advances in Artificial Intelligence – IBERAMIA 2014. Lecture Notes in Computer Science 8864*. Cham: Springer.

Wilske, Sabrina and Geert-Jan Kruijff. 2006. Service robots dealing with indirect speech acts. *Proceedings of the International Conference on Intelligent Robots and Systems (IROS)*.

Wilson, Deirdre and Dan Sperber. 1988. Mood and the analysis of non-declarative sentences. In Jonathan Dancy, Julius M. E. Moravcsik and Charles C. W. Taylor, eds., *Human Agency: Language, Duty and Value*. Stanford, CA: Stanford University Press, 77–101.

Yin, Chun-Po and Feng-Yang Kuo. 2013. A study of how information system professionals comprehend indirect and direct speech acts in project communication. *IEEE Transactions on Professional Communication* 56 (3): 226–41.

Zaefferer, Dietmar. 1990. On the coding of sentential modality. In Johannes Bechert, Giuliano Bernini and Claude Buridant, eds., *Toward a Typology of European Languages. Proceedings of the Workshop Held at Consiglio Nazionale delle Ricerche, Rome, 7–9 January 1988*. Berlin: Mouton de Gruyter, 215–37.

Zanuttini, Raffaella. 2008. Encoding the addressee in the syntax: evidence from English imperative subjects. *Natural Language and Linguistic Theory* 26 (1): 185–218.

Index

ability, 5, 16, 18, 21, 26, 32–6, 38–9, 74–5, 82, 84–5, 87, 95, 97, 105, 108, 114, 116–17, 119–20, 122, 127, 130, 134, 159, 183, 189–90, 194, 199
abstract-performative hypothesis, 8
acceptability judgements, 9, 38
achievability, 49
affectivity *see* distance
agent, 47, 73, 78, 182, 192–6
agonist, 77, 79
ambiguities, 7, 10–11, 25, 39, 95, 107, 112, 122, 127, 129, 132, 138–9, 145, 153, 157, 167, 171–2, 182, 189–90, 193, 195–6, 198–9
answers, 16–19, 26, 28, 34, 37–8, 40, 51–5, 57–9, 66–71, 73–4, 79, 89, 96, 108, 117, 125–6, 130, 143–4, 177, 182, 193, 204
antagonist *see* agonist
AOI *see* areas of interest
apologies, 30, 167
areas of interest, 132, 202
artificial intelligence, 100, 181, 205
assertions, 9, 13, 25–7, 32, 53, 64, 67, 69, 80, 84, 126, 172, 174, 202
attitudes, 22–4, 30, 100, 102, 105
Austin, John L., 5, 11–14, 21, 24, 205
authority, 45, 77, 148

Bach & Harnish, 21–3, 36, 75, 127
background, 18, 78, 98, 157
bad news, 197
begging, 86
Blum-Kulka, Shoshana, 31, 33, 81, 142, 159, 161, 163–4, 207
BNC, 52, 54, 77, 98, 127
Bolinger, Dwight, 8, 63–4
brain activation, 110, 116, 129, 131

bribes, 148–9, 162–3
Brown & Levinson, 29–31, 81, 142–3, 147, 153, 169–71, 173, 176, 185, 203–5
business communication, 100, 162, 168

Chinese, 113, 200
Clark, Herbert, 33–4, 36, 52, 72, 84, 94, 116–18, 120, 127, 129, 143, 148, 193
closeness, 151, 163–4, 166, 170
COCA, 8, 10, 15, 19, 33, 44, 47, 52, 60, 66–7, 70, 76, 104
cognitive effects, 57, 90–3, 98, 101, 103, 105, 202, 205
cognitive environment, 91
cognitive linguistics, 3, 33, 85, 87, 89–90, 104–5
coherence theory, 37
commands, 8, 19, 25–6, 34, 45, 49, 88, 106, 129
commitment, 46, 146
complaints, 30, 141, 172–9, 199
completeness, 58, 61, 64, 73
completion, 57, 60–1, 67, 164, 202
compliance, 18–19, 28, 71–2, 102, 117, 119, 188, 190, 193, 204, 207
compliments, 6, 30, 180
computer-mediated communication, 128
conditions
 answer conditions, 28
 availability conditions, 25, 25, 26, 202
 essential conditions, 17, 32, 56
 felicity conditions, 17, 32, 82, 84
 obedience conditions, 28
 preparatory conditions, 17–18, 32–3, 37, 39, 54, 71, 84, 106, 116, 159, 161–2, 191, 194–5, 205

221

conditions (cont.)
  propositional content conditions, 17, 32, 54
  satisfaction conditions, 28–9, 84
  sincerity conditions, 17, 32, 84, 191
  truth conditions, 28
constitutive components, 173–6, 178, 203
consultative devices, 155
conventions, 12, 32–3, 35, 37–9, 61, 84–5, 116–18, 120, 134
  conventions of means, 32–4, 36, 39–40, 81, 84–5, 116–17, 119–20, 122–3, 129, 134, 139, 194, 199
  conventions of use, 35–6, 61
  extralinguistic conventions, 12
conventionality, 32, 34, 41, 81, 83–5, 87, 89, 104, 107, 116, 122–3, 134, 139, 144, 181, 198
  conventionality of form, 32, 89
  conventionality of means, 32, 34, 87, 89, 107, 116, 122–3, 139, 144, 181, 198
conversational analysis, 70
conversational presumptions, 21, 23
cooperation, 5, 14, 16, 18, 21, 23, 37, 41
Cooperative Principle, 14
corpus, 40, 71, 104, 120, 122, 157, 160–1, 167–8, 174, 176–80, 191
cortical motor areas, 110, 202
costs
  processing costs, 90–4, 98–9, 103, 105, 107, 110, 113, 116, 128, 130, 139, 200, 205
coupling, 72
courtroom, 149
cross-cultural speech act realization project, 159, 164
Culpeper, Jonathan, 100, 142, 176, 180
customer, 71–2, 118, 173–6, 178, 182
Czech, 161, 200

Danish, 99, 165
declaratives, 6–7, 9, 13, 22, 27, 39, 41, 45, 47, 52, 55, 57, 60, 62–5, 68–9, 73–6, 79, 81, 86, 94, 97, 102–3, 124, 126, 132–4, 185, 202, 204–5
  rising declarative, 52
Decock & Depraetere, 169, 173–5
deep structure, 7–11
default, 97, 151, 190, 193, 200, 202

deniability, 148–9, 199, 202, 204
deontic necessity, 78
deontic reasons, 185
desirability, 49, 57, 94, 96–7, 102, 105
desires, 22–3, 27, 32, 39, 44, 53, 70, 75, 84, 102–3, 121, 159
diachronic process, 37, 40, 89, 120
directive-commissives, 150
discourse completion task, 146, 164, 202
discourse representation theory, 37, 205
dissatisfaction, 173–4, 176, 178
distance
  affective distance, 153, 170–2, 179, 200
  social distance, 31, 151–2, 155, 158, 160, 163–6, 168–9, 171, 200, 205
downgraders, 88, 162, 164
downtoners, 168
Dutch, 7, 109–10, 167

electrical brain activity, 109, 203
emails, 100, 158, 160–2, 164, 168, 205
emojis, 127–8
emoticons, 127
enablement, 73–4, 103
English
  American English, 117, 164, 170
  British English, 162
enrichment, 94–5
ERPs see event-related potentials
Escandell-Vidal, Victoria, 98–100
events, 47, 49, 64, 78, 109, 148, 172, 203–4
event-related potentials, 109
explicatures, 94–6, 98, 100
  higher-order explicatures, 94–6, 98
expressive speech acts, 19, 42, 172
eye-tracking, 107, 112, 131–4, 199, 202–3

f0 see fundamental frequency
face
  face management, 146
  negative face, 29–30, 102, 142, 146, 149, 158, 167, 203
  positive face, 29, 102, 142, 144, 146, 150, 167, 172, 203

Index

face-threat, 29–31, 101, 142, 144, 146, 149, 152–4, 156, 164, 166, 170, 172, 175–6, 179, 199, 203, 205
Fiengo, Robert, 6, 52, 61–3, 66–7, 70
figurative language, 104, 129, 140, 151, 210
force
  force dynamics, 73, 77, 80, 203
  force exertion, 73, 77–8, 80
formality, 151
Francik & Clark, 71, 117–18, 193
French, 7, 52, 62, 65, 118, 120, 132, 157, 167, 174–5, 189, 200
fundamental frequency, 136

gender, 146, 158, 165–70, 179, 200
generality of form, 32–3
generative semantics, 5, 11, 41
generative syntax, 7, 44
Gibbs & Colston, 21, 129, 140, 151, 200
Gibbs, Raymond, 21, 71, 105, 113, 115, 118–19, 129, 140, 151, 193, 195, 200
Giora, Rachel, 104
good wishes, 10, 19, 203
graded salience, 104–5
Greek, 142
greetings, 159, 191
Grice, H. Paul, 5, 13–16, 20–1, 41, 91, 97, 114, 147, 204
Groefsema, Marjolein, 39, 95–7
Groenendijk & Stokhof, 51–2, 54
GSH *see* graded salience

Han, Chung-Hye, 44–5, 52–3, 68
hints, 31, 145, 155, 161
Holtgraves, Thomas R., 122, 124–6, 145, 152–3, 156, 167, 169
HRI *see* human–robot interactions
human–robot interactions, 181, 186, 189–90, 195

idealized cognitive model, 87
illocutionary forces
  illocutionary force salience, 32, 88–9, 107, 116, 126–8, 134, 139, 144, 181, 198
  illocutionary types, 6, 75
imperatives, 5–11, 13–14, 16–18, 21–3, 27–30, 35, 38–9, 41, 43–50, 52–3, 55–6, 61, 75–7, 79, 81, 85, 88, 92–4, 96–103, 105, 107, 111–13, 117–19, 124, 126, 129, 131, 135, 139, 143, 154, 173, 188–9, 198, 203, 205
implicatures, 39, 99, 103, 183–4, 203
  conventional implicatures, 14
  conversational implicatures, 14–15, 31
impoliteness, 99–100, 103, 176–7, 180
imposition, 30–1, 152, 160–4, 169, 179, 200, 203
inferences
  short-circuited inferences, 36, 75, 183–4, 196
informativeness, 43, 63–5, 68–9, 79
inquisitive semantics, 56, 59, 204
inquisitiveness, 60, 63–5, 69
instructions, 45–6, 76, 189, 199
intentions
  communicative intentions, 27, 30–1, 91
  informative intentions, 91
interrogatives *see* questions
interrogativity, 65
intimacy, 150–1
intonation, 51–3, 56, 62, 65, 68, 79, 136, 203–4
invitations, 136, 148–9, 151, 177
  ostensible invitations, 149
irony, 20–1
IS *see* inquisitive semantics
ISI, 125–6
Italian, 65

Japanese, 142
Jary, Mark, 12, 50, 99, 102–3

Kissine, Mikhail, 24, 26, 50
Korean, 155, 164, 170

Lao, 65
late positive components, 109, 204
L-compatibility *see* locutionary compatibility
Lepore & Stone, 37–8, 95
Levinson, Stephen, 30–1, 42, 64, 70, 142, 169, 176

lexical activation, 125–6
lexical decision, 124–6
literalism, 6, 16–22, 26–9, 41–6, 53, 134, 198, 204
locutionary acts, 12–13, 21–4, 204
locutionary compatibility, 22
logical form, 44, 57, 61, 94, 204

Mastop, Rosja, 45–7, 50, 52, 76
maxims
  maxim of Manner, 14
  maxim of Quality, 14
  maxim of Quantity, 14–15
  maxim of Relation, 15–16
meaning
  primary meaning, 25–6, 36, 41, 74, 83–4, 89, 114, 116, 120, 127, 134, 139, 148, 178, 199, 202
  secondary meaning, 25–6, 41, 54, 74, 83–4, 114–16, 120, 127, 134, 139, 202
  sentence meaning, 17, 19, 35, 46
memory, 109, 119–20, 122–4, 154–5, 200
  verbatim recall, 123
mental states, 197, 204
metaphor, 21, 39
metonymic illocutionary scenarios, 82, 84
misunderstanding, 135, 145, 153
mitigation, 31, 85–7, 106, 142, 147, 158, 168, 187, 204
modal verbs, 7, 32–3, 39, 74–6, 78, 95–6, 103, 117, 184
mood, 17, 94–7, 105
Morgan, Jerry L., 33, 35–6, 68, 75, 183–4
must, 32, 43, 75–8, 80, 84
mutual knowledge, 151, 195

natural language processing, 182
negative state remarks, 81, 84, 109–10, 122, 129, 132, 136–8, 150–1, 156, 158–9, 161, 163, 173, 184, 191, 194–5, 204
Nepali, 142
NLP *see* natural language processing

obligation, 34, 43, 75–8, 80, 82–4, 117, 159, 191–2, 194
obstacle hypothesis, 71–2, 117, 119, 204

Occam's razor, 36
off-record speech acts, 30–1, 142, 147–9, 161, 164, 170, 204
Ogiermann, Eva, 142, 158, 167, 176
on-record speech acts, 30–1, 142, 147, 149, 204
opinion disclosure, 128, 144–7, 154, 166–7
optionality, 38, 49, 86–7, 106
orders, 12, 24, 26–7, 30, 34, 71, 113, 187

Panther & Thornburg, 82–5
paraphrases, 36, 39, 115, 122, 128, 156
parentheticals, 9–10
partition theory, 58–9, 63–4, 68, 204
Pérez Hernández, Lorena, 85, 87–8
performatives, 8–10, 12, 34–5, 204–5
  hedged performatives, 35, 112, 162
perlocutionary effects, 100, 103, 175, 205
permission, 35, 44–5, 129
Persian, 158
personality, 152, 170–1, 179, 200
Pinker, Steven, 103, 147, 149, 162
plan-based model, 182–4, 196
please, 11, 37–8, 48–9, 71–2, 85–9, 113, 127, 130, 139, 152, 187, 191
Polish, 142
politeness, 5, 21, 29–31, 99–101, 103, 105, 135, 140–4, 146, 149, 153–5, 158–62, 164–6, 169–70, 176, 178, 181, 191–3, 199–200, 203–5
  negative politeness, 30
  positive politeness, 30
Portner, Paul, 44–5, 77–8
potentiality, 49–50, 94, 96–7
power, 31, 45, 73, 101, 153, 168, 205
pragmatic routines, 98
praise, 112
pre-frontal cortex, 110
pre-requests, 30, 70–2, 193
presuppositions, 55, 145, 174, 205
pretence, 148–9
probe recognition task, 124–5
processing times, 108, 122, 130, 134, 139, 156
promises, 6, 42, 80, 89, 180
pronouns, 9, 32, 48–9, 124, 145, 160, 184

Index

propositions, 7, 17, 22, 24, 32, 44–5, 49, 54, 57, 59–61, 63, 67–8, 70, 76, 95–6, 182, 205
prosody, *see* intonation
proto-illocutionary acts, 27
prototypes, 85, 87, 89, 104, 106, 125
pupil, 110, 205
pupillometry, 110, 205

questions
 exam questions, 58
 expository questions, 55, 58
 guess questions, 55, 58
 ordinary questions, 58
 question under discussion, 63
 rhetorical questions, 43, 55, 58, 66–9, 74–5, 80, 121
 self-addressed questions, 58
 sensitive questions, 144
 speculative questions, 55
 surprise questions, 55, 58
 survey requestions, 11

rational reconstruction, 16, 18, 69, 96
rationality, 32, 37
recall *see* memory
Recanati, François, 12, 24–6, 41
recommendations, 76
redress, 30, 101, 205
relevance
 maximal relevance, 92–3, 98, 101–3
 optimal relevance, 101–3
relevance theory, 39, 56–8, 90–1, 94, 97–8, 101, 105–6, 129, 205
reminders, 66, 68, 124–5
replies
 evasive replies, 146, 154
 indirect replies, 128
 irrelevant replies, 128, 146, 154, 163
 laconic replies, 130
request forms, 10–11, 29, 35–6, 81, 83, 100, 118, 131, 134–5, 143, 155, 159–61, 163, 165, 174, 187, 189, 191
requestions *see* questions
response times, 108, 110, 113, 115, 129–30, 198–9
responsibility, 31, 147, 150, 167

robots, 168, 181, 186, 188–92, 195–7, 200
RT *see* relevance theory
rudeness, 49, 100, 177–8
Russian, 142

Sadock & Zwicky, 6, 52
Sadock, Jerrold M., 6–11, 38, 52, 86, 127
sarcasm, 31, 115, 128, 142, 177
Searle, John R., 5, 9, 11, 16–18, 20–2, 24–5, 27, 32–4, 41, 52, 54, 75, 79, 84–5, 96, 114, 142, 150, 169, 181, 185, 195, 198, 205
sentence recognition paradigm, 118
sentence-types, 6–7, 13, 16–19, 21, 26–9, 41, 43, 45–6, 51–3, 56, 61, 63–4, 69, 74, 79–81, 93–4, 97, 103, 105, 126, 132, 168, 172, 198, 200, 202, 204
sexuality, 148–9
should, 15, 23, 32, 39, 43, 75–6, 78, 80, 123, 128, 146, 185, 187
Spanish, 7, 65
 Peninsular Spanish, 162
speech act theory, 5, 11–12, 16, 18–21, 25–7, 29, 41–2, 79, 198, 205
Sperber & Wilson, 49, 57, 91
standard pragmatic model, 114, 116, 198
standardization, 32, 36–7, 39–41, 85, 87–9, 98, 107, 120–3, 126, 134, 139, 159, 181, 183, 194, 196, 198
state of affairs, 25, 49, 51, 73, 79, 85, 88, 94, 96, 204
subject, 9, 47–9, 61, 111, 124, 203
suggestions, 85, 88–9, 136
surface form, 7, 131

tags, 7, 47, 65, 205
Talmy, Leonard, 73, 77
temporo-parietal junction, 110
Terkourafi, Marina, 98, 100–1, 150–1
theory of mind, 129, 195
to-do list, 44–5, 77
Twitter, 141, 172, 174–9
typology, 56, 65, 185–6

uncertainty, 168, 187, 193, 196
update semantics, 45

upgraders, 88
uptake, 72, 129

variables
  social variables, 151–2, 170

verbal aggression, 165
verbatim recall *see* memory

warnings, 23, 75, 136, 172
willingness, 34, 118, 122, 159, 190
Wilson & Sperber, 49, 52, 55, 94

CPSIA information can be obtained
at www.ICGtesting.com
Printed in the USA
LVHW011608030821
694401LV00006B/383